Golden Advice from Global Icons

Golden Advice
from
Global Icons

135 Acclaimed Leaders and Legends
Share Their Insights on How Best
to Journey Through Life

Schuyler W. Huck, Ph.D.

Published by
Notaed Press
Sweetwater, Tennessee, USA

ISBN: 978-1-951677-13-8

Cover design by Janiel Escueta
Edited by Angelina Collake

Published by Notaed Press
Sweetwater, Tennessee, USA

Publishing Consultant: Matt Deaton, Ph.D.
E-mail: matt@mattdeaton.com

The photo on front cover was taken by the author while he was in Florida on a family vacation. The photo of the author on the back cover was taken by a friend of the author while both were on a biking trip in New Mexico.

Dedication

The author (whose nickname is "Sky") dedicates this book to his wife, Kathryn (whose nickname is "Kathy")

The Peasant, the Queen, and the King

A host of things in life make little sense
Like when the poor get little from the rich
Or when twixt homes, you'll often see a fence
Or why no man is ever called a witch.

There's one main thing that's baffling in Sky's life.
One day he got a gift that was pure gold—
A lass agreed to be his loving wife;
Said she: "We're 'one' from now until we're old."

What's strange about this Queen that Sky did wed
Was that she could have had most any man;
Those with great wealth (and looks) who were well-bred,
And countless more, each one a "Kathy-fan."

But Kathy chose to take and wear Sky's ring,
And that changed Sky from Peasant to a King

Preface

You're a good person, right? In all likelihood, you possess a slew of positive traits. That's why your friends and relatives, if asked, would probably describe you as a competent and worthy individual. But is there "room for improvement"? Yes, of course, there is, for no one is perfect. Even the best of us can widen or deepen our "goodness" in one way or another.

So, realizing that you are a good but not fully perfected person, here's the crucial question: *Would you like to *improve* the person you see in the mirror?* If you say "no," close this book and go do something else. On the other hand, if you say "yes" to this all-important initial query, continue reading!

If you absorb even a sliver of what is in this book's "core," you'll become an even better person than you are now. No matter how many positive attributes you currently possess, this book has the power to help you improve the way you think and act. It can do this through the wise advice you'll find located in the coming pages. This advice is not mine. It comes, instead, from a group of revered icons from around the globe.

What You'll Encounter Inside this Book

This book contains 135 two-page write-ups. Although these "mini-mini-chapters" are totally different in terms of their content, they all have the same basic structure. As you will see, each write-up has three main ingredients:

1. A quotation.
2. A biographical sketch.
3. A photo.

The Quotes, Bios, and Photos

The first thing you'll see in any two-page write-up is a boxed quotation. Collectively, these quotes vary in length and topic. They are similar, however, in that every quote provides one or more meaningful tips for improving your thinking or behavior. For example, one of the quotes you'll encounter says:

> *It's one of the greatest gifts you can give yourself, to forgive. Forgive everybody.*

Just as important as the quotes are the biographical sketches of the people responsible for them. Each "bio" is well worth considering. Though short, they'll give you a glimpse into the life stories of 135 amazing human beings. Once you read about their achievements and honors, you'll be more likely to remember and be influenced by the advice they offer.

Many of the quotes you'll see come from people with positive reputations that span the globe. Examples of such luminaries are Anne Frank, Mahatma Gandhi, Florence Nightingale, and Martin Luther King, Jr. Even though you already know at least a little about such world-famous icons, their bios will give you new insights into why they are so widely admired.

Whereas you'll be familiar with most of this book's quotation authors, there will be others you've never heard of. I suspect the typical reader of this book won't know anything at all about Knud Rasmussen (from Greenland), Kartini (Indonesia), Gabriel Garcia Márquez (Colombia), Mary MacKillop (Australia), or Denis Mukwege (the Democratic

Republic of the Congo). One nice feature of this book is that the bios will introduce you to these and other accomplished individuals from countries other than your own. You'll have a broader worldview after you learn a bit about these people who are revered figures in distant lands.

Quotes from and bios about Rasmussen, Kartini, and other lesser-known people are not in this book by accident. Nor were they intentionally inserted as "fillers" to make the book longer. Instead, they were painstakingly sought out and purposefully included to help you (and me) overcome any ethnocentric biases or xenophobic prejudices we may have acquired during our upbringing or in later seasons of our lives.

Consider the world map shown below. The 52 darkly shaded areas are the home countries of the people whose golden

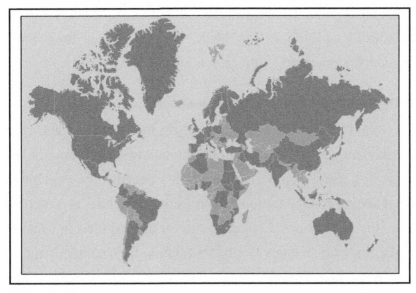

gems of wisdom are located in this book's boxed quotes. This map shows that the advice embodied in these quotes comes from people spread out across the globe. Hence the term: "global icons."

The third and final component of each two-page write-up is a photo of the quote's author. When this book project began, I had no plans to include such photos. However, a friend who had seen early drafts of a few of the two-page write-ups suggested that I include pictures of the quotation authors. At first, I balked at this suggestion because several of the book's quotes come from people who lived centuries ago. "How," I asked myself, "could I include a photo of someone like Plato or Catherine the Great who lived long before cameras were invented?"

As you will see, I found a creative solution to my "photo dilemma." As a result, an image exists for each of the book's 135 global icons. I hope you find these photos to be, as I do, a wonderful addition to the book. They allow us to become "visually acquainted" with each advice-giver.

How Best to "Consume" this Book

With most books, you begin on page 1 and read subsequent pages, in order, until you end up on the book's last page. It's usually important to do this because the content of most books, be they fiction or non-fiction in nature, is presented in a "linear" manner. Chapter 2 is built upon what's in Chapter 1; the first two chapters lay the foundation for Chapter 3; and so on. With many books, and especially with mysteries and documentaries, you actually cheat yourself if you read chapters out of order.

This book is different. Its content is not linear. Because the 135 write-ups are independent of each other, they could have been arranged in any number of possible orders. In fact, the order of the write-ups could have been determined randomly. Had that been done, little, if anything, would have been lost.

Feel free to begin reading wherever you want. Also, you may want to skip around as you take in the advice from and information about this book's global icons. If you wish, use the alphabetized *Index of Quotation Authors*—located near the back of the book—to find the two-page write-ups of the global icons whose names already are familiar to you. (But don't forever overlook the write-ups focused on individuals you've never heard of.) Or, use the *Index of Quotation Topics*—also located at the back of the book—to help you find bits of advice that focus on specific areas of concern, such as friendship, nature, gratitude, money, perseverance, etc.

My Hope

I hope you will remember the sage advice embodied in one or more of the boxed quotations in this book. More importantly, I hope you'll be influenced by these words of wisdom. If that happens, I am confident that you will consider yourself to be an improved human being.

I'd now like to share two examples of how the book's quotes have helped me. I don't do this to pat myself on the back. Rather, I simply want to illustrate how the quotes can impact one's thoughts and actions. (I could provide many more such examples, but two are sufficient, I think, to show that the quotes can function as useful guideposts as we travel through life.)

Some of this book's quotes encourage us to alter the way we *think*. For example, I now am more forgiving, in my mind, when I think someone has been rude to me. Why? Because I once saw and chose to remember the quotes from Maya Angelou and Charles Dickens. You saw Maya Angelou's "forgive everybody" quote earlier in this Preface. Now, consider what Charles Dickens has to say about remembering occasions when we've been "wronged":

> *May I tell you why it seems to me a good thing*
> *for us to remember wrong that has been*
> *done us? That we may forgive it.*

The quotes from Maya Angelou, Charles Dickens, and several other icons encourage us to adopt a more helpful mindset about other people, events, and things. A different set of quotes in this book nudges us to actively *do* something (or to alter what we're inclined to do). For instance, the great Lebanese author Khalil Gibran offers us this advice:

> *You give little when you give of*
> *your possessions. It is when you*
> *give of yourself that you truly give.*

Gibran's words have prompted me to stop giving store-bought items as gifts. Instead, the presents I now prefer to give are joint experiences, such as a lunch together or a shared walk in the park, or something I create, such as a poem about the other person. In one way or another, I now try to have my gifts be "me giving me."

I hope that you, too, will be influenced—in both your thinking and actions—by one, a few, many, or all of this book's quoted words of wisdom. If that happens, you legitimately can take pride in telling yourself that you "walk with the wise"!

Acknowledgments

I want to express my deep and sincere appreciation to several individuals who made it possible for this book to come into existence. Without the important contributions of these people, this seven-year project would never have reached its conclusion. In fact, without their help, this project would never have begun.

First and foremost, I am indebted to the 135 icons (some living, some deceased) whose advice to us is contained in this book's boxed quotations. If I could, I'd like to personally thank these global leaders and legends for providing their golden words of wisdom. The world would be a better place, I believe, if everyone would follow these 135 tips for becoming more other-centered, helpful, and satisfied. I, for one, am trying my best to remember and to be influenced by their suggestions.

Next, I want to thank a large group of my friends and relatives. They helped me select the final set of quotes; they counseled me to include photos of the advice-givers; they assisted me in crafting the book's title; they provided emotional support. These invaluable "helpers" were Alex Huck, Allison Huck, Andrew Huck, Ann Eyssen, Anne Lee, Bill Poppen, Bob Lee, Charlie Chmielewski, Cindy Payne, David Huck, David Turner, Elle Kate Huck, Ellen Turner, Emily Huck, Gary Howe, Hadley Huck, Janine Barnett, Jared Howe, Jeannine Studer, Jim Studer, John Peterson, Jordan Howe, Kathy Huck, Lori Chmielewski, Martha Albertson, Nancy Huck, Pat Huck, Penny Gruen, Schuyler James Huck, Ted Payne, Tim Barnett, Tom McClain, Turner Huck, and Yvonne Poppen.

In addition to the people mentioned in the previous paragraph, two others deserve special recognition: Michael Carter and Matt Deaton. Michael kept me on my toes by asking questions that challenged me to think deeply about my goals, my initial decisions, and my fundamental reasons for embarking on, and staying with, this multi-year project. Michael also introduced me to his good friend, Matt. For some unexplained reason, Matt—an experienced book author and first-rate publishing consultant—took me under his wing. He offered clear answers to my naïve questions about how to get a book published; he made me aware of design and formatting options, always encouraging me to choose freely what I felt would be best; he put me in contact with experienced and trusted professionals to edit my manuscript and create my book's cover.

Without the crucial assistance provided by Michael and Matt, this book project would have withered on the vine. What I say next may seem overly sappy and sentimental, but it's true. Matt and Michael functioned as a two-person team of guardian angels who watched over me, guided me, and believed in me as I sought to create a book that might help its readers.

Finally, I want to thank my wife, Kathy. She always responded honestly when I asked for her opinion about the book's length, content, and cover design. More importantly, Kathy—my life partner and soulmate—put up with me spending lengthy periods of time thinking about and working on this book. I thank her for her inordinate patience. And, I apologize to her for it taking me so long to complete this project.

SWH

> *Find things beautiful as much as you can.*
> *Most people find too little beautiful.*

Vincent Van Gogh, 1853-1890. Born in the Netherlands, Van Gogh was a prolific painter who is now considered one of the greatest artists the world has ever seen.

During a recent 12-month period, nearly two million people visited the Van Gogh Museum in Amsterdam. Most came from foreign countries. People flock to see Van Gogh's paintings in other world-class museums, such as the Metropolitan Museum of Art in New York, the National Gallery in London, the Musée d'Orsay in Paris, and the Art Institute in Chicago. Simply stated, Van Gogh's works are among the world's most viewed artistic gems.

Van Gogh started to paint when he was 27 years old, but he died when just 37. During those ten years, he produced an incredible amount of artwork, including over 850 oil paintings. Art critics consider Van Gogh's best works to include *The Starry Night, Sunflowers, The Potato Eaters,* his various paintings of cypress and olive trees, *Wheatfield with Crows,* and a large number of self-portraits. Many of these items contain Van Gogh's vibrant colors (especially yellow), movement, and broad brushstrokes.

Sadly, Van Gogh led a troubled life. His paintings were not popular while he was alive, and he earned little money from his creations. He drank heavily and was involved with prostitutes. Van Gogh also had severe bouts of depression.

1

When Van Gogh was 35, he and Paul Gauguin shared a studio in southern France and worked together. This arrangement did not last long due to their opposing ideas and personalities. After two months, they got into a heated argument. Van Gogh was so upset he used a razor blade to cut off a part of his own left ear. Soon after that, Van Gogh entered an asylum in Saint-Rémy, France. He was institutionalized there for about a year. Two years after leaving the asylum, Van Gogh committed suicide by shooting himself in the chest with a handgun.

Van Gogh's paintings had a noticeable influence on other famous painters, especially Henri Matisse. According to several sources, Matisse's paintings were conservative during the early portion of his career. However, when he was introduced to Van Gogh's paintings in 1897, Matisse is said to have experienced "an artistic about-face," subsequently using— as in *The Dance*—the intense colors characteristic of Van Gogh's many masterpieces.

In the opinion of many art critics, Van Gogh's best painting is *The Starry Night*. Ironically, Van Gogh himself considered this work to be a failure!

Boxed Van Gogh quotation at top of previous page: Excerpt from a letter he sent in January, 1874, to his brother. Letter located in the Van Gogh Museum in Amsterdam, Netherlands.

Photo credit/attribution: Title: Photo of Van Gogh's colorful painted self-portrait; Photographer: unknown; Photo is in the public domain; Source: https://commons.wikimedia.org/wiki/File:Vincent_van_Gogh_-_Self-Portrait_-_Google_Art_Project_(454045).jpg; Original color photo has been cropped and made black-and-white.

> *The best remedy for those who are afraid, lonely, or unhappy is to go outside. ... Go outside and try to recapture the happiness within yourself. Think of all the beauty in yourself and in everything around you and be happy.*

Anne Frank, 1929-1945. During World War II, teenager Anne Frank's family hid from Nazi Germans for over two years in a concealed apartment in Amsterdam. Eventually, Anne and the others sequestered in the "Secret Annex" were discovered. All but one of them were put to death in Nazi concentration camps.
Although Anne was killed, her famous diary lives on yet today.

Beyond those well-known facts about Anne Frank, five other aspects of her life are noteworthy:

- After moving from Frankfurt to Amsterdam in 1934, Anne enrolled in a Montessori school where she had above-average skills in reading and writing.
- Anne's father tried, in 1940, to move his family to the United States. His visa request was not approved.
- Foreshadowing her enormous, enduring fame, Anne put these words in her diary on April 4, 1944: "I want to be useful or bring enjoyment to all people, even those I've never met. I want to go on living even after my death!"
- After the Franks' Secret Annex was raided and its occupants arrested, the Gestapo police deported Anne to Auschwitz, where she was a prisoner for two months. She was then relocated to the Bergen-Belsen

concentration camp. Anne died there only a short time before the Allies liberated that death camp.

- After World War II ended, Anne's father (who had survived his confinement in Auschwitz) gave Anne's diary to a historian who tried unsuccessfully to get it published. She showed the diary to her husband, who wrote a newspaper article describing Anne's life. That article was seen by a book publisher who was quite impressed. Soon, Anne's diary took the form of a book.

Anne Frank is one of the most famous and inspiring girls who has ever lived. Is there any convincing evidence to support this opinion? Yes, there exists an abundance of evidence!

To gauge Anne's status, consider these facts. Her *Diary* has been translated into more than 70 languages and is one of the most widely read books in the world. In 1999, *Time* magazine included Anne in its list of "The Most Important People of the Century." The United Nations made 1995 the International Year of Tolerance, commemorating the 50th anniversary of Anne Frank's death. Over a million people annually visit the Anne Frank Museum (housed in the original building that contained the Secret Annex where Anne Frank's family hid). Impressively, more than 270 schools—located on four continents—bear Anne Frank's name.

Boxed Anne Frank quotation at top of previous page: Excerpt from entries on March 2 and March 7 in the 1952 book, *The Diary of a Young Girl*, Garden City, New York: Doubleday & Company.

Photo credit/attribution: Title: Anne Frank passport photo, 1942; Photographer: unknown; This photo is located at the Anne Frank House, Amsterdam; Photo is in the public domain; Original photo has been cropped; Source: https://commons.wikimedia.org/wiki/File:Anne_Frank_passport_photo,_May_1942.jpg.

> *Be like the bird who, pausing in her flight awhile*
> *on boughs too slight, feels them give way beneath her,*
> *and yet sings, knowing she hath wings.*

Victor Hugo, 1802-1885. Born in Eastern France, Hugo grew up to become one of his country's best-known authors. Extremely versatile, he wrote historical accounts, poems, speeches, dramas, and books. He also was an artist, creating thousands of drawings. His best-known and most admired works are his two  novels, *The Hunchback of Notre-Dame* and *Les Misérables*.

Hugo wrote the first of his two well-known novels because he wanted the people of Paris to appreciate and care for the Cathedral of Notre Dame, the then neglected and defaced masterpiece of Gothic architecture. In this story, the hunchback Quasimodo is the 20-year-old half-deaf, half-blind bell-ringer of the Cathedral who falls in love with Esmeralda, a beautiful young Gypsy street dancer. The novel's evil antagonist is Frollo, the Cathedral's Archdeacon and Quasimodo's mean "guardian." Nearly as bad is the soldier, Phoebus. Though Esmeralda is kind and compassionate, she is unfairly executed near the end of the story. Seeing her killed, the distraught Quasimodo pushes Frollo off a Cathedral tower to his death.

In *Les Misérables*, the primary plot involves the struggles of ex-convict Jean Valjean to be a force of good in a world filled with injustice and social misery. The other main characters are police inspector Javert, who obsessively stalks Valjean; the beautiful but destitute Fantine, abandoned by her husband; Cosette, Fantine's daughter; and Marius, a law student who falls in love with the grown-up Cosette. This book was 17 years in the making.

Although Hugo is famous for what he wrote, he also was passionately involved in politics. He was a statesman, speaking out against social injustice and the death penalty. He argued for freedom of the press, free education for all children, and voting rights for everyone. Hugo's beliefs put him at odds with Napoléon, who seized power in a coup. After accusing Napoléon of being a traitor to France, Hugo went into exile. Nearly 20 years later, he returned to Paris as a national hero.

Hugo's achievements have been honored in many ways. For example, his portrait has appeared on French currency, statues of him can be found in Rome and Beijing, an important street in Paris bears his name, and he is considered a saint in one of Vietnam's many religions. However, the most significant honor came to Hugo at his funeral. This Paris ceremony was an official state affair, with two million people walking behind his casket as it was carried from the *Arc de Triomphe* to the Pantheon. He was buried there, joining luminaries such as Voltaire, Antoine de Saint-Exupéry, Louis Braille, Marie Curie, and Jean-Jacques Rousseau.

Boxed Hugo quotation at top of previous page: Excerpt from "In the Church of ***
[Dans l'eglise de ***]," Songs of Dusk [Les chants du crepuscule], #33 sec. 6 (1836).
Photo credit/attribution: Title: Cabinet Card Photo of Victor Hugo; Photographer: Bacard Fils; Source: https://commons.wikimedia.org/wiki/File:Victor_Hugo_by_Bacard_Fils_c1880.jpg; Date of photo: Between 1871 and 1885; Photo is in the public domain {{US-PD}}; Original tinted photo has been cropped and made black-and-white.

> *Life is not a spectator sport.*
> *If you're going to spend your whole life*
> *in the grandstand just watching what goes on,*
> *in my opinion you're wasting your life.*

Jackie Robinson, 1919-1972. Born in a small town in southern
Georgia, Robinson was the youngest of five
children. After his father abandoned the
family, Robinson and his remaining family
members moved to a poor area of Pasadena,
California. Robinson's athletic ability was
apparent, and his older brothers encouraged

him to play sports. Not just one sport. All sports.

In high school, Robinson lettered in four sports: football
(where he played quarterback), basketball (guard), baseball
(shortstop), and track (broad jump). He also was on the tennis
team. After graduating, Robinson attended Pasadena Junior
College. There, he again was a four-sport star. Next, Robinson
enrolled in UCLA, where, once more, he stood out in four
sports. While there, he was NCAA champion in the long jump.
After college, the talented Robinson could have pursued and
excelled in just about any sport he wanted. He chose baseball.

After serving two years in the military and three in
baseball's minor leagues, Robinson was given a chance to play
on the Brooklyn Dodgers. With that move, he became the first
African American player in the major leagues, thus breaking the
so-called "color barrier." Being black in a white man's sport,
Robinson endured racist slurs from fans and opposing team
members. Despite that abuse, he simply let his playing ability

speak for itself. In his first year with the Dodgers, he won the Rookie-of-the-Year award. Two years later, he was named the National League's MVP (most valuable player). He went on to play in six All-Star games and six World Series, and he ended his career with a .311 batting average. He later became the first black player inducted into baseball's Hall of Fame.

Robinson's baseball success helped advance the Civil Rights Movement, but so did his work in other areas. Robinson was the first black person to serve as the VP of a major American corporation. He chaired the NAACP Freedom Fund Drive. Robinson helped establish the Harlem-based Freedom National Bank. He created the Jackie Robinson Construction Company, which built housing for low-income families. In addition, he openly criticized segregated restaurants and hotels.

Because of Robinson's achievements, he was widely honored. *Time* magazine put him on its list of the "100 Most Influential People of the 20th Century." He received the Presidential Medal of Freedom and the Congressional Gold Medal. Perhaps the most treasured honor that came Robinson's way was the comment from Martin Luther King, Jr., who said that Robinson was "a legend and a symbol [who] challenged the dark skies of intolerance and frustration."

Boxed Robinson quotation at top of previous page: Excerpt from "Jackie Robinson, Civil Rights Advocate" in the Educator Resources section of the U.S. National Archives and Records Administration.

Martin Luther King, Jr. comment about Robinson: Excerpt from Rachel Robinson and John F. Kerry's article "A Pioneer in Civil Rights" published on March 2, 2005, in *The Boston Globe*.

Photo credit/attribution: Title: 1950 photo of Jackie Robinson in his Brooklyn Dodgers Uniform. Photographer: Unnamed employee of the United States Information Agency; Photo is in the public domain; Original photo has been cropped; Source: https://commons.wikimedia.org/wiki/File:Jackie_Robinson_1950_(cropped).jpg.

> *Never see a need without*
> *trying to do something about it.*

Mary MacKillop, 1842-1909. In July of 2008, Pope Benedict XVI traveled to Australia and visited MacKillop's shrine. Once there, he asserted that she was one of the most outstanding figures in her country's history. He went on to say that her "perseverance in the face of adversity, her plea for justice on behalf of those unfairly treated, and her practical example of  holiness have become a source of inspiration for all Australians." Two years later, the Pope officiated the ceremony in the Vatican during which MacKillop officially became a saint.

Living her entire life in Australia, MacKillop grew up in a low-income family. It was in that setting that she, the eldest of eight children, realized that the disadvantaged often need help. She spent the rest of her life providing assistance to others.

When MacKillop was 16, she worked in a stationery store to help her family's unstable finances. Two years later, she became the "governess" in charge of teaching her wealthy aunt and uncle's children. Sensitive to the plight of the poor, she also taught the children of the farmworkers who were employed on her relatives' estate.

At the age of 24, MacKillop was invited (along with two of her sisters) to help open a new Catholic school in a small town called Penola. Housed in a remodeled stable, the school had over 50 students. News of this new school spread, and soon several other women joined the instructional staff. These teachers called themselves the Sisters of Saint Joseph of the Sacred Heart. Their nickname was the Josephites, and their goal was to educate the poor.

MacKillop and her fellow Josephites adopted a "Rule of Life" that emphasized poverty, disallowed ownership of any personal belongings, and required a willingness to go wherever they might be needed. Many went into the Aboriginal outback. As time went on, more and more women joined the Josephites. Their focus became twofold: teaching poor children and helping destitute and socially disadvantaged women. Their dedicated work led to the creation of new schools and charitable institutions in both Australia and New Zealand. The undisputed leader of the Josephites was Mary MacKillop.

In 1925, 16 years after MacKillop died, many of her admirers began an effort to have her declared a saint. That goal was achieved in 2010, eight and a half decades after the effort had been initiated. Once canonized, MacKillop acquired a new name: Saint Mary of the Cross. She became the first Australian to be elevated by the Catholic Church to the status of a Saint.

Boxed MacKillop quotation at top of previous page: Excerpt from page 183 of Ann Neven and Patricia Thompson's 2011 article "The Educational Mission of the Sisters of Saint Joseph of the Sacred Heart in Aotearoa New Zealand: 1880s to 2010," *International Studies in Catholic Education*, Vol. 3, No. 2.

Pope Bennedict comment about MacKillop: Excerpt from the document "Welcoming Ceremony Address of His Holiness Benedict XVI." Government House, Sydney. Thursday, 17 July 2008.

Photo credit/attribution: Title: Photo of St. Mary Mackillop painting; Artist: Unknown; Photographer: Unknown; Source: https://commons.wikimedia.org/wiki/File: Painting_of_St_Mary_Mackillop-1_(5099044082).jpg; Photo is used here under the Creative Commons Attribution-Share Alike 2.0 Generic license: (https://creativecommons.org/licenses/by-sa/2.0/deed.en) [CC BY-SA 2.0]; Original color photo has been cropped and made black-and-white.

> *You conquer self-centeredness by coming to the point of seeing that you are where you are today because somebody helped you to get there.... No matter where you stand, no matter how much popularity you have, no matter how much education you have, no matter how much money you have, you have it because somebody in this universe helped you to get it.*

Martin Luther King, Jr., 1929-1968. Most people know that King was a Civil Rights leader; that he delivered his stirring "I Have a Dream" speech to 250,000 people who were in Washington, D.C., protesting racial discrimination; that he received the Nobel Peace Prize; and that he was assassinated at  the Lorraine Motel in Memphis, Tennessee, by James Earl Ray.

Beyond the more well-known facts about King's life, there are 10 lesser-known things worth knowing about this highly admired human being:

- In his youth, King both observed and experienced racial discrimination. He heard a white police officer refer to his father as "boy." He and his dad were told to move to the back of a shoe store. The white parents of King's best friend stopped allowing their son to play with King because King was black. He had to vacate his seat on a bus so a white passenger could sit.

- In school, King was an outstanding student. He skipped two years of high school, graduated from Morehouse College when just 19, and then earned a Ph.D. in theology from Boston College.

- When 29, King nearly died when a woman stabbed him in the chest at a book signing event in Harlem.
- Just as he worked to eliminate prejudice toward blacks, King tried to upgrade the status of Native Americans.
- King was frustrated by the "white moderate," the person who is more devoted to "order" and the absence of tension than to true justice for all.
- King felt that many white people in the United States treated blacks no better than India's "untouchables," who were shunned and considered dangerous.
- The preliminary, typed version of King's "I-Have-a-Dream" speech did not include the famous words: "I have a dream today." He improvised and added those words on the spot when a friend nearby shouted during his speech: "Tell them about the dream, Martin!"
- King was encouraged to run for President in 1968.
- King asked that his many awards not be mentioned at his funeral. Instead, he wanted to be remembered simply as one who did his best to "feed the hungry, clothe the naked, and love/serve humanity."
- A life-size statue of King stands above the west entrance to Westminster Abbey in London.

Boxed King quotation at top of previous page: Excerpt from a sermon (entitled "Conquering Self-Centeredness") King delivered at Dexter Avenue Baptist Church in Montgomery, Alabama, on August 4, 1957.

Comment about King's "I Have a Dream" speech: See page 107 of M. P. Vicaro's article "Haunting Dreams: Time and Affect in the Neoliberal Commemoration of 'I Have a Dream'" located in the 2018 book (edited by R. C. Aden) *Rhetorics Haunting the National Mall*, Lanham, Maryland: Rowman & Littlefield.

Photo credit/attribution: Title: 1964 photo of Martin Luther King, Jr.; Source: https://www.nobelprize.org/prizes/peace/1964/king/facts/; Artist: Unnamed photographer for the Nobel Foundation; Photo is in the public domain {{PD-US}}; Original photo has been cropped.

> *Never, for the sake of "peace and quiet,"*
> *deny your own experience or convictions.*

Dag Hammarskjöld, 1905-1961. Born in southern Sweden, Hammarskjöld had an illustrious ancestry. His father was Prime Minister, and his more distant relatives had served the Monarchy of Sweden since the 17th century.

After earning philosophy and law degrees, Hammarskjöld spent the rest of his life being a public servant. For 21 years, he was employed by the Swedish government in various jobs dealing mainly with economics. Then, at age 46, Hammarskjöld became one of his country's representatives to the United Nations General Assembly. A year later, he was elected to the UN's top position: Secretary-General.

As the leader of the United Nations, Hammarskjöld worked to defuse tensions in the world's "hot spots" (particularly in the Middle East and Central Africa). Less visible to people outside the UN was his humble and unpretentious approach to his day-to-day work routine. He made an elevator in the UN, previously reserved only for the Secretary-General, available to any UN worker. He ate in the "regular" UN cafeteria as often as possible. And he created a "meditation room" in the UN where employees of any faith could decompress and pray for peace.

Tragically, the widely respected Hammarskjöld died in a plane crash near the city of Ndola in Zambia. He was just 56 years old. On the day his plane plummeted from the sky,

Hammarskjöld was on his way to negotiate a cease-fire between opposing forces in the Republic of Congo.

Hammarskjöld authored only one book, *Markings*. It contained reflections from his diary. (He began writing in his journal when he was 20 years old; his final entry was dated the month before he died.) Many readers of Hammarskjöld's book have found one particular passage to be especially meaningful: "We are not permitted to choose the frame of our destiny; but what we put into it is ours."

Before he died, Hammarskjöld received honorary degrees from Oxford, Harvard, Yale, Princeton, John Hopkins, and several other universities. The library in the UN headquarters is named after him, as are streets in Sweden, Denmark, Norway, the Netherlands, Germany, Canada, Tunisia, and Argentina. Perhaps the grandest honor bestowed on Hammarskjöld was the Nobel Peace Prize (awarded posthumously). Almost as impressive is the comment made by President John F. Kennedy following Hammarskjöld's death: "I realize now that in comparison to him, I am a small man. He was the greatest statesman of our century."

Boxed Hammarskjöld quotation at top of previous page: Excerpt from Andrew Gilmour's article "Dag Hammarskjöld: Statesman of the Century." *The Nation*, September 9, 2013.

Hammarskjöld's passage from his diary: Page 63 of Hammarskjöld's 1964 book, *Markings*, London: Faber and Faber.

Kennedy comment about Hammarskjöld: Excerpt from Hans Göttel's online article "Diplomacy and Mysticism." *Wiener Zeitung*, Sunday, September 17, 2017.

Photo credit/attribution: Title: 1953 photo of Dag Hammarskjöld.; Source: https://commons.wikimedia.org/wiki/File:Dag-Hammarskjold-1953.jpg; Photographer: Caj Bremer; Photo is in the public domain; Original photo has been flipped horizontally and cropped.

> *Aim high and resist cynicism, even in the face of ample opportunity to become jaded and cynical.*

Ellen Johnson Sirleaf, 1938-. Born and raised in Liberia's capital city of Monrovia, Sirleaf has a life story that shows how education, courage, and determination can produce leaders who play important roles on the world's stage.

After graduating from high school in Monrovia, Sirleaf traveled to the U.S., where she first earned her B.A. in Accounting in Madison, Wisconsin. Next, she garnered a diploma in economics from the University of Colorado. Finally, she secured a Master's Degree in Public Administration from Harvard's Kennedy School of Government.

Upon returning to Liberia, Sirleaf took a job in the Ministry of Finance. Over time, she assumed various roles having more and more responsibility. Finally, she was asked to manage Monrovia's country-wide economy as the Minister of Finance. Following a military coup, Sirleaf fled Liberia and worked for five years at international financial institutions and the United Nations. In 1985, she returned to Liberia and became involved in politics. Sirleaf was outspoken about corruption and unfair elections, and she was twice imprisoned. In 1997, she ran for president, lost, and again went into exile.

After Liberia's second civil war ended in 2005, Sirleaf returned to Liberia and again ran for president. This time she won. This made her the first elected female head-of-state on the African continent. She was reelected six years later. During her

12 years as her country's leader, she worked to end discrimination toward women, improve education, expand health care, reduce the national debt, and strengthen relations with other countries. In working toward these goals, Sirleaf became a leading promoter of peace, justice, and democracy.

Because of her lengthy and impactful public service, Sirleaf received a wide variety of coveted awards and honors. She won the prestigious Indira Gandhi Prize and the equally meritorious Ibrahim Prize for African Leadership. She was awarded honorary doctoral degrees from Harvard, Yale, Dartmouth, and several other universities. She received the U.S. Presidential Medal of Freedom. She was named by Forbes magazine as one of the most powerful women in the world. Most notably, Sirleaf received the Nobel Peace Prize.

After Sirleaf's second presidential term ended, she was 80 years old. Did she retreat to her home to sit and savor her many honors and awards? No. She continues her life's work through her appointed positions on influential international boards and by means of the stirring commencement addresses she delivers worldwide.

Boxed Sirleaf quotation at top of previous page: Excerpt from Sirleaf's commencement address at Harvard University on Thursday, May 26, 2011. (Her remarks "as prepared for delivery" were published in *The Harvard Gazette*; also, her address was videotaped.)

Photo credit/attribution: Title: 2015 photo of the Liberian President at the U.S. Pentagon; Original color photo has been cropped and made black-and-white; Image is used here under the Creative Commons Attribution 2.0 Generic license (https://creativecommons.org/licenses/by/2.0/deed.en) [CC-BY 2.0]; Source: https://commons.wikimedia.org/wiki/File:Ellen_Johnson_Sirleaf_February_2015.jpg; Photographer: Sean Hurt.

> *We don't need to worry about what happens after this life, as long as we do our duty here to love and to serve.*

Albert Einstein, 1879-1955. Born and raised in Germany, young Einstein was exceptionally talented in math and physics. At age 12, he created his own proof of the Pythagorean theorem. He also taught himself calculus. After graduating from college, Einstein worked in a Swiss patent office where he evaluated others' claims of new inventions and discoveries.

Einstein published several groundbreaking papers while in his early 20s. Noting this, the University of Bern in Switzerland hired him. Later, as a 32-year-old professor at the University of Berlin, he developed his theory of relativity, successfully predicting that gravity could bend light. At the age of 43, he won the Nobel Prize "for his service to theoretical physics, and especially for his discovery of the law of the photoelectric effect."

Einstein, of course, was (and still is) considered to be a scientific genius. However, that reputation might not have been what *he* thought was his most important life accomplishment. Most likely, he felt best about his role as a humanitarian.

During World War II, Einstein's other-centered concerns saved the lives of many Jewish people who otherwise would have been murdered by the Nazi regime. He met with Winston Churchill and convinced him to invite German Jewish scientists to relocate to British universities. He wrote to

17

Turkey's Prime Minister with the same request, thus saving the lives of more than 1,000 people. Einstein even met with President Roosevelt and recommended that the United States develop the atomic bomb to prevent Germany from becoming a dominant and evil world power.

This advice Einstein gave FDR was not easy to give, for Einstein was a pacifist. However, he knew what the Germans were doing to Jews. Einstein evaluated two "negatives"— German atrocities vs. weapons development—and decided that the latter, though bad itself, was needed to deal with the former.

On a lighter note, most people do not know that Einstein loved music. He played the piano and the violin and once said: "I often think in music. I live my daydreams in music. I see my life in terms of music…. I get most joy in life out of music." He even nicknamed his violin "Lina"!

A surprising anecdote about Einstein concerns his response, when he was older, to a reporter's question. The reporter had asked if he would have been happy in a different profession. In response, Einstein said, "I think I would have enjoyed being a plumber." Learning of that statement, the Plumbers and Steamfitters Union in Washington, D.C., immediately made Einstein an honorary member of its group!

Boxed Einstein quotation at top of previous page: Excerpt from page 94 of William Hermanns' 1983 book, *Einstein and the Poet*, Brookline Village, MA: Brandon Press.

Nobel Prize quotation: https://www.nobelprize.org/prizes/physics/1921/summary/.

Einstein's music comment: Excerpt from M. Waldrop's *National Geographic* article, "Inside Einstein's Love Affair with 'Lina'—His Cherished Violin." Feb. 3, 2017.

Einstein's plumber comment: Excerpt from page 40 of John Brockman's 2006 book, *My Einstein*, New York: Vintage Books.

Photo credit/attribution: Title: Official Nobel Prize in Physics; Photographer: Unknown; Source: https://commons.wikimedia.org/wiki/File:Albert_Einstein_(Nobel).png; Photo is in the public domain {{PD-US}}. Original photo has been cropped.

> *Realize what the true object is in life—*
> *that it is not pleasure, not knowledge, not even*
> *fame—but that it is the development of character,*
> *the rising to a higher, nobler, purer standard.*

Lewis Carroll, 1832-1898. Born into a family with ten younger brothers and sisters, Carroll received his early education at home. From age 12-17, he attended a grammar school and then Rugby School (where the game of rugby originated). From there, Carroll followed in his father's footsteps and went to college at Oxford. He  graduated with honors in mathematics at age 22. Immediately, Carroll was given a lectureship at his alma mater, where he wrote and taught for the next 47 years.

In 1856, a new dean arrived at Carroll's Oxford college, Christ Church. Carroll became friends with the dean's family, often taking the dean's children on rowing trips. On one such excursion, he told the girls a story, and one of them—the 10-year-old Alice—begged him to write it down. The children of another friend of Carroll's also were enthusiastic about this same story. Such encouragement prompted Carroll to research his story's animals (and their natural habitat), elaborate on the plot, and add his own illustrations to the text he wrote.

In 1865, Carroll published his story with the title being *Alice's Adventures in Wonderland.* It was an instant success, and its popularity quickly spread far beyond the borders of England. In 1871, Carroll published a sequel, *Through the Looking-Glass, and What Alice Found There.* (This second book in the Alice series contains Carroll's famous poem, "Jabberwocky.")

Most people know that Lewis Carroll wrote *Alice's Adventures in Wonderland*, but they don't know that Carroll had other interests and talents besides story-telling. He was a top-notch mathematician who contributed to the evolving disciplines of geometry, algebra, and mathematical logic. (One of his 11 mathematical works was titled *An Elementary Treatise on Determinants, With Their Application to Simultaneous Linear Equations and Algebraic Equations*.) Carroll also was an inventor, creating, among many other things, a case for postage stamps, a writing tablet for taking notes in the dark, and a game that foreshadowed *Scrabble*. Not to be overlooked is the fact that Carroll was an adept photographer who made portraits of famous people such as the scientist Michael Faraday and the poet Alfred Lord Tennyson.

It is worth noting that Carroll's real name was Charles Lutwidge Dodgson. Dodgson's pen name was Lewis Carroll, a play on his real first and middle names. The Latin versions of those names, when translated into English and reversed in order, produce the name Dodgson is known by: Lewis Carroll.

Boxed Carroll quotation at top of previous page: Excerpt from page xx in the Preface of Carroll's 1890 book, *Sylvie and Bruno*, London: Macmillan and Company.

Photo credit/attribution: Title: 1863 photo of a portrait painting of Charles Lutwidge Dodgson; Artist: Oskar Gustav Rejlander; Photo is in the public domain {{PD-US}}; Source: http://www.educ.fc.ul.pt/docentes/opombo/seminario/alice/lewis_carroll.htm; Photo has been cropped.

> *Take things always by their smooth handle.*

Thomas Jefferson, 1743-1826. Born in the colony of Virginia, Jefferson started school when he was five years old. At age nine, he began to study French, Greek, and Latin. He loved to read, and he devoured books from his father's library.

At age 16, Jefferson entered the College of William and Mary. While there, he developed a strict daily routine that involved 15 hours of study and just six hours of sleep. He studied philosophy, physics, mathematics, logic, ethics, and rhetoric. Jefferson's broad knowledge—gained by what he was taught and what he learned on his own—laid the foundation for his impressive political career.

Upon leaving W&M, Jefferson studied law (under jurist George Wythe) and was admitted to the bar. He worked as a lawyer and was chosen to be a delegate to Virginia's House of Burgesses. He soon became a state senator, then Virginia's governor, and then a representative to the U.S. Congress.

Following terms as Minister to France (where Benjamin Franklin mentored him) and Secretary of State (having been appointed by George Washington), Jefferson ran for president in 1796. He lost that race to John Adams but became vice president because he had the second-most electoral votes. Jefferson ran again in 1800 and won, then four years later, he was re-elected president.

As most people know, Jefferson wrote the Declaration of Independence and designed Monticello, his majestic home and gardens in Virginia. People who visit Mount Rushmore in South Dakota (or see pictures of it) know that Jefferson's face is there—along with those of Abraham Lincoln, George Washington, and Teddy Roosevelt.

Beyond what is commonly known about Jefferson, six additional facts about this revered American are worth noting:

- During the presidential election of 1800, the House of Representatives broke a tie in the Electoral College and chose Jefferson over Aaron Burr to be president. It took the House six days and 36 ballots to reach this decision!
- When Jefferson acquired the Louisiana Purchase from France, he negotiated the price with Napoléon.
- Jefferson died on July 4th, 1826—the 50th anniversary of the Declaration of Independence.
- Jefferson's will stipulated that his headstone should note that he authored the Declaration of Independence, that he fought for religious freedom, and that he created the University of Virginia.
- The Jefferson Memorial in Washington, D.C., was dedicated on the 200th anniversary of Jefferson's birthday.
- A likeness of Jefferson appears on both the $2 bill and the nickel.

Boxed Jefferson quotation at top of previous page: Excerpt from his "Canons of Conduct in Life" contained in an undated letter Jefferson sent to his granddaughter, Cornelia Jefferson Randolph. This letter is contained in the Thomas Jefferson Papers, Special Collections, University of Virginia Library.

Photo credit/attribution: Title: Photo of 1801 portrait painting of Thomas Jefferson; Artist: Rembrandt Peale; Photo is in the public domain {{PD-US}}; Source: https://commons.wikimedia.org/wiki/File:Thomas_Jefferson_by_Rembrandt_Peale,_1800.jpg; Original color photo has been flipped horizontally, cropped, and made black-and-white.

> *To wall off your own suffering*
> *is to risk being eaten from the inside.*

Frida Kahlo, 1907-1954. Born in Mexico City, Kahlo is considered by art historians to be one of the greatest Mexican artists to have ever lived. Evidence of her stature is impressive. The world-famous Louvre Museum in Paris purchased one of her paintings. She was the first Hispanic woman to have her image  appear on a U.S. postage stamp. The $500 commemorative Mexican banknote bears her portrait as well as one of her paintings. In 2016, one of her paintings sold for eight million dollars.

Clearly, Kahlo is a renowned painter. Her fame is all the more impressive because she endured two highly traumatic events in her youth. At age six, she contracted polio and was confined to a bed for nine months. This disease caused her right leg to be shorter and thinner than her left leg, resulting in a limp that plagued her for the rest of her life.

Kahlo's second tragedy occurred when she was 18 years old. She was on a bus that had a horrible accident. Several other passengers were killed. Kahlo survived, but a steel beam impaled her and severely injured her spine and hip. After the accident, it took 40 surgeries to fix her body. During her lengthy recovery, Kahlo's childhood interest in painting resurfaced.

Although Kahlo initially painted works that aped European artists, she soon changed her subjects and style. From age 25 on, Kahlo chose a motif and topics that reflected

23

Mexican culture. Kahlo's signature works are her 55 engaging self-portraits, all of which display her prominent, dark eyebrows.

Several of Kahlo's self-portraits, as well as many of her other 88 paintings, are surreal. They depict topics emanating from her dreams, her unrelenting physical pain, and her belief that government and religious institutions are often selfish and dishonest. When asked why she painted so many self-portraits, Kahlo replied: "I paint myself because I am so often alone, and I am the subject I know best."

While Kahlo was living, her works were included in prestigious exhibitions, and she also earned money whenever her paintings were sold. Nevertheless, Kahlo's high-level popularity did not come until 20 years after she died. Then, it soared. She is now considered to be one of the most significant artists of the 20th century and someone who "left a heritage of some of the finest works of art in human history."

In 2002, a movie about this great painter was released. Its one-word title: *Frida*. This film was nominated for six Academy Awards and won two Oscars.

Boxed Kahlo quotation at top of previous page: Excerpt from page 420 of Carmen Fernández Díaz's article "La 'Escritura' Surrealista de Frida Kahlo" located in *Estudios Románicos*, Vol. 126, 2007-2008, pages 417-424.

Kahlo's explanation for her many self-portraits: Excerpt from page 96 of Susie Hodge's 2022 book *ArtQuake: The Most Disruptive Works in Modern Art*, London: Frances Lincoln Publishing.

Quote regarding the status of Kahlo's art: Excerpt from a scholarly paper entitled "Toulouse Lautrec and Frida Kahlo: Women, Pain, Death and Joie de Vivre" delivered by Roger Hollander on March 12, 1999, at the 2nd Symposium in Celebration of International Women's Day held in Guayaquil, Ecuador.

Photo credit/attribution: Title: Photo of Frida Kahlo; Artist: Guillermo Kahlo; Source: https://commons.wikimedia.org/wiki/File:Frida_Kahlo,_by_Guillermo_Kahlo.jpg; Photo is in the public domain {{PD-US-1996}}; Original photo has been flipped horizontally and cropped.

> *As you pay your water bill, think of others.*
> *Think of those who only have*
> *clouds to drink from.*
> *As you go home, your home, think of others.*
> *Don't forget those*
> *who live in tents.*
> *As you sleep and count the planets, think of others.*
> *There are people*
> *who have no place to sleep.*

Mahmoud Darwish, 1941-2008. Born in a small town near the Mediterranean Sea just south of Lebanon, Darwish grew up to become Palestine's most eminent poet. His first book of poetry was published when he was 19. He followed that with 29 additional volumes of poetry.

Darwish won several international awards for his poetry. These included the Lotus Prize from the Afro-Asia Writers' Association, the Forum for Arabic Poetry Prize, the Golden Wreath Award at ·Macedonia's Poetry Festival, Morocco's Prize for International Poetry, the Prince Claus Award from the Netherlands, and France's Knight of Order of Arts and Belles Lettres Medal. According to award-winning Arab-American poet Naomi Shihab Nye,

> *Darwish is the essential breath of the Palestinian people, the eloquent witness of exile and belonging, exquisitely tuned singer of images that invoke, link, and shine a brilliant light into the world's whole heart. What he speaks has been embraced by readers around the world—his in an utterly necessary voice, unforgettable once discovered.*

Darwish did more than write poetry. He also spoke out and wrote on behalf of those with little or no political power or wealth. Simply put, Darwish was a human rights advocate. In 1983, Darwish received the Lenin Peace Prize. With that high honor, he joined Nelson Mandela, Pablo Picasso, Linus Pauling, and W.E.B. DuBois, who, in other years, also were recognized for their work in "strengthening peace among peoples." In 2001, Darwish won the Cultural Freedom Prize—from the Lannan Foundation in Santa Fe—for "his courage in speaking out against injustice and oppression, while eloquently arguing for a peaceful and equitable coexistence between Palestinian Arabs and Israeli Jews."

Despite the many awards and accolades bestowed upon Darwish (including being regarded as Palestine's Poet Laureate), he was an incredibly humble human being. In an interview, he once stated: "I would not want to appear as a patriot or as a hero [but rather] as a modest poet."

Boxed Darwish quotation at top of previous page: Excerpt from page viii in Mohammad H. Tamdgidi's article, "Editor's Note: Mahmoud Darwish's Parting Gift," *Human Architecture: Journal of the Sociology of Self-Knowledge*, Vol. VII, Special Issue, 2009.

Comment about Darwish from the Lannan Foundation: Excerpt from page 67 of the 2002 article, "A Love Story Between an Arab Poet and His Land: An Interview with Mahmoud Darwish," *Journal of Palestine Studies*, Vol. 31, Issue 3.

Darwish's humble self-assessment: Excerpt from an interview Darwish had with Dalia Karpel published in *Haaretz Newspaper*, July 12, 2007.

Photo credit/attribution: Title: Photo of Mahmoud Darwish; Photographer: Don Usner (of Don J. Usner Photography, 222 March Street, Suite 7, Santa Fe, New Mexico); Source: Private correspondence on June 10, 2022, between Usner and this book's author; Original photo has been flipped horizontally and cropped.

> *Write injuries in dust, benefits in marble.*

Benjamin Franklin, 1706-1790. Most people know that Franklin was a scientist, politician, diplomat, and author. If pressed to be more specific, many people would respond by saying that Franklin invented the lightning rod and bifocals, that he was one of the "Founding Fathers" of the United States, that he was America's first Ambassador to France,  and that he published *Poor Richard's Almanack.* Some might add that Franklin was his country's first Postmaster General and that his face is on the $100 bill.

Unfortunately, most people are unaware of these other accomplishments of Franklin:

- He assisted in creating America's first public library: the Library Company of Philadelphia.
- Franklin was an educator and helped establish the academy that became the University of Pennsylvania.
- He studied population growth and influenced the thinking of Adam Smith and Thomas Malthus.
- He studied ocean currents and coined the term "gulf stream."
- Franklin had an interest in music. He played the violin and harp, composed music, and invented a glass harmonica. Impressively, both Ludwig van Beethoven and Wolfgang Amadeus Mozart composed music for this new Franklin creation!

- Franklin co-founded Philadelphia's Union Fire Company, referred to by many as the "bucket brigade." (It was the first community-focused all-volunteer fire company in North America.)
- Whereas Franklin supported slavery early in his life, he became a firm abolitionist by the time he died. In the last public action of his life, he sent Congress a petition requesting an end to slavery and the slave trade.

In addition to wanting America to become better, Franklin tried to become a better person himself. To do this, he paid attention to 13 virtues, such as frugality, sincerity, and justice. (For the virtue of industry, Franklin said: "Lose no time; be always employ'd in something useful; cut off all unnecessary actions.") He didn't concentrate on all 13 personal-improvement goals simultaneously; instead, he focused on just one a week. In the end, Franklin felt he was a better person because of his work on these 13 virtues. His attention to them contributed much, he thought, to his success and happiness.

It is interesting to note that Franklin—an avid chess player (who liked to play against and learn from better players)—is a member of the U.S. Chess Hall of Fame!

Boxed Franklin quotation at top of previous page: Excerpt from the book *Poor Richard, An Almanack for the Year of Christ 1747* authored by Richard Saunders (Franklin's pseudonym), Philadelphia: printed and sold by Benjamin Franklin.

Franklin's comment about the virtue of industry: Excerpt from page 76 of the 1914 book, *The Autobiography of Benjamin Franklin*, London: Henry G. Bohn.

Photo credit/attribution: Title: Photo of 1767 portrait painting of Benjamin Franklin; Artist: David Martin; Source #1: The White House Historical Association; Source #2: https://commons.wikimedia.org/wiki/File:Benjamin_Franklin_1767.jpg; Photo is in the public domain; Original color photo has been cropped and made black-and-white.

> *When one door of happiness closes, another opens;*
> *but often we look so long at the closed door that we*
> *do not see the one which has been opened for us.*

Helen Keller, 1880-1968. Born in Alabama, Keller was 19 months old when she contracted a severe illness. It may have been scarlet fever or meningitis. Whatever it was, Keller became unable to see or hear. As she later recounted in her autobiography, the disease made her feel like she was "at sea in a dense fog."

The daughter of the family's cook helped Keller learn over 50 "home signs" that allowed her to communicate with others. Upon seeing a doctor in Baltimore, Keller was referred to Alexander Graham Bell, who, at that time, was working with deaf children. Based on Bell's referral, Keller was next seen at Boston's Perkins School for the Blind. After meeting Keller, the School's director asked 20-year-old Anne Sullivan, an alumna who herself was visually impaired, to help the 6-year-old Keller.

Sullivan accepted the challenge of assisting Keller. Doing so became Sullivan's "life work." She lived with the young Keller, taught her to communicate, and helped her with schoolwork. Sullivan was incredibly successful in that role, for Keller went through grade school, graduated from high school, and gained admission to Radcliffe College. Keller became the first deaf and blind person in America to earn a B.A. degree (graduating *cum laude* with membership in Phi Beta Kappa).

Keller went on—with Sullivan functioning as her mentor and companion—to become an influential author, political activist, and lecturer. She traveled to 25 countries giving motivational speeches. After one of her talks—delivered on January 22, 1916, at the Mabel Tainter Memorial Building in Menomonie, Wisconsin—a story in the local newspaper stated that:

> *Helen Keller spoke of the joy that life gave her. She was thankful for the faculties and abilities she did possess and stated that the most productive pleasures she had were curiosity, imagination, the joy of service, and the happiness that came from doing things for others.*

Three additional facts about Helen Keller's amazing life are worth noting:

- In addition to advocating for people with disabilities, Keller argued for women's right to vote.
- One of Keller's many admirers and friends was Mark Twain.
- Keller's autobiography, *The Story of My Life*, was one of her 12 published books. With a focus on Anne Sullivan, it became the basis of the impressive play and movie entitled, *The Miracle Worker*. The film was nominated for five Academy Awards and won two Oscars.

Boxed Keller quotation at top of previous page: Excerpt from page 23 of Keller's 1929 book *We Bereaved*, New York: Leslie Fulenwider Publishers.

Keller's "dense fog" comment: Excerpt from page 21 in Chapter IV of Keller's 1904 book, *The Story of My Life*, New York: Doubleday, Page & Company.

Newspaper report about Keller's talk: Excerpt from page 41 of Jennifer Moss' 2016 book *Unlocking Happiness at Work*, London: Kogan Page Publishers.

Photo credit/attribution: Title: Photo of Helen Keller; Photographer: unknown; Source https://commons.wikimedia.org/wiki/File:Helen_Keller_circa_1920_-_restored.jpg; Image located at the *Los Angeles Times* Photographic Archive at the University of California, Los Angeles (UCLA); Photo is in the public domain; Original photo has been flipped horizontally and cropped.

> *Be not hasty to envy the condition of others.*

Aesop, around 620-564 BCE. Scholars know few verifiable facts about Aesop, and some doubt he even existed. Those who believe Aesop was an actual person have used information from Aristotle and others to surmise that Aesop was a Greek slave who earned his freedom because of his storytelling ability.

Despite differing beliefs about Aesop's life, most literary historians acknowledge that many of the stories referred to as "Aesop's Fables" have existed for a long time. How long? For over 2,500 years!

The typical Aesop story has two parts. First, there is a concise story written in language that is understandable by children. Some stories contain just two sentences; the longer ones have no more than a dozen.

The second part of an Aesop story is a one-sentence moral of the story. For example, the fable entitled "The Mischievous Dog" tells the story (in just five sentences) of a dog who mistakenly thinks the big bell hanging from his neck is a status symbol when, in fact, the dog's master put it there to warn people of the dog's tendency to nip at their heels. The fable's moral: "Those who achieve notoriety often mistake it for fame."

Three of Aesop's most famous fables are "The Tortoise and the Hare," "The Boy Who Cried Wolf," and "The Miser and His Gold." The first of these fables shows why we should not overlook an adversary's tenacity. The second points out how false claims of danger can cause others to disbelieve later reports of genuine peril. The last of these fables teaches that poor use of valuable possessions is no better (and possibly worse) than not having the prized belongings in the first place.

Most of Aesop's stories involved one or more animals. There are grasshoppers, ants, eagles, dogs, cats, beetles, foxes, mice, storks, goats, horses, lions, swans, bears, crabs, fish, ants, weasels, frogs, oysters, bees, snakes, wolves, and donkeys. These animals are unusual in that they talk. Their conversations with each other or with human characters provide the essential grist for each fable.

Initially, the fables passed from generation to generation via oral storytelling. Then, beginning around 400 BC, the stories attributed to Aesop took written form, first in Greek, then in Latin. Over time, more and more tales entered the collection, with writers adapting content to comply with contemporary language and customs. The fables also migrated from Greece to Europe, Asia, the Americas, and Africa.

The content of Aesop's Fables has been used as the basis of religious sermons and books, art, pieces of classical music, songs, fancy dinner plates, and theatrical plays. Aesop's Fables most assuredly are not restricted to use by children. They can be enjoyed by people of all ages!

Boxed Aesop quotation at top of previous page: Excerpt from page 49 of the book *Aesop's Fables* (translated by R. Worthington), The Floating Press, 2009.

Photo credit/attribution: Title: Statue of Aesop located in the Art Collection of Villa Albani, Roma (from century 1-5 A.D.); Artist: unknown. Photographer: Unknown; Source: https://commons.wikimedia.org/wiki/File:Aesop.jpg; Photo is in the public domain {{US-PD}}; Original color photograph has been cropped and made black-and-white.

> *Keep close to Nature's heart, yourself, and break clear away, once in a while, and climb a mountain or spend a week in the woods.... Nature's peace will flow into you as sunshine flows into trees.*

John Muir, 1838-1914. Born in Scotland, Muir was 11 when his family moved to America's Midwest. For a decade, he worked on his parents' farm and engaged in self-study. Then, Muir enrolled at the University of Wisconsin. Though there for only two years, Muir's college experience had a  dramatic impact on him. His studies in botany and geology ignited in him a life-long interest in the outdoors.

For the next few years, Muir worked at odd jobs (and had adventures) in the northern U.S. and Canada. He also took an unconventional trip, choosing off-road routes through forests and pastures on a hike from Indiana to Florida. At age 30, Muir's wanderlust years ended when he sailed from Cuba to San Francisco. From that point forward, California was his home.

Muir first visited the Yosemite area when he was 40. He was captivated by the vistas and diverse flora. Enamored by what he saw, Muir built a small cabin and inhabited it for two years. He became a well-known expert guide and valuable source of natural history, and many scientists and artists visited him, seeking his knowledge. One was Ralph Waldo Emerson. In Yosemite, Muir studied geology, but his main love was botany—especially the giant sequoia.

Worried about the mistreatment of nature by humans, Muir was an activist. He argued that Yosemite should become a national park, opposed the commercial use of such treasures, and lobbied against a proposal to form a reservoir in Yosemite. When President Theodore Roosevelt went to see Yosemite, Muir was his host for four days as they talked, rode mules through forests, and camped in the backcountry. The President ended his visit in agreement with Muir's concerns.

Besides being an explorer, naturalist, and activist, Muir was a prolific and exquisite writer. His detailed descriptions of the natural settings he saw and cared for filled 12 books and over 300 articles. Muir called America's virgin land its "home," and he always capitalized the first letter of the word, "Nature." Muir's writing inspired environmentalists, private citizens, and government officials.

Muir was called "the Patron Saint of America's Wilderness" and "a role model [for] conservationists around the world." Perhaps the highest compliment came from President Teddy Roosevelt, who said that Muir was "a man able to influence contemporary thought and action on the subjects to which he devoted his life."

Boxed Muir quotation at top of previous page: Excerpt from pages XX and 677 in the 1996 book (edited by Terry Gifford) *John Muir: His Life and Letters and Other Writings*, London: Bâton Wicks Publications.

Patron saint comment: Excerpt from page 134 of James C. Clarke's 1979 book *The Life and Adventures of John Muir*, San Francisco: Sierra Club Books

Theodore Roosevelt comment about Muir: Excerpt from page 27 of Roosevelt's article "John Muir: An Appreciation" published in *Outlook*, Vol. 109, January 16, 1915.

Photo credit/attribution: Title: 1902 photo of John Muir; Photo is in the public domain; Source: https://commons.wikimedia.org/wiki/File:John_Muir,_full-length_portrait,_facing_right,_seated_on_rock_with_lake_and_trees_in_background_LCCN95514008.jpg; Original photo has been flipped horizontally and cropped.

> *Cheerfulness, it would appear, is a matter which depends fully as much on the state of things within, as on the state of things without and around us.*

Charlotte Brontë, 1816-1855. Born in a small village in northwestern England, Charlotte had a sad family life. When she was five years old, her mother died of cancer. The following year, two of Charlotte's four sisters died of tuberculosis. Her brother was an alcoholic who died when he was 31. Despite these  enduring and sorrowful events, Charlotte and her two surviving sisters became famous authors.

Charlotte's career began with her being a teacher, and she tried to open a new school when she was in her 20s. When this school venture did not materialize, she worked for two years as a governess, a job that made her miserable. At age 30, she shifted her focus to what had long been her main passion: writing.

Charlotte had penned her first poem by the time she was 13, and her love of poetry prompted her to write more than 200 poems over her lifetime. She and her sisters self-financed the publication of their poetry, but this effort was fruitless. They sold only two copies. Moreover, publishing houses showed no interest in Charlotte's first novel, *The Professor*.

Despite the failure of *The Professor*, Charlotte did not give up. That was a wise decision, for her second novel, *Jane Eyre*, eventually made her famous. In this book, Charlotte described Jane's difficult childhood, education, work as a governess, and romantic involvement with Mr. Rochester. Charlotte discussed both the moral and spiritual concerns of her characters, and this may explain why the novel was not popular at first. It simply was out of step with the morality of mid-19th-century England. Today, however, this book is considered a masterpiece, and high schools worldwide either encourage or require students to read it.

Because of the lasting popularity of *Jane Eyre*, most people think of Charlotte Brontë as just a novelist. Her poetry is often overlooked. This is unfortunate, as her poems embody many valuable pearls of wisdom. For example, in "Pleasure," she advises her readers to enjoy and appreciate nature; in "Parting," she points out that fond memories of friendship can soften the pain and sorrow of being apart. Here, in four lines taken from her poem, "Life," she admonishes her readers to appreciate the relatively small amount of time they have to be alive on Earth:

Rapidly, merrily
Life's sunny hours flit by,
Gratefully, cheerily
Enjoy them as they fly!

Boxed Brontë quotation at top of previous page: Excerpt from chapter 3 of Brontë's 1849 novel, *Shirley*, London: T. Nelson & Sons.

Excerpt from Brontë's poem "Life": Located on page 94 of the 1848 book *Poems by Currer, Ellis, and Acton Bell*, Philadelphia: Lea and Blanchard.

Photo credit/attribution: Title: 1850 photo of George Richmond's chalk portrait of Charlotte Brontë; Photo is in the public domain {{PD-US}}; Source: https://commons.wikimedia.org/wiki/File:Charlotte_Bronte_by_George_Richmond.j pg; Photographer: Unknown; Location of portrait: National Portrait Gallery, Washington, D.C. Original color photo has been flipped horizontally and made black-and-white.

> *Do not let yourself be forced into*
> *doing anything before you are ready.*

Wilbur Wright, 1867-1912. As most U.S. citizens know (as do
many people who live elsewhere), Wilbur
Wright and his younger brother, Orville,
constructed and flew the first heavier-than-
air, machine-powered airplane. It also is well-
known that their plane's inaugural and brief
flight took place on a sandy beach in eastern
North Carolina. That famous place is called Kitty Hawk.

Although most people are familiar with what Wilbur
accomplished, few know very much about the personality and
character of this elder Wright brother. Fortunately, Ivonette
Miller, a niece of Wilbur, gives us a glimpse into her "Uncle
Wil's" traits through her recorded talks and authored accounts.
Ivonette is a trusted source of information, as she knew her
uncles well. She flew in a Wright Flyer plane in 1911, delivered
more than 100 lectures on the Wright family, received a
"Trailblazer" award from the Aviation Trail Association, and
wrote a book entitled *Wright Reminiscences*.

According to Ivonette Miller's many detailed
descriptions:
- Wilbur very much liked working with his younger
  brother in their pre-flight printing business and in their
  joint effort to build, fly, and improve the first motorized
  airplane. Ever since he was a young boy, Wilbur had
  enjoyed doing things with Orville.

- Wilbur shared many traits in common with Orville, for both had a passionate desire to discover the unknown, patience when trying to solve problems, a commitment to careful scientific experimentation, and enjoyment of children, music, and animals.
- Wilbur read widely (with a near-photographic memory for what he had seen in print) and wrote clearly.
- Wilbur was adept at arranging facts into a logical sequence.
- A leader and independent thinker, Wilbur sometimes (but not often) made decisions without first consulting with Orville.
- Wilbur's lifelong sense of humor was apparent even when he was dying of typhoid fever.
- Wilbur realized that he had a significant advantage while young: parents who encouraged intellectual curiosity.

In a letter sent in 1899 to the Smithsonian Institution, Wilbur wrote: "...human flight is possible and practicable [but] birds are the most perfectly trained gymnasts in the world and are specially well fitted for their work, and it may be that man will never equal them."

Boxed Wright quotation at top of previous page: Excerpt from page 178 of David McCullough's 2015 book *The Wright Brothers*.

Wright's letter to the Smithsonian: Excerpt from page 4 in the 1953 book (edited by Marvin Wilks McFarland) *The Papers of Wilbur and Orville Wright: Vol. 1*, New York: McGraw-Hill.

Photo credit/attribution: Title: 1905 photo of Wilbur Wright; Photographer: Orville Wright; Source: https://commons.wikimedia.org/wiki/File:Wilbur_Wright-crop.jpg; Photo is in the public domain {{PD-US}}; Original photo has been cropped.

> *Indifference is one of the worst attributes a human can have. To combat indifference, ask yourself "What can I do for another? How can I support another?" The answer ... is to choose love.*

Denis Mukwege, 1955-. Born and raised in what now is the Democratic Republic of the Congo (DRC), Mukwege is one of Africa's most well-known and celebrated individuals. To many, he is a gift from God.

Mukwege has won the Nobel Peace Prize. He has received honorary degrees from Harvard and universities in Scotland, Portugal, Belgium, France, Canada, and Sweden. He has been the recipient of a host of other prestigious awards, including the United Nations Human Rights Prize, the Four Freedoms Award, Sweden's Olof Palme Prize, and the Seoul Peace Prize. Mukwege also has been named "Hero for Africa" and "African of the Year."

You might be wondering how Mukwege has achieved such wide-scale admiration. Is it because he—a Ph.D. recipient—wrote scholarly books and articles? No. Is it because he—a Pentecostal minister—delivers memorable sermons to thousands of listeners? No. Is it because he—a trained surgeon—has invented a new medical device? No.

Mukwege never sought to be famous. He never wanted to be in the spotlight. He just did what he felt he was called to do. He used his calming demeanor, faith, and gynecological expertise to help thousands of women and girls who sustained injuries while being raped by armed rebels.

In 1999, Mukwege founded the Panzi Hospital in DRC's city of Bukavu. That hospital has treated tens of thousands of female survivors of violence, most of whom were sexually abused. Following Mukwege's lead, doctors and nurses there give patients more than just medical treatment; they provide holistic care for the trauma each patient has endured.

Mukwege does not simply treat rape victims. He also speaks out about the root cause of the rape problem. During a formal lecture in 2015, Mukwege said

> *I am calling upon us men to take responsibility, because those who rape are men. Although only a minority of men rape, the majority does not denounce. Although we may not be rapists ourselves, we do become accomplices of the crimes by not denouncing them.*

Saying such things puts Mukwege at risk. On one occasion, four armed men broke into his home and tried to assassinate him. Since then, Mukwege has received many death threats. Undeterred, he continues to argue that rapists should be incarcerated and shamed by men who treat women honorably.

Despite the many awards Mukwege has received, he likely is most proud of the moniker his patients have bestowed upon him. They call him "Dr. Miracle."

Boxed Mukwege quotation at top of previous page: Excerpt from a videotaped interview of Dr. Denis Mukwege by Emma Watson at the Emmanuel Centre in London on May 15, 2019.

Mukwege comment about men's responsibility: Excerpt from his November 11, 2015, speech in New York when he accepted the "Champion of Peace Award."

Photo credit/attribution: Title: 2018 photo of Dr. Denis Mukwege; Source: https://commons.wikimedia.org/wiki/File:Denis_Mukwege_2018.jpg; Photographer: Unknown member of UK's Foreign and Commonwealth Office; Photo is used here under the Creative Commons Attribution 2.0 Generic license (https://creativecommons.org/licenses/by/2.0/deed.en) [CC BY 2.0]. Original color photo has been cropped and made black-and-white.

> *It's one of the greatest gifts*
> *you can give yourself, to forgive.*
> *Forgive everybody.*

Maya Angelou, 1928-2014. Angelou was an extraordinarily talented human being. She received a Presidential Medal of Freedom, more than 50 honorary degrees, a National Medal of Arts, three Grammy Awards, and nominations for both a Tony Award and a Pulitzer Prize.

Angelou is remembered mainly for having been a poet, an author, and a civil rights activist. These were the three primary arenas in which she gained fame. (She was highly talented, however, in other domains as well).

Angelou's poetry focused on various topics, such as the human spirit, love, the strength of women, and the experience of being Black. One particular poem, "When Malindy Sings," points out that certain people have special gifts that others can't acquire, no matter how hard they try. Notably, Angelou was asked to read one of her poems at the presidential inauguration of William Jefferson Clinton.

As an author, Angelou focused on herself, sharing her thoughts about the events of her life. The most famous of her six autobiographies was *I know Why the Caged Bird Sings*. In it, Angelou described her horrid life as a child. When she was three, her parents divorced, and she was sent away to live with her grandmother. As an eight-year-old girl, she was raped by her mother's boyfriend. She reacted to this trauma by choosing not to talk to anyone for five years. The other books in this series focused on different phases of her adult life.

Regarding civil rights, Angelou was outspoken. She called for an end to racial discrimination and economic injustice. She argued for religious tolerance and marriage equality. Angelou did more, though, than just voice opinions. She participated in marches, raised money for organizations, and used her artistic talent to nudge others to become less ethnocentric. She also gave funds (and her name) to the Maya Angelou Center for Health Equity at Wake Forest University.

Angelou had a remarkable life for reasons other than her poems, books, and civil rights advocacy. At 16, she was a cable car conductor in San Francisco. In her 20s, she danced in a nightclub and toured Europe as a cast member in the opera, *Porgy and Bess*. In Ghana, Angelou worked as a newspaper editor. When she was 50 years old, she wrote, produced, and narrated a TV series. At 60, she directed a London play.

At the memorial service for Angelou, lofty praise for her came from two notable speakers. First Lady Michelle Obama stated that Angelou was "one of the greatest spirits our world has ever known." Former President Bill Clinton asserted that "God loaned her His voice; she had the voice of God."

Boxed Angelou quotation at top of previous page: Excerpt from an interview published in *O, The Oprah Winfrey Magazine*, May, 2013, Vol. 14, Issue 5.

Michelle Obama comment about Angelou: Office of the First Lady, Obama White House Archives, June 7, 2014.

Bill Clinton comment about Angelou: *USA Today*, June 7, 2014.

Photo credit/attribution: Title: Maya Angelou reciting her poem *On the Pulse of the Morning* at President Bill Clinton's 1993 inauguration; Source: https://commons.wikimedia.org/wiki/File:Angelou_at_Clinton_inauguration_(cropp ed_2).jpg; Photographer: Unnamed member of the U.S. government; Photo is in the public domain; Original color photo has been cropped and made black-and-white.

Leonardo da Vinci, 1452-1519. Almost everyone knows three things about the great Leonardo. The first well-known fact is that he was a renowned artist who painted the *Mona Lisa.* The second fact is that Italy was his homeland. The third thing most people know about this famous painter is that he lived during the Renaissance.

Leonardo is one of history's most celebrated painters. He was famous when alive, and his reputation has only grown in the centuries since his death. One is wise, therefore, to know the following things about this widely admired individual:

- The middle and last parts of his name, "da Vinci," mean "from Vinci," that is, "from his birth town." Vinci is located about 15 miles west of Florence.
- Known primarily for his paintings, Leonardo generated only about 30 such works during his lifetime.
- Although *Mona Lisa* is the most renowned painting in the world, it is just 30 inches tall by 21 inches wide. Leonardo worked on this famous painting for 14 years.
- Believing that music and the visual arts are symbiotic, Leonardo played the flute, sang, and composed music.
- Leonardo's revered religious work, *The Last Supper*, is the most reproduced painting in the world.
- The *Vitruvian Man* is Leonardo's drawing of a naked man, shown in two standing positions, inscribed within a circle and a square. It gets its name from an ancient

Roman architect, revealing Leonardo's belief that art, geometry, architecture, and anatomy are important.

- Leonardo was not just an artist. He had advanced skills and knowledge in several areas, including science, architecture, music, anatomy, mathematics, history, and astronomy. His breadth of interests and talent made him an authentic "Renaissance Man" (i.e., polymath).
- Leonardo invented, among other things, a helicopter, a machine gun, a tank, hydraulic pumps, musical instruments, and floating snowshoes.
- Prior to his death, Leonardo said that 60 beggars should walk behind his casket on its trip to the gravesite.

What do historians say about Leonardo? In 1568, Vasari wrote that he "cultivated his genius so brilliantly that all problems he studied he solved with ease." Nearly 500 years later, the curator at New York's Metropolitan Museum of Art praised Leonardo as "a supreme icon in Western consciousness ... whose work as an artist, scientist, inventor, and theorist has spoken across the centuries with an astonishing modern voice."

Boxed Leonardo quotation at top of previous page: Excerpt from page 41 in the 1906 book *Thoughts on Art and Life by Leonardo da Vinci* (translated by Maurice Baring), Boston: The Merrymount Press.

Vasari comment about Leonardo: Excerpt from page 291 of Jackson J. Speilvogel's 2016 book, *Western Civilization: A Brief History*, Boston: Cengage Learning.

Curator comment about Leonardo: Excerpt from page 3 of Carmen C. Bambach's 2003 book (that she edited), *Leonardo da Vinci: Master Draftsman*, New York: Metropolitan Museum of Art.

Photo credit/attribution: Title: George Cook's line engraving of Leonardo da Vinci; Original tinted photo has been cropped and made black-and-white. Source: https://commons.wikimedia.org/wiki/File:Leonardo_da_Vinci._Line_engraving_by_ G._Cooke._Wellcome_V0006064.jpg; Photo is used here under the Creative Commons Attribution 4.0 International license (https://creativecommons.org/licenses/by/4.0/deed.en) [CC BY 4.0].

> *If you want others to be happy, practice compassion.*
> *If YOU want to be happy, practice compassion.*

Tenzin Gyatso, 1935 -. Born into a farming family living in a tiny Chinese town, Gyatso was just four years old when he became the 14th Dalai Lama. This event occurred without a vote or a genealogical connection between Gyatso and the deceased 13th Dalai Lama. Instead, Gyatso was chosen following a search by  senior Tibetan Buddhist monks. As had been customary for generations, those monks used a combination of predictions, tests, and signs to lead them to Gyatso.

When Gyatso was old enough after being named the Dalai Lama, his monastic education began. He studied ten subjects, including Buddhist philosophy, logic, medicine, poetry, and drama. When he turned 15, Gyatso became the spiritual leader of the Tibetan people. He continued his studies, and at 23, he earned the equivalent of a Ph.D. in Buddhist philosophy.

As Dalai Lama, Gyatso promotes Buddhist values and traditions, and he works to unify different religious sects. In addition to being Tibet's spiritual leader, he also functions as "head of state." In this latter role, Gyatso represents the Tibetan people in their struggle to be independent of Chinese rule.

The 14th Dalai Lama has authored over 110 books and an impressive essay entitled: *The Ethic of Compassion.* In this essay, he argues that we all have a responsibility to be compassionate to everyone, not just those we like or love. He also states that to have genuine compassion, you must have feelings of equality with those with whom you are trying to be compassionate. Gyatso shares a simple technique he uses to achieve this goal: "I try to treat whoever I meet as an old friend…. It is the practice of compassion."

Gyatso has traveled to more than 67 countries on six continents to give talks to both Buddhist and non-Buddhist groups. The topics of these talks have included peace, ethics, the environment, the empowerment of women, other social issues, and the danger of nuclear weapons. Gyatso is always exceedingly well-received wherever he goes.

In recognition of his work, Gyatso has received a slew of awards, ceremonial citizenships, prestigious prizes and medals, and honorary degrees from a host of universities. Moreover, he has met with kings and queens, presidents and prime ministers, scientists and philosophers, and religious leaders worldwide. Impressively, he received the 1989 Nobel Peace Prize for his non-violent struggle to liberate Tibet from control by China.

Boxed Gyatso quotation at top of previous page: Excerpt from "Educating the Heart" posted online by the Dalai Lama Center for Peace+Education, December 8, 2013.
Gyatso comment about compassion: Excerpt from the Dalai Lama's online message entitled "Compassion and Human Values/Compassion and the Individual."
Photo credit/attribution: Title: Circa 2015 photo of the Dalai Lama; Source: https://commons.wikimedia.org/wiki/File:Hh_Dalai_Lama_(153287781).jpeg; Photo is used here under the Creative Commons CC0 1.0 Universal Public Domain Dedication (https://creativecommons.org/publicdomain/zero/1.0/deed.en) [CC0 1.0]; Photographer: Lonyi; Original color image has been cropped and made black & white.

> *If one by one we counted people out*
> *for the least sin, it wouldn't take us long*
> *to get so we had no one left to live with.*
> *For to be social is to be forgiving.*

Robert Frost, 1874-1963. Born in San Francisco but raised mainly in New England, Frost had various jobs as a teenager. Even then, however, his love was poetry. His first "public" poem appeared in his high school magazine. Soon after that, he sold a different poetic verse (about a butterfly) to a weekly periodical published in New York City.

During the early part of his adult life, Frost was a teacher, and he also worked on his family's farm. In that period, though, he was happier when he was able to spend time writing poetry. Few of his poems, however, were accepted for publication. To get more exposure for his poetry, Frost and his family moved to London in 1912, where they stayed for three years. There, critics considered his work to be outstanding.

Upon returning to Boston, literary critics viewed him as a bright new star among American poets. Frost's reputation grew until he was considered to be one of his country's greatest poets. His most well-known poem is *The Road Not Taken*. It ends with the famous lines: "Two roads diverged in a wood, and I— / I took the one less traveled by, / And that has made all the difference."

During his life, Frost wrote poetry about rural settings, farm life, and people's connections with—and alienation from—one another. His poem, *The Mending Wall*, focuses on the literal and figurative barriers people erect to keep others at a distance, often without realizing the consequence of their actions. Midway through this powerful poem, Frost sets forth some advice for his reader: "Before I built a wall I'd ask to know / What I was walling in or walling out / And to whom I was like to give offense."

Frost earned four Pulitzer Prizes and a Congressional Gold Medal. He was Vermont's first Poet Laureate. He received honorary doctoral degrees from over 40 colleges and universities, including Oxford, Cambridge, and Princeton. At Harvard, he was made an honorary member of Phi Beta Kappa.

When Frost turned 75 years old, the U.S. Senate passed a resolution in his honor stating that: "His poems have helped to guide American thought and humor and wisdom, setting forth to our minds a reliable representation of ourselves." Perhaps Frost's grandest honor came in 1960 when he was chosen to read one of his poems at President John F. Kennedy's inauguration.

Boxed Frost quotation at top of previous page: Excerpt from Frost's poem *The Star-Splitter* located in his 1923 book *New Hampshire*, New York: Henry Holt and Company.

U.S. government resolution honoring Frost: Senate Resolution No. 233, March 24, 1950, located in box 4 of the Robert Frost Family Collection at the Special Collections Research Center, University of Michigan., Ann Arbor, Michigan.

Photo credit/attribution: Title: Photo of Robert Frost about 40 years old; Source: https://commons.wikimedia.org/wiki/File:Robert_Frost,_1910s.jpg; Photographer: Unknown; Location of photo: Library of Congress; Photo is in the public domain; Original photo has been cropped.

> *Life is not easy for any of us. But what of that?*
> *We must have perseverance and above all*
> *confidence in ourselves.*

Marie Skłodowska-Curie, 1867-1934. Born and raised in Poland, Curie grew up to become one of the world's leading scientists of her time. After earning her Ph.D. in France, Curie remained there to work. Her pioneering scientific achievement involved radiation (where she coined the term "radioactivity").

Curie founded and served as the first Director of the Radium Institute at the University of Paris. As Director of the Red Cross Radiology Service, she helped save thousands of lives in World War I by creating mobile vehicles and hospital units that took x-rays. Her research also led to the use of radiation therapy in medicine.

Because of Marie Curie's groundbreaking work—including the discovery of two radioactive chemical elements: Polonium (named in honor of her beloved homeland, Poland) and Radium—she became the first woman to win the Nobel Prize. She also was the first person, male or female, to win two Nobel Prizes: one in chemistry, the other in physics. Curie also received several honorary academic degrees and prestigious medals.

After she died, Curie was honored by having three radioactive minerals named after her, by being voted the most inspirational woman in science, and by having museums and universities renamed after her. Perhaps her highest honor came when she was buried at the Panthéon in Paris. It is the final resting place of luminaries such as Voltaire, Victor Hugo, Rousseau, Louis Braille, Alexandre Dumas, and Saint-Exupéry.

Though known best because of her brilliant scientific mind, "Madame Curie" possessed three lesser-known yet highly admirable traits: honesty, humility, and other-centeredness. She returned money to a scholarship fund after she began making a living. She distributed much of the money she received from her first Nobel Prize to research associates, students, family members, and friends. She chose not to patent her radium-isolation process so others could use it. She refused to accept many awards and medals or accepted them with the stipulation that the associated monetary funds be given to scientific institutions, not her.

One of the highest compliments to Curie came from the theoretical physicist Albert Einstein. In a personal letter addressed to "Highly esteemed Mrs. Curie," Einstein wrote:

> *I am impelled to tell you how much I have come to admire your intellect, your drive, and your honesty, and that I consider myself lucky to have made your acquaintance.*

Boxed Curie quotation at top of previous page: Excerpt from a letter she sent to her brother, Joseph, on March 18, 1894. Located on page 222 in Eve Curie's 1937 book *Madame Curie: A Biography* (translated by Vincent Sheean), New York: Doubleday, Doran & Company.

Einstein comment about Curie: Excerpt from the letter sent by Einstein to Curie on November 23, 1911. That letter is contained in Volume 8 of *The Collected Papers of Albert Einstein.*, Princeton, New Jersey: Princeton University Press.

Photo credit/attribution: Title: Photo of Marie Curie circa 1920; Photographer: Henrie Manuel; Photo is in the public domain {{PD-US}}; Source: https://commons.wikimedia.org/w/index.php?search=marie+curie&title=Special:Me diaSearch&go=Go&type=image; Original photo has been cropped.

> *People say: "Oh, if I were only rich, I would do great things to help people." But we all can be rich in love and generosity. Moreover, if we give with care, if we find out the exact wants of those who need our help the most, we are giving our own loving interest and concern, which is worth more than all the money in the world.*

Albert Schweitzer, 1875-1965. Born in a small village in Germany, Schweitzer was a highly educated and multi-talented individual who earned two advanced degrees. He was admired by those who knew him. He was a true "Renaissance Man" with wide-ranging, awe-inspiring accomplishments.

Schweitzer is remembered most for his other-centered medical work in Africa. In the town of Lambaréné, in what now is the country of Gabon, Dr. Schweitzer founded a hospital that treated thousands of poor people, many of whom were lepers. Citing Schweitzer's "altruism, reverence for life, and tireless humanitarian work," the Norwegian Nobel Committee awarded him its 1952 Peace Prize.

In addition to being a humanitarian who worked in Africa, Schweitzer was a philosopher. Having earned a Ph.D. in philosophy, he wrote two books, *The Religious Philosophia of Kant* and *The Philosophy of Civilization*. In these and his other philosophical writings, Schweitzer focused on ethics. His work led him to say that people should live in service to all living creatures, both human beings *and* animals.

Schweitzer also was an acclaimed musician. Adept when playing different instruments, his specialty was the organ. When he was 18, he played it in front of the French master Charles-Marie Widor. The Frenchman was so impressed with Schweitzer that he agreed to teach him for free. The two became life-long friends and professional colleagues. The Widor-Schweitzer duo helped create the Paris Bach Society, and they published a definitive six-volume treatise on Bach's organ compositions.

Besides his humanitarian, philosophical, and musical achievements, Schweitzer was a theologian. Trained at and then hired by the Theological College of Saint Thomas in Strasbourg, Schweitzer was a New Testament scholar. One of his two most famous theological books focused on Jesus, the other on Paul the Apostle.

Schweitzer's work did not go unnoticed. He received several honorary degrees from universities in Europe and America. Queen Elizabeth II made him an honorary member of England's Order of Merit, a group of honorees that even today cannot have more than 24 living members. Einstein compared Schweitzer to Gandhi, and Winston Churchill referred to him as "a genius of humanity."

Boxed Schweitzer quotation at top of previous page: Excerpt from page 309 in the 1947 book, *Albert Schweitzer: An Anthology* (edited by Charles R. Roy), Boston: The Beacon Press.

Churchill comment about Schweitzer: Page 64 of Michael J. Thate's 2013 book *Remembrance of Things Past?* Tübinger, Germany: Mohr Siebeck.

Photo credit/attribution: Title: 1955 photo of Albert Schweitzer; Source: https://commons.wikimedia.org/wiki/File:Albert_Schweitzer_1955.jpg; Photographer: Rolf Unterberg; Photo is used here under the Creative Commons Attribution-Share Alike 3.0 Germany license (https://creativecommons.org/licenses/by-sa/3.0/de/deed.en) [CC BY-SA 3.0 DE]; Original photo has been flipped horizontally and cropped.

> *Always be on the lookout for*
> *the coming of wonders.*

E. B. White, 1899-1985. Born in a suburb of New York City, White joined a family of high-achievers. His father was a prominent piano manufacturer; an older brother became a professor and inventor. Both served as success-oriented role models.

While a student at Cornell University, White was editor of his school's newspaper and a member of the exclusive Quill and Dagger Society. After graduation, he worked for newspapers and an advertising agency in Seattle. Following those jobs, White moved east and was hired by *The New Yorker* magazine. He contributed well-liked essays, poetry, and cartoons to its pages for nearly 60 years, thus helping it develop the stellar reputation it has today.

In addition to his magazine contributions, White wrote beloved books. Among these works are his two children's classics, *Charlotte's Web* and *Stuart Little*, books that are cherished still today by young and old alike. These works repeatedly show up in surveys as the most popular children's books of all time. The last of White's triad of children's books is *The Trumpet of the Swan*.

In addition to his children's stories, White is widely known for his relatively thin but highly useful book (co-authored with William Strunk) that teaches how to write clearly, effectively, and concisely. This easy-to-read classic, entitled *The Elements of Style*, is a goldmine of clearly articulated tips for any author, with advice given for good grammar, effective composition, and wise choice of words. Not to be overlooked, White published three different anthologies of his work: *Writings from the New Yorker 1927-1976*, *E. B. White on Dogs*, and *E. B. White on Democracy*.

Understandably, White's accomplishments brought him prestigious awards and recognition. These included a Newbery Honor, the Laura Ingalls Wilder Medal, the Presidential Medal of Freedom, a Gold Medal from the American Academy of Arts and Letters, and a Pulitzer Prize Special Citation. White was also a two-time U.S. nominee for the Hans Christian Andersen Award, the highest international recognition given to authors of children's books.

Two other interesting facts about White are connected to his name:

- Most people aware of White's work have no idea what his initials stand for. They are, surprisingly, nothing but proxies for his first and middle names: Elwyn Brooks.
- While attending college at Cornell, White acquired the nickname "Andy." Why? Because it was a tradition there among students to use that nickname for anyone whose last name was White, thereby honoring Cornell's co-founder, Andrew White.

Boxed White quotation at top of previous page: Excerpt from page 85 in his 1952 book *Charlotte's Web*, New York: Harper & Row.

Photo credit/attribution: Title: Family photo of E. B. White; Source: https://commons.wikimedia.org/wiki/File:EB_White_(headshot).png; Photo is used here under Creative Commons Attribution-Share Alike 3.0 Unported license (https://creativecommons.org/licenses/by-sa/3.0/deed.en) [CC BY-SA 3.0]; Photographer: unknown; Original tinted photo has been rotated slightly, cropped, and made black-and-white.

> *You say, "If I had a little more,*
> *I should be very satisfied." You make*
> *a mistake. If you are not content with what you*
> *have, you would not be satisfied if it were doubled.*

Charles Haddon Spurgeon, 1834-1892. Born in Southeast England, Spurgeon had a religious "conversion" when he was 16 years old. Within 12 months, he had become a Sunday school teacher and had delivered his first sermon. At age 19, Spurgeon took a job as the head preacher at a large church in London that  had seen a downturn in membership and Sunday attendance. He became popular, and before long, he was a renowned preacher, orator, and author. In 1861, the church moved to a newly-built, gigantic building.

Spurgeon's sermons reportedly kept parishioners spellbound in London's Metropolitan Tabernacle. The typical attendance was 5,000 people seated in pews, with an additional 1,000 standing. On occasion, he preached to more than 10,000 listeners. Because of his popularity, Spurgeon became known as "the Prince of Preachers."

Although Spurgeon wrote out the entirety of each of his sermons, he never read them on Sunday mornings. Instead, he spoke extemporaneously, referring only to brief notes. His message was recorded by stenographers, quickly printed, translated into more than 30 languages, and then widely circulated. Over time, this produced the most extended continuous publication of weekly sermons in history.

In addition to preaching, Spurgeon was a prolific writer. His works included books, poetry, magazine articles, hymns, and an autobiography. Within these various works (and during his sermons), Spurgeon shared thousands of his maxims. Most were about God, faith, and prayer, but several were nonreligious in nature. Two such maxims said, "An ounce of heart knowledge is worth a ton of head learning" and "We waste far too much of our time upon trifles."

As Alex DiPrima noted, Spurgeon was a social activist, for he was "an outspoken advocate for the oppressed, the poor, and the disenfranchised of almost every conceivable variety." He also was a staunch abolitionist, corresponding with Frederick Douglass and speaking out about the travesty of slavery in America.

Spurgeon's legacy is embodied in two of the organizations he founded. They operate even now, long after his death. One is "Spurgeon's," a charitable organization in the UK that helps vulnerable families and children. The other is Spurgeon's College, a London-based educational institution that provides theological training to both men and women.

Boxed Spurgeon quotation at top of previous page: Excerpt from page 154 of his 1894 book *Sermons Preached and Revised by Rev. C. H. Spurgeon, Minister of the Chapel, During the Year 1859* (Vol. V), London: Passmore & Alabaster.

Spurgeon's maxim about heart learning: Excerpt from the October 14/Morning entry in the 2010 book *Mornings and Evenings with Spurgeon* (edited by Larry and Marion Pierce), Green Forest, Arkansas: New Leaf Publishing Group.

Spurgeon's maxims about time spent on trifles: Excerpt from a sermon he delivered July 7, 1872.

DiPrima comment about Spurgeon: Excerpt from his online article "What Did Charles Spurgeon Think About Social Activism?" June 18, 2020

Photo credit/attribution: Title: 1934 photo of Charles Haddon Spurgeon; Source: https://commons.wikimedia.org/wiki/File:Spurgeon.png; Photographer: unknown; Photo is in public domain; Original tinted photo has been flipped horizontally, cropped, and made black-and-white.

> *There are many persons ready to do what is right*
> *because in their hearts they know it is right.*
> *But they hesitate, waiting for the other fellow*
> *to make the first move and he, in turn, waits for you.*

Marian Anderson, 1897-1993. Born into a low-income family
in Philadelphia, Anderson was a gifted
singer, even at a young age. She sang in
church and anywhere else where she
could gain experience and learn from
others. Following high school, she applied
to the Philadelphia Music Academy but
was denied admission because she was black. Undeterred,
Anderson sought out private teachers. Her persistence paid off.

When Anderson was 28, she won 1st place in a singing
competition sponsored by the New York Philharmonic. A year
later, she was invited to sing in New York City's Carnegie Hall.
Soon after that, she sang in Chicago's Orchestra Hall.

Anderson's performance in Chicago was so good that
she was encouraged to seek financial support. She applied and
was awarded a fellowship, using its funds to study and perform
in Europe. She sang in Salzburg, London, Helsinki, and other
cities. High-powered musical gurus—like Sibelius and
Toscanini—heard her and immediately recognized that
Anderson had incredible musical talent.

Back in America, Anderson held an open-air concert in
1939 at the Lincoln Memorial in Washington. Over 75,000
people attended this event, and millions more heard Anderson's
performance on the radio. First Lady Eleanor Roosevelt helped

set up this concert after the white-only members of the Daughters of the American Revolution, in a racist-motivated decision, refused to let Anderson sing in Constitution Hall. (Roosevelt had been a DAR member but resigned—as did thousands of others—over the organization's bigoted decision.)

At her alternative Washington venue, Anderson stood at a microphone in front of Abraham Lincoln's statue. Many expected her to comment on the DAR's decision that prevented her from singing in Constitution Hall. She didn't say a word about that. Instead, she just sang, like only she could, with a voice that stirred the emotions of all who listened. With patriotic emotion, her opening song began with these 13 words: "My country, 'tis of thee, sweet land of liberty, of thee I sing."

Anderson's accomplishments brought her many awards and honors. She was asked to sing at the Eisenhower and Kennedy inaugurations. She was the first African-American to sing at the Metropolitan Opera in New York. She served as a Goodwill Ambassador for the U.S. and as a delegate to the United Nations Human Rights Committee. She received the United Nations Peace Prize. Significantly, Anderson was the first person to receive the U.S. Presidential Medal of Freedom.

Anderson's ancestry should not go unnoted. She was the great-granddaughter of an enslaved person.

Boxed Anderson quotation on previous page: Excerpt from page 310 of her 1956 book, *My Lord, What a Morning: An Autobiography*, New York: Viking Press.
Photo credit/attribution: Title: 1933 photo of Marian Anderson; Source: https://commons.wikimedia.org/wiki/File:Marian_Anderson_1933_(121327138).jpg; Photo is used here under the Creative Commons Attribution 2.0 Generic license (https://creativecommons.org/licenses/by/2.0/deed.en) [CC BY 2.0]; Original photo has been cropped.

> *When you witness an injustice: Don't stand idly by. When you hear of a person or group being persecuted: Do not stand idly by. When there is something wrong with the community around you or far away: Do not stand idly by. You must intervene. You must interfere.*

Elie Wiesel, 1928-2016. Wiesel was born in Sighet, a picturesque Romanian mountain town located next to the country's northern border. In 1940, Wiesel's hometown became part of Hungary after a territorial dispute. Soon, Hungary sided with Germany in World War II, and Nazi forces infiltrated Hungarian territories, including Sighet.

When Wiesel was 15 years old, his family was put into a confinement ghetto along with nearly 13,000 other Jews from towns and cities in what had been northern Romania. From there, Wiesel's family was deported to the Auschwitz concentration camp, wherein Wiesel's mother and a sister were immediately killed in a gas chamber. Wiesel and his father were transferred to the Buchenwald concentration camp. There, Wiesel's father was beaten and killed.

Elie Wiesel survived the Holocaust when the U.S. Army liberated Buchenwald in April, 1945. For 10 years after World War II ended, Wiesel would not talk or write about his Holocaust experience. During that period, he studied and worked as a journalist in France. A close friend eventually convinced him to "open up." Wiesel did so, writing a 900-page memoir entitled *Night*. This book has sold more than 10 million copies in the U.S. and has been translated into 30 languages.

After Wiesel moved to New York in 1956, he penned more than 60 books. Most are non-fiction "insider" descriptions of the Holocaust. These works often are advertised as having been written by "The Conscience of the World."

In addition to being an author, Wiesel was a political activist, a teacher, and a speaker. In all three roles, he opposed nuclear weapons, supported the oppressed, and argued that being silent, neutral, and uninvolved allows tyranny and injustice to prevail. In Wiesel's 1986 Nobel Lecture, he said, "There may be times when we are powerless to prevent injustice, but there must never be a time when we fail to protest."

Not surprisingly, Wiesel was asked to be chairman of the U.S. Presidential Commission that guided the construction of the Holocaust Museum in Washington. He also received numerous prestigious awards and honors for his work. These included the Nobel Peace Prize, the U.S. Presidential Medal of Freedom, the French Legion of Honor's Grand Croix, and more than 100 honorary doctoral degrees.

Boxed Wiesel quotation at top of previous page: Excerpt from his May 20, 2011 commencement address (entitled "Memory and Ethics") at Washington University in St. Louis.

Wiesel's Nobel Lecture quote: Excerpt from page 81 of Heather Lehr Wagner's 1977 book *Elie Wiesel: Messenger for Peace,* New York, NY: Chelsea House Publishing.

Photo credit/attribution: Title: Undated photo of Elie Wiesel; Source: https://commons.wikimedia.org/wiki/File:Dr._Mashkevitch_and_Nobel_Peace_Priz e_Winner_Elie_Wiesel.JPG; Photographer: Sbakuria; Photo is in the public domain; Original color photo has been cropped and made black-and-white.

> *You give little when you give of your possessions.*
> *It is when you give of yourself that you truly give.*

Khalil Gibran, 1883-1931. Born in what now is Lebanon, Gibran's early life was a struggle. His father gambled, drank heavily, went into debt, and was imprisoned for embezzling. Authorities then confiscated the family's property. After he and his mother moved to the slums of Boston, his mother was a peddler selling linen and lace.

When Gibran was 15, his mother sent him back to their homeland to continue his formal education at Beirut's Collège de la Sagesse. There, things began to improve. He started a collegiate literary magazine and was elected "college poet." After graduating (with honors), Gibran returned to Boston and became an accomplished artist and writer. Greenwich Village in New York City was his next destination, and there he associated with many artists and writers.

Gibran's literary career took off when he was about 30. Initially, he expressed himself via "prose poems" published in newspapers. Gibran also wrote short stories and books, some of which contained parables from, and philosophical dialogue between, the characters. He also penned plays, political essays, and fables.

In 1923, Gibran published his most well-known work, *The Prophet*. This book's fictional story focuses on Almustafa, a prophet who has lived away from home for 12 years. He is now about to board a ship to return to his birth island. Before departing, several of the city's residents ask Almustafa to share his wisdom concerning "great issues" of human existence. Almustafa then reveals his thoughts on 26 topics, such as love, friendship, beauty, giving, freedom, and death. This beloved book has been translated into more than 100 different languages.

Despite *The Prophet*'s immense and enduring popularity, most people are unaware that Gibran was an artist as well as an author. Among his hundreds of drawings are portraits of William Butler Yeats, Carl Jung, and Auguste Rodin. Several museums—such as New York's Metropolitan Museum of Art, the Gibran Museum in Lebanon, and the Harvard Art Museums in Cambridge, Massachusetts—display Gibran's oil and watercolor masterpieces.

Is Gibran's first name "Khalil" or "Kahlil"? The first of these spellings is what Gibran's parents bestowed upon him at birth. According to one source, Gibran was forced (by a teacher at the Boston school he attended from 1895 to 1897) to change "Khalil" to "Kahlil." The latter of these spellings is what one often sees in places where English is the spoken and written language.

Boxed Gibran quotation at top of previous page: Excerpt from page 23 of his 1925 book *The Prophet*, New York: Alfred A. Knopf.

Photo credit/attribution: Title: Photo of self-portrait of Khalil Gibran during his youth; Source: https://commons.wikimedia.org/wiki/File:Khalil_Gibran_Self_Portrait.png; Photographer: unknown; Original tinted image has been flipped cropped and made black & white.

> *Happiness is a state of mind.*
> *You can be happy or you can be unhappy.*
> *It's just according to the way you look at things.*

Walt Disney, 1901-1966. Almost everyone knows about Disney movies (such as *The Lion King, Beauty and the Beast,* and *Frozen*) and Disney theme parks (like those in California, Florida, Paris, and Hong Kong). However, most people know very little about Walt Disney, the man who created a worldwide entertainment empire.

What made Disney so successful? Biographers highlight eight personality characteristics that collectively provide an answer to that question.

- As he pursued an adult career, he never turned his back on the talent and passion he had as a child: a love for drawing (especially cartoons), trains, and photography.
- Disney was a perfectionist, and as such, he wanted those who worked for him to have the highest possible standards for the quality of their work.
- He took risks. He invested vast amounts of money on projects that might fail. Some of his projects *did* fail. However, he learned from his mistakes and kept moving forward, taking more risks when necessary.
- Disney adapted to changing times and new developments in film-making, especially animation.
- Disney was a charismatic leader. He was energetic, lively, and enthusiastic about his company's projects.

(Those traits influenced others to be optimistic, upbeat, and innovative.) Along with those attributes, Disney exuded honesty, confidence, courage, and persistence.

- Disney partnered with his brother, Roy, who had a complementary set of skills. Walt was the artist, the creative genius, the visionary; Roy, on the other hand, was a financial expert who enjoyed dealing with numbers, accountants, and lawyers.
- He went out of his way to support his employees in personal ways. Many people who worked for Disney viewed him as their protector and defender.
- Disney never sat back and "rested on his laurels" after a project turned out to be an immense success. He had an insatiable appetite for creating the "next" new entertainment item for people.

Disney was human, of course, and he wasn't perfect in either his personal or professional life. Nonetheless, Walt Disney was and remains (long after his death) a cultural icon. Most likely, the vast majority of the people living on Earth are familiar with the word "Disney."

Boxed Disney quotation at top of previous page: Excerpt from comments made by Walt Disney while being interviewed by Fletcher Markle on September 25, 1963. (This remark appeared on page 102 of Kathy Merlock Jackson's edited book, *Walt Disney: Conversations*, Jackson, Mississippi: University Press of Mississippi.)
Photo credit/attribution: Title: 1946 photo of Walt Disney; Photographer: Unknown; Source: https://commons.wikimedia.org/wiki/File:Walt_Disney_1946.JPG; Photo is in the public domain; Original image has been flipped horizontally and cropped.

> *In the pursuit of wealth,*
> *the main design of its acquisition*
> *should be to expend it for noble purposes.*

Moses Maimonides, 1135-1204. Born in Spain to highly educated Jewish parents, Maimonides and his family moved to Morocco when the Islamic empire expanded in the Mediterranean region and eliminated religious freedom. The family moved again before ending up in Egypt.

Maimonides spent most of his adult life in a town near Cairo. There, he became an acclaimed Middle Ages physician, scientist, and philosopher. More importantly, he was an eminent rabbi and scholar who wrote extensively on the Jewish religion. Maimonides was considered to be "a thinker for the ages."

Of the vast array of written works produced by Maimonides, the most famous were *Mishneh Torah* and *Guide for the Perplexed.* It took Maimonides 10 years to prepare the first of these works, and he continued to edit it until his death. It took that long to write it because of its massive content: nearly 1,000 chapters spread across 14 books. The focus of this gigantic work was the totality of Jewish Law. The philosophical basis of the Jewish religion was considered, but so too were practical matters. For example, in the section called "Gifts to the Poor," Maimonides wrote:

> *One who reaps his field should not reap the whole field entirely but rather should leave a little bit of standing grain for the poor.*

On the surface, *Guide for the Perplexed* was written for a former pupil who had become confused and bewildered about religious matters. However, this work was actually aimed at Jewish intellectuals who posed, and then tried to answer, esoteric, philosophical/religious questions (e.g., "Can we prove that God exists?"). In addressing such questions, Maimonides assumed his readers to be highly educated, able to follow complex arguments involving logic, thoroughly knowledgeable of what is in the Old Testament, and familiar with Aristotelian ideas. Lacking these attributes, a reader of *Guide for the Perplexed* likely would become even more perplexed!

Today, one might ask, "How important were/are the works of Maimonides?" The clear answer is: profoundly important. Maimonides influenced other luminaries such as Saint Thomas Aquinas and Sir Isaac Newton, and his works are studied even now, more than 800 years after he died.

In 1985, a UNESCO-sponsored scholarly conference held in Paris focused on just one topic: Maimonides. Highly respected Professor Shlomo Pines summed up the thoughts of most attendees when he stated: "Maimonides is the most influential Jewish thinker of the Middle Ages, and quite possibly of all time."

Boxed Maimonides quotation at top of previous page: Excerpt from page 70 the 1912 book (edited and translated by Joseph Isaac Gorfinkle) *The Eight Chapters of Maimonides on Ethics*, New York: Columbia University Press.

Comment about Maimonides from Professor Pines: Excerpt from Richard J. Ostling's article in *Time* magazine "Religion: Honoring the Second Moses: Muslims and Jews Unite in Paying Tribute to a Medieval Sage," Monday, December 23, 1985.

Photo credit/attribution: Title: Medieval engraving of Moses ben Maimonides; Source: https://commons.wikimedia.org/wiki/File:Maimonides.jpeg; Photo is in the public domain {{PD-US}}. Original tinted photo has been cropped and made black-and-white.

> *Do not judge any deed,*
> *never mind how base it may appear,*
> *till you know all of the causes that led to it.*

Kartini, 1879-1904. In the country of Indonesia, the government formally recognizes certain of its citizens as "National Heroes." In 1964, this esteemed honor was awarded posthumously to Kartini. This recognition was long overdue, for Kartini's achievements were well-known early in the 20th century. As one scholar in 1920 pointed out:

> *The influence of her life and teachings is perhaps greater than that of any other woman of modern times because it reaches all of the millions of Javanese and extends to some extent throughout the entire East.... She is a national heroine, almost a patron saint.*

Living her entire, shortened life on the island of Java (the fourth largest of Indonesia's 15,000+ islands), Kartini was—and still is—widely admired for three main reasons: her efforts to educate girls, her advocacy of women's rights, and the extensive and persuasive letters she wrote.

Kartini's concern for education was tied to the fact that most native Javanese girls in the late 19th century were not permitted to attend school after turning 12 years old. Kartini opposed this practice. In 1903, she established the first primary school for native Indonesian girls. Kartini also wanted the children of Javanese nobility to be educated. She believed that teachers should be trained and that the content of education should focus on both intellectual and moral matters.

As for her advocacy for women's rights, Kartini protested societal obstacles that prevented women from developing and helping others. She opposed the tradition of young girls being forced into polygamous marriages with restricted roles for the rest of their lives. "The development of the Javanese people," she argued, "can never adequately advance if women are excluded." Kartini paved the way for the later emergence of the Indonesian Women's Movement.

Regarding her letters, Kartini wrote to Dutch officials, telling them of the oppressive and exploitative laws imposed by the Dutch East Indies Colonial System. After her death, Kartini's influential letters were published as a book: *Letters of a Javanese Princess*. Scholars Paul Bijl and Grace Chin contend that this work "made Kartini, after Anne Frank, the most well-known Dutch-language author in the world."

Kartini is not forgotten. Several "Kartini" schools for girls have been constructed across Java. Impressively, "Kartini Day" is celebrated in Indonesia on April 21, Kartini's birthday.

Boxed Kartini quotation at top of previous page: Excerpt from the letter she wrote on August 23, 1900, to Dr. J. H. Abendanon and his wife. Located in the 1921 book *Letters of a Javanese Princess*, London: Duckworth & Co.

Quoted comment about Kartini's influence: Excerpt from Chapter 8 (written by Susan MacFarland) in Mary Ann Tétreault's 1994 edited book *Women and Revolution in Africa, Asia, and the New World*, Columbia, South Carolina: University of South Carolina Press.

Photo credit/attribution: Title: Portrait of Kartini; Photographer: Tidak Diketahui; Location of artwork: Tropenmuseum, Amsterdam, Netherlands; Source: https://commons.wikimedia.org/wiki/File:COLLECTIE_TROPENMUSEUM_Portre t_van_Raden_Ajeng_Kartini_TMnr_10018776.jpg; Photo is used here under the Creative Commons Attribution-Share Alike 3.0 Unported license (https://creativecommons.org/licenses/by-sa/3.0/deed.en) [CC BY-SA 3.0]; Original photo has been flipped horizontally and cropped.

> *Be as a tower, that, firmly set,*
> *Shakes not its top for any blast that blows!*

Dante, 1265-1321. Born in Florence in what now is Italy, Dante was and is a famous poet. His work influenced other authors such as Chaucer and Tennyson. Pope Benedict XV once referred to him as "the pride and glory of humanity."

Regarding Dante's youth, he was self-educated (or perhaps taught in a church school). He studied poetry, religion, philosophy, and politics. In his 20s, Dante served in the military, earned an apothecary certificate, and worked as a politician. Because of political infighting and an unfair fine levied against him (with death the option if he did not pay the fine), Dante, at age 37, left Florence and went into exile far from home. He remained in exile for the rest of his life.

Although Dante wrote many books and poems during his exile, he is known mainly for his religious work, *Divine Comedy*. This epic poem—containing 14,233 lines—is considered by many to be "the most important poem of the Middle Ages and the greatest literary work in the Italian language." Dante spent 12 years creating this masterpiece. It describes Dante's vision of his afterlife via his imagined experience traveling through Hell, Purgatory, and Paradise. Helping Dante on these travels are three fellow pilgrims: Virgil (the Roman poet), Beatrice (the ideal woman), and Saint Bernard. They represent human reason, divine knowledge, and devotion, respectively.

In Hell (i.e., the Inferno), Dante comes to know various sins of action, such as anger and greed. In Purgatory, psychological sins are discussed, like envy and pride. In Paradise, the travelers become aware of seven virtues, such as prudence, justice, and faith. In this third portion of the work, Dante has a vision of Heaven.

Initially, this monumental work had the one-word title, *Comedy*. In the Middle Ages, this word meant something different than it does now. In Dante's days, poems were put into two categories: "high" if written in an elevated style or "low" if presented in everyday language. Synonyms for these two categories were "Tragedy" and "Comedy," respectively. Because Dante wrote this poem to make it accessible to anyone who could read, it was called *Comedy*. After Dante's death, someone added the word "Divine" in front of the word "Comedy."

Today's educated people are familiar with the name "Dante" and the term "Dante's Inferno." Few of them, however, can correctly pronounce or spell Dante's last name: Alighieri. (It is pronounced, "ah' li gay ree.")

Boxed Dante quotation at top of previous page: Excerpt from lines 14-15 within Canto V of "Purgatory" in Dante's masterpiece *The Devine Comedy*.

Claim that Dante's major work is widely considered to be "the most important poem....": Footnote 66 on page 172 of Giorgio Agretti's 2021 book, *To Believe in God? To Hope ... Maybe*, Eugene, Oregon: Wipf and Stock Publishers.

Photo credit/attribution: Title: Photo of portrait painting of Dante; Artist: Sandro Botticelli; Photo is in the public domain; Source: https://commons.wikimedia.org/wiki/File:Dante_Alighieri%27s_portrait_by_Sandro _Botticelli.jpg; Original color photo of painting has been cropped and made black-and-white.

> *You oughta be thankful,*
> *A whole heaping lot,*
> *For the places and people*
> *You're lucky you're not!*

Dr. Theodore S. Geisel, 1904-1991. Born and raised in Massachusetts, Geisel earned a B.A. degree from Dartmouth College. He then enrolled at Oxford in England, hoping to get trained in English literature so he could become a teacher. His plans changed, however, when a classmate at Oxford (who later became his  wife) saw his drawing ability. She encouraged him to change career aspirations and refine his already good artistic skills.

Upon returning to the U.S., Geisel worked as a magazine writer and cartoonist. He also drew ads for General Electric and NBC. During World War II, Geisel penned cartoons and posters that supported FDR's efforts. He then joined the Army, where, among other things, he helped develop films that explained why American forces were on foreign soil.

At age 53, Geisel authored *Cat in the Hat,* the first of his "Dr. Seuss" books. In creating this book, his goal was to reduce illiteracy among school children by giving them something that was both easy and fun to read. To accomplish this objective, Geisel used only 236 simple words appropriate for beginning readers, and he put humorous characters into the story. This book's enormous success led to other books such as *Green Eggs and Ham* and *How the Grinch Stole Christmas.*

Over time, Geisel authored more than 60 children's books, with some being translated into a slew of different languages. The last book he wrote—*Oh, the Places You'll Go*—appears on the surface to be a children's book. However, its content focuses on the "journey of life." Parents (and other adult relatives) of college graduates often give this book as a "bon voyage" gift to young men and women who are about to embark on a new chapter of their lives.

Because of his contributions to children's literature, Geisel received the Laura Ingalls Wilder Medal, the Lewis Carroll Shelf Award, three Caldecott Honor Awards, a special Pulitzer Prize, and an honorary doctorate from Dartmouth. But, perhaps most meaningful to Geisel would be the fact that March 2nd, his birthday, has been designated by the National Education Association as "National Read Across America Day."

It is interesting to note how Geisel become Dr. Seuss. As an undergraduate, he was caught drinking gin and told by Dartmouth's administration to abandon his involvement with the college's popular humor magazine. Undeterred, Geisel secretly kept involved by using the pen name Seuss, his little-known middle name. A few years later, he added the title "Dr."

Boxed Geisel quotation at top of previous page: Excerpt from his 1973 book, *Did I Ever Tell You How Lucky You Are?* New York: Random House Children Books.

Photo credit/attribution: Title: Ted Geisel at his desk; Photographer: Al Ravenna; Source: https://commons.wikimedia.org/wiki/File:Ted_Geisel_NYWTS_2_crop.jpg; Photo is in the public domain; Original photo has been cropped.

> *We can easily manage, if we will only take each day, the burden appointed for it. But the load will be too heavy for us if we carry yesterday's burden over again today, and then add the burden of the morrow to the weight before we are required to bear it.*

John Newton, 1725-1807. Born in London, Newton was an English clergyman, hymnist, and writer. He is best known for writing the words for a world-famous hymn known today as "Amazing Grace."

Newton was introduced to seafaring early in his life. He went to sea six times before he was 17, as his father was a shipmaster. When 23, Newton sailed on a ship headed to West Africa to trade its cargo of goods for slaves. Then, for five years, he continued to be involved in the slave-trading business as a ship captain and an investor.

When in his 30s, Newton turned his attention to religious matters. At first, he was just a lay minister. In 1764, however, he became an ordained priest in the Church of England. Newton became well-known for his preaching and outreach to the poor. In 1779, Newton collaborated with his poet friend, William Cowper, on writing a popular book called *Olney Hymns*, with the first word of the title denoting Newton's village. This hymnal included "Amazing Grace."

In 1788, Newton became an abolitionist and wrote a widely-circulated pamphlet entitled, *Thoughts Upon the African Slave Trade*. In it, he first apologized for his earlier involvement in the slave trade, saying, "It will always be a subject of humiliating reflection to me, that I was, once, an active instrument, in a business at which my heart shudders." Newton then described the horrible conditions on ships:

- The ship's crew members considered slaves to be their savage enemies.
- Slaves were tightly shackled together in pairs.
- If drinking water was in short supply, some slaves were tossed overboard so fewer of them needed to drink water.
- So many slaves were put on a ship that they would lie "like books upon a shelf...so close, that the shelf would not, easily, contain one more."
- The air in the slave quarters was hot and putrid.
- Epidemic fevers and diarrhea among slaves were common occurrences.

Conditions were so bad that as many as half the slaves would die on board.

In the latter part of his life, Newton worked with William Wilberforce to get the British Parliament to prohibit England's involvement in the slave trade. In 1807, Parliament voted 283-16 to do just that. Newton died a few months later, his anti-slavery work in England completed.

Boxed Newton quotation at top of previous page: Excerpt from page 336 of the 2009 book, *The Amazing Works of John Newton* (edited by Harold J. Chadwick), Alachua, Florida: Bridge Logos.

Newton's apology for being involved in the slave trade: Excerpt from page 2 of his 1788 pamphlet, *Thoughts Upon the African Slave Trade*, London: J. Buckland Publisher.

Photo credit/attribution: Title: Circa 1788 engraving of Rev. John Newton; Source: https://commons.wikimedia.org/wiki/File:Portrait_of_John_Newton_(4672661).jpg; Artist: William Ridley; Location: National Library of Wales; Photo is in the public domain {{PD-US}}; Original photo has been cropped.

> *I [want] to persuade each of you to concern himself less with what he has than what he is.*

Socrates, 469-399 BC. No books or other manuscripts were written by Socrates. Nevertheless, insights into what this great Greek philosopher said and did come from the written works of his pupils, especially Plato and Xenophon.

Following mandatory military duty, most men of ancient Athens worked to earn a living. Not Socrates. He embraced poverty and would not accept others' money. So, what did he do? He simply engaged people in conversation! He did this to help others gain insights—gleaned from dialogue—into matters such as courage, love, friendship, honor, beauty, and moderation. In these conversations, Socrates was not a didactic lecturer; instead, he merely asked questions and helped people see, at times, the inconsistencies in their logic.

The contemporary term "Socratic method" refers to this dialogic method of assisting others in clarifying their thinking. The key element of this kind of teaching is called "elenchus." It occurs when an initial thesis (e.g., always be truthful) is shown to be in conflict with a subsequent thesis (e.g., don't give names of friends or relatives to corrupt, murderous police officers), thereby bringing forth a new thesis (e.g., it's usually good to be truthful, but not good if doing so puts other people in danger). Socrates had these conversations with those who were willing to talk with him, be they young or old, rich or poor, male or female, slave or master.

In his teachings, Socrates wanted others to grapple with the fundamental question: How can a person live a good and virtuous life? As one contemporary scholar put it, Socrates wanted everyone

> *to reflect upon what we believe, account for what we know and do not know, and ... to seek out, live in accordance with, and defend those views that make for a well-lived and meaningful life.*

This is what Socrates meant when he famously said that "an unexamined life is not worth living."

When 69 years old, Socrates was arrested and accused of corrupting the youth of Athens, siding with enemy Sparta, and being guilty of impiety (i.e., irreverence for Athenian gods). A childhood friend named Crito pleaded with Socrates to escape. Socrates refused, for he considered himself to have done what he was accused of, and his commitment to moral behavior compelled him to serve whatever sentence he received. The verdict was death. Accordingly, Socrates willingly drank from a cup containing the poison, hemlock, and died. So ended the life of the "Father of Western philosophy."

Boxed Socrates quotation at top of previous page: Excerpt from page 90 of Pierre Hadot's 1995 book (translated by Michael Chase), *Philosophy as a Way of Life: Spiritual Exercises from Socrates to Foucault*, Oxford, England: Blackwell.

Socrates' goal when in dialogue with people: Excerpt from James M. Ambury's article "Socrates (469-399 B.C.E)" located in the *Internet Encyclopedia of Philosophy*.

Photo credit/attribution: Title: Marble Bust of Socrates; Artist and photographer: Unknown; Location of bust: Galleria degli Uffizi, Florence, Italy; Source: https://commons.wikimedia.org/wiki/File:Portrait_bust_of_a_man_on_a_Herm_(known_as_Socrates)-Uffizi.jpg; Photo is used here under the Creative Commons Attribution-Share Alike 4.0 International license (https://creativecommons.org/licenses/by-sa/4.0/deed.en) [CC BY-SA 4.0]; Original color photo has been flipped horizontally, cropped, and made black-and-white.

> *In the child is much knowledge, much wisdom. If we do not profit from it, it is only because of neglect on our part to become humble and to see the wonder of this soul and learn what the child can teach.*

Maria Montessori, 1870-1952. Born and raised in Italy, Montessori established a form of education that bears her name: the Montessori Method. Far from being a little old lady who played with children on her front porch, she was an accomplished professional. She was respected in academic circles, a prolific  author of books, a lecturer who spoke to standing-room-only audiences, and a person who translated texts from French into Italian.

Being an educator was not Montessori's first career goal. Interested in both physics and mathematics, Montessori initially studied to be an engineer. At age 20, she changed direction and decided to become a doctor. Three years later, she earned her MD degree (from the University of Rome) and began work in a hospital. Montessori also started a private practice. Her specialty in both arenas was children with mental illness or other disabilities. Montessori was especially interested in the education of such children, and she became well-known as an expert.

Montessori focused her additional studies on philosophy, psychiatry, and pedagogy, and she was soon asked to investigate how best to educate normal children. Her findings—based primarily on careful observation of children during periods of independent play—led to many of the educational ideas and practices that later made Montessori famous. To create more time for her research into childhood education, she gave up her two medical positions.

Her signature book, *The Montessori Method,* led to over 4,000 Montessori classrooms operating worldwide. The bedrock assumption of this teaching strategy is that young children develop and learn best when driven by their own natural abilities and initiative. Children are viewed as acquiring skills, at their own pace, via "practical play," with little need for direct instruction, rewards, or punishments. The teacher's job is to set up special environments that meet the developmental needs of students, with a concern for getting the child to explore, manipulate objects, repeat successful strategies, use abstraction, and communicate with others. Montessori also emphasized that being in (and appreciating) nature is critical to any child's education.

By any measure, Montessori had an enormous impact on education. Her image has appeared on stamps, coins, and paper currency. Montessori schools currently operate on six continents. Ironically, her early school record includes this three-word evaluative comment of Montessori: "Not particularly noteworthy."

Boxed Montessori quotation at top of previous page: Excerpt from page 108 of Paula Polk Lillard's 1972 book *Montessori: A Modern Approach,* New York: Schocken Books.

Montessori's school-record comment: Excerpt from Paola Trabalzini's 2011 book *Maria Montessori Through the Seasons of the Method,* NAMTA Journal, Vol. 36, No. 2.

Photo credit/attribution: Title: Photo of portrait of Maria Montessori; Photographer: Unknown; Location: Nationaal Archief (Dutch National Archives); Source: https://commons.wikimedia.org/wiki/File:Maria_Montessori_(portrait).jpg; Photo is in the public domain; Original photo has been flipped horizontally and cropped.

> *Unite with anybody to do right;*
> *and with nobody to do wrong.*

Frederick Douglass, 1818-1895. Born into slavery on a Maryland plantation, Douglass grew up to become a highly influential abolitionist and statesman. He spoke and wrote on behalf of African-Americans, women, immigrants, Native Americans, and the poor. Some say he was the most significant African-American of the 19th century.

As a slave boy, Douglass was separated from his family, beaten, and discouraged from learning how to read. When 20, Douglass escaped, traveling mainly by train and boat, and ended up in New York City. He became an anti-slavery speaker and wrote an autobiography—*Narrative of the Life of Frederick Douglass, an American Slave*—that quickly became a bestseller. It sold more than 10,000 copies within three years; it also appeared in French and Dutch languages.

Following a two-year tour of Europe, Douglass returned to New York and began publishing an abolitionist newspaper. Known to be a great orator, he gave talks denouncing slavery, supporting education for African Americans, and promoting women's right to vote. He became so famous that he met with presidents Abraham Lincoln and Andrew Johnson to discuss black suffrage.

It is worth noting that Douglass, in the early part of his adult life, did not like Abraham Lincoln. That's because Douglass thought Lincoln was not doing enough to help

African-Americans. In time, Douglass changed his opinion and came to admire Lincoln. Evidence of this change of heart shows up in three events. As Mary Todd Lincoln removed personal belongings from the White House, she gave Douglass her husband's favorite walking cane, saying: "I know of no one that would appreciate this more than Fred. Douglass." In 1876, Douglass was the keynote speaker at the unveiling ceremony of the Emancipation Memorial in Washington. Later, in a book he wrote, Douglass said: "While in his presence, I felt I was [with] a very great man, as great as the greatest, I felt as though ... I was in the presence of a big brother, and there was safety in his atmosphere."

One tidbit of information about Douglass is somewhat surprising. In 1872, the Equal Rights Party nominated him to be Vice President of the United States. However, he didn't know he had been so designated, he did not run, and he never acknowledged that he was a nominee!

Boxed Douglass quotation at top of previous page: Excerpt from page 33 of Douglass' 1855 book, *The Anti-Slavery Movement: A Lecture by Frederick Douglass before the Rochester Ladies' Anti-Slavery Society*, Rochester, New York: Lee, Mann & Co.

Mary Todd Lincoln comment about Douglass: Excerpt from page 325 of Allen Thorndike Rice's 1909 book, *Reminiscences of Abraham Lincoln by Distinguished Men of His Time*, New York: Harper & Brothers Publishers.

Douglass comment about Lincoln: Excerpt from page 327 of *The Frederick Douglass Papers, Series Four, Volume I: Journalism and Other Writings* (edited by John R. McKivigan), New Haven, Connecticut: Yale University Press, 2021.

Photo credit/attribution: Title: Photo of Frederick Douglass; Source #1: Frontispiece of 1897 book *In Memoriam: Frederick Douglass* (edited by Helen Douglass), Philadelphia: John C. Yorston & Co., Publishers; Source #2: https://commons.wikimedia.org/w/index.php?search=Frederick+Douglass&title=Special:MediaSearch&go=Go&type=image; Photo is in the public domain; Photographer: Unknown; Original color photo has been flipped horizontally, cropped, and made black-and-white.

> *Act in such a way as to treat humanity,*
> *whether in your own person or in that of anyone else,*
> *always as an end and never merely as a means.*

Immanuel Kant, 1724-1804. Scholar Matthew McCormick contends that Kant was "one of the most influential philosophers in the history of western philosophy." That assessment comes from an authoritative source, for McCormick wrote his Ph.D. dissertation on Kant, won the Rockefeller Prize for his essay  about Kant, and penned the lengthy, detailed article about Kant that appears in the *Internet Encyclopedia of Philosophy.* Historian C. L. Fernow went further, asserting that "God spake: Let there be light; and there came—the Kantian philosophy."

Kant was born in the Prussian town of Königsberg, now the city of Kaliningrad, in the Russian territory between Poland and Lithuania. After graduating from a prestigious gymnasium (i.e., high school), Kant attended the University of Königsberg. Following graduation, he worked as a tutor in neighboring towns. Eventually, he became a professor at his collegiate alma mater.

One of the subfields of philosophy that Kant wrote about was ethics, and within that area, he specialized in moral philosophy. He authored three influential books on this topic. Those writings contain his famous Categorical Imperative, a way to decide whether or not an action is moral. Kant argued that your behavior can be deemed moral if it passes three simple tests:

- It must be something that you would want all other people to do.
- It must not use anyone as a stepping stone to your goal.
- You must freely choose the behavior.

Suppose you, by yourself, are first in line to be seated in a crowded luncheon eatery. Behind you is a single parent holding a fidgety infant. Giving up your turn and allowing the person behind you to be seated at the first available table would be deemed ethically moral because that act passes the three tests: (1) Should anyone in your position allow the single parent to be seated first? Yes. (2) Are you in any way using the single parent for your own personal gain? No. (3) Would you be freely choosing to give up your place in line? Yes.

Although most people know that Kant was a philosopher, few are aware that he was brilliant in other domains. He wrote books and won awards in astronomy, mathematics, anthropology, politics, and religion. He truly was a "polymath" (i.e, a person with wide-ranging knowledge).

In 2005, the University of Königsberg became the Immanuel Kant State University of Russia. It is now called the Immanuel Kant Baltic Federal University.

Boxed Kant quotation at top of previous page: Excerpt from page 163 of Samuel Kerstein's 2009 article "Treating Others Merely as Means" located in the scholarly journal *Itilitas*, Vol. 21, No. 2, pages 163-180.

Photo credit/attribution: Title: Photo of 1768 painting of Immanuel Kant; Artist: Johann Gottlieb Becker; Source #1: Page 307 of the 1910 book *Masters of Achievement*; Source #2: https://commons.wikimedia.org/wiki/File:Immanuel_Kant_3.jpg; Image is in the public domain; Original photo has been cropped.

> *May I tell you why it seems to me a good thing*
> *for us to remember wrong that has been done us?*
> *That we may forgive it.*

Charles Dickens, 1812-1870. Born and raised in England, Dickens was a voracious reader as a child. He also had a vivid memory of the people and places of his childhood. Many of those locations and individuals became settings and characters in the stories and plays he penned as an adult.

Five of his most famous works include *A Tale of Two Cities, Great Expectations, Oliver Twist, David Copperfield*, and *A Christmas Carol.* The last of these is his most famous work, as it includes well-known characters—Ebenezer Scrooge, the Ghosts of Christmas Past/Present/Future, Bob Cratchit, and Tiny Tim—and one of literature's most famous end-of-story lines: "God bless us, Every One!" In his written body of work, these five and other items caused Dickens to be considered nothing short of a literary mastermind.

It should be noted that Dickens used his stories as a vehicle for pointing out the immorality of having people in upper levels of society steeped in wealth while those in less prominent sectors were bogged down in poverty. He succeeded, for many of his well-heeled readers were surprised when they discovered, in *Oliver Twist*, that begging and crime together were part of a necessary "line of work" for many lower-class residents of London. Readers also learned that workhouses had horrid conditions for their inhabitants and that England was awash in social inequality.

Dickens was a social critic, with his opinions aired primarily through his stories. He showed, as in *A Christmas Carol*, that good people can be found among the poor. He shared this point of view—perhaps recalling the painful economic conditions of his own family of origin—in a lecture he once gave, stating that "virtue shows quite as well in rags and patches as she does in purple and fine linen."

Not surprisingly, Dickens has been honored in many ways since his death. Artists have created life-size statues of him, his portrait has appeared on the Bank of England's £10 note, postage stamps in a wide array of countries have carried his image (or that of his works), and certain of his books' terms—such as "scrooge" and "bah, humbug"—are seen and heard, yet today.

Dickens is interred in the Poets Corner of London's Westminster Abbey. His gravesite is marked with a stone bearing just his name and the dates he was alive. In his will, that's all he said he wanted, stating that "I rest my claim to the remembrance of my country upon my published works."

Boxed Dickens quotation at top of previous page: Excerpt from pages 161-162 of Dickens' 1848 book *The Haunted Man and the Ghost's Bargain*, London: Chapman and Hall, LTD.

Dicken's comment about virtue: Excerpt from a speech Dickens made in February of 1842 in Boston. Located on page 345 of Peter Ackroyd's 1990 book *Dickens*, London: Sinclair-Stevenson.

Dickens' passage from his will: Excerpt from page 286 of William Richard Hughes' 1891 book, *A week's Tramp in Dickens-Land*. London: Richard Clay & Sons.

Photo credit/attribution: Title: Circa 1860 photo of Dickens; Source: https://commons.wikimedia.org/wiki/File:Charles_Dickens_portrait_c1860s_restore. png; Photographer: Unknown; Photo is in the public domain {{PD-old}}; Original color photo has been cropped and made black-and-white.

> *In order for love to be genuine,*
> *it has to be above all a love for our*
> *neighbor. ... It is not always easy to love*
> *those who live right next to us. ... I want you*
> *to be concerned about your next-door neighbor.*
> *Do you know who your neighbor is?*

Mother Teresa, 1910-1997. Born in Macedonia, Teresa seemed destined to be the world icon she became. As a child, she was interested in the work and dedication of missionaries. By age 12, she knew she wanted to devote her life to religion. When 18, Teresa went to Ireland to learn English, the language spoken at the  Sisters of Loreto Abbey in India. After a year, she returned to India.

In Calcutta, Teresa worked as a teacher in a convent school (and eventually became its headmistress). In 1946, she felt called to leave the convent in order to help the poor in Calcutta. For the rest of her life, she worked to serve, in her words,

> *the hungry, the naked, the homeless, the crippled,*
> *the blind, the lepers, all those people who feel*
> *unwanted, unloved, uncared for throughout*
> *society, people who have become a burden to the*
> *society and are shunned by everyone.*

Her first year was a test of her conviction. She had no income, begged for food, and was lonely. She was tempted to return to the comforts of convent life. Despite the challenges she faced and the temptation to chart an easier life path, she persisted.

Soon, 12 nuns joined Mother Teresa in staffing her Missionary of Charity. Over time, thousands of workers came to staff a network of 517 such missionary facilities in over 100 countries. The goal of each of these missionaries was to serve the "poorest of the poor." In both India and many foreign countries, Mother Teresa herself went into war zones and disease-ridden communities to help others. She did this with little fear for her own safety; her main concern was for others.

For her charitable work, Mother Teresa received honorary degrees, the Albert Schweitzer International Prize, India's highest civilian award, and sainthood in the Catholic Church. In 1999, she earned the top spot in Gallop's list of the most widely admired people of the 20th century. Fittingly, the United Nations designates September 5th—the anniversary of Mother Teresa's death—as the International Day of Charity.

Notably, Mother Teresa received the Nobel Peace Prize in 1979. She declined to attend the costly ceremonial banquet for laureates, and she used all of her prize money to help India's poor. After receiving her prestigious medal at the awards ceremony in Norway, she stated in her acceptance speech: "Never turn your back on the poor."

Boxed Mother Teresa quotation at top of previous page: Excerpt from page 27 of the 2001 book, *No Greater Love: Mother Teresa* ("Commemorative Edition" edited by B. Benenate and J. Durepos), Novato, California: New World Library.

Mother Teresa's goal of helping "the hungry, the naked, ...": Excerpt from page 20 of the 2014 book *Mother Teresa: Symbol of Kindness*, New Delhi, India: Om Books International.

Photo credit/attribution: Title: 1980 photo of Mother Teresa; Source: https://commons.wikimedia.org/wiki/File:Kay_Kelly_of_Liverpool_%26_Mother_Teresa_in_1980_(cropped).jpg; Photographer: Unknown; Photo is used here under the Creative Commons Universal Public Domain Dedication (https://creativecommons.org/publicdomain/zero/1.0/deed.en) [CC0 1.0]; Original photo has been cropped.

> *You have to live with what you are given.*
> *Who knows what God is dreaming for us?*

Manute Bol, 1962-2010. The well-attended funeral of Manute Bol took place in the National Cathedral in Washington, D.C. This service honored Bol for what he had accomplished in two distant countries, the United States and Africa's Sudan.

After coming to the U.S., Bol played basketball for a year in college and then a decade in the NBA. He possessed something quite valuable that no teammate or opponent had. His size. He was 7 feet, 7 inches tall, with a "wingspan" of 8½ feet.

Bol used his extraordinary physical characteristics to become an imposing and dominant defensive force on the court. He could sense when an opponent was about to shoot a short jump shot or a layup, and he then would jump up (or simply stand) and swat the ball away as it headed upwards toward the basket. He set and still holds the NBA career record for the most blocks per 48 minutes of playing time. Moreover, he is the only player to have more blocked shots in a career than points scored.

Bol towered over players, coaches, and referees, leading fans to call him a basketball "giant." Although Bol's athletic prowess was impressive, what he did *away* from basketball is even more noteworthy. Simply stated, Bol was a first-class humanitarian. He used his fame and most of his NBA salary money to help others who lived in, or were refugees from, his native homeland, the war-torn and poverty-stricken country of

Sudan. Bol gave money to charities and built schools for children. He started the Ring True Foundation, a mission designed to bring food, medicine, and hope to those in need. According to Sudan's former ambassador to the U.S., Bol "gave his time to children, to the poor, to the displaced, to the helpless, to the sick everywhere." A United States senator said, "I can't think of a person that I know of in the world who used his celebrity status for greater good than what Manute Bol did."

Bol worked tirelessly to bring about reconciliation between enemies from warring factions in Sudan. That he did this is awe-inspiring, for 250 members of his extended family died in Sudan's country-splitting, north-versus-south civil war. Yes, Bol was a giant on the basketball court. More importantly, he was—as noted by a Pulitzer prize-winning journalist—"a moral giant who leveraged his fame on behalf of the neediest people on Earth."

An interesting tidbit of information about Bol concerns his third year in the NBA when he played for the Washington Bullets. One of his teammates was Muggsy Bogues, the shortest player in NBA history. Photos of Bol and Bogues standing next to each other made Buogues look like he was five-year-old boy who just entered kindergarten!

Boxed Bol quotation at top of previous page: Excerpt from Leigh Montville's article (entitled "A Tall Story") in *Sports Illustrated*, December 17, 1990, pages 62-70.

Comments about Bol from Akec Khoc (Sudan's U.S. Ambassador) and Sam Brownback (Kansas senator): *Voice of Africa*, June 28, 2010.

Comment about Bol by Pulitzer prize-winning Nicholas Kristof: Excerpt from Kristof's article "Most Valuable Helper" that appeared on page 33, Section A of the *New York Times,* June 24, 2010.

Photo credit/attribution: Title: Manute Bol's Funeral Servive; Photographer: David Byrd; Original color photo has been cropped and made black-and-white. Source: https://commons.wikimedia.org/wiki/File:Manute_Bol%27s_funeral_at_National_C athedral_2010-06-29_1.jpg; Photo is in the public domain.

> *School yourself to savor most*
> *Joys that have but little cost;*
> *Prove the best of life is free,*
> *Sun and stars and sky and sea;*
> *Eager in your eyes to please,*
> *Proffer meadows, brooks and trees;*
> *Nature strives for your content,*
> *Never charging you a cent.*

Robert Service, 1874-1958. Born in England, Service lived his youth in Scotland. He moved to Western Canada when he was 21, spending 18 years there working as a cowboy, a bank clerk, and a writer. At age 39, he moved (with his newfound wealth) to France, which became his home for the rest of his life. Living in these  various places—along with trips to California, Cuba, the Soviet Union, and other destinations—gave Service an insight into people's joys and fears, hopes and disappointments, work and play.

Although Service had been trained to work in banks, his passion was writing. He became a prolific author, and he acquired the moniker "Bard of the Yukon" for the popular items he wrote while in Canada. Of these, the most well-liked piece was his narrative poem, *The Shooting of Dan McGrew.*

During his life, Service wrote six novels, words and music for ballads, and two autobiographies. His enormous popularity and income, however, came mainly from the vast number of poems he produced. He wrote his first poem when he was six and continued penning poetry throughout his life.

Altogether, he wrote 854 poems. His 1907 collection of poems, *Sounds of a Sourdough*, was an immediate success and earned him more than $100,000 (over $2.5 million in today's money).

Literary critics have used terms such as "simplistic and pedestrian" to describe what Service wrote. This criticism mattered little to Service. He intended his written efforts for the common man and woman. Service once asserted that

> *What I was after [was] something the man in the street would take notice of and the sweet old lady would paste in her album; something the schoolboy would spout and the fellow in a pub would quote.... I belonged to the simple folks I tried to please.*

Prior to spending his final years in Monaco, Service lived in Paris. While there, he was considered to be the city's richest man. He did not, however, retire from his line of work. Always trying to gain inspiration for new poems to write, he often would dress in old, tattered clothes and walk through the city's run-down districts. From the poor people he watched, he discovered topics for poems that came to be liked by rich and poor alike. Prime examples of such verses are his poetic gems, "The Joy of Little Things" and "The Pencil Seller."

Boxed Service quotation at top of previous page: Excerpt from his poem "Learn to Like" located on pages 198-199 in the book *The Best of Robert Service* (reprinted by Penguin in 1989), New York: The Berkley Publishing Company.

Comment from Service regarding his poetic intentions: Excerpt from page 291 of the 2012 book *Robert W. Service: Selected Poetry and Prose* (edited by Michael Gnarowski), Toronto, Canada: Dundurn Press Limited.

Photo credit/attribution: Title: Circa 1905 photo of Robert Service; Source: https://commons.wikimedia.org/wiki/File:Robert_W._Service.jpg; Photo is in the public domain in both Canada and the U.S. {{PD-US}}{{PD-Canada}}; Original photo has been cropped.

> *Make it thy business to know thyself,*
> *which is the most difficult lesson in the world.*

Miguel de Cervantes, 1547-1616. Born to poor parents in a small town near Madrid, Cervantes grew up to become Spain's most celebrated author. Some historians contend that Cervantes was the greatest Spaniard who has ever lived.

Before writing his most famous work, *Don Quixote*, Cervantes worked as a purchasing agent for Spain's navy and then as a tax collector. Because of alleged irregularities in his accounts and his bankruptcy, authorities put Cervantes in prison. Scholars believe that it was there, in prison, that he developed the idea for the novel for which he is best known.

In his masterpiece, Cervantes describes the adventures of the "knight-errant" Don Quixote de la Mancha and his squire sidekick, Sancho Panza. Because the central figure, Don Quixote, has read so many books about chivalry, he and his squire set out, in a knightly manner, to "undo wrongs and bring justice to the world." Unfortunately, Don Quixote's passion for doing this causes him to have a distorted view of what he encounters. He believes, for example, that windmills are ferocious giants, that an inn is a castle, and that a farm girl is his "Lady Love," who he renames Dulcinea.

Literary scholars consider *Don Quixote* to be one of the greatest works of fiction ever written, and it stands as one of the most-translated books of all time. Interestingly, three English words and an idiom have their roots in this fabled book that

Cervantes wrote. According to the *Merriam-Webster Dictionary*,

- *Quixotic* means "foolishly impractical, especially in the pursuit of ideals; marked by rash lofty romantic ideas or extravagantly chivalrous action."
- *Dulcinea* means "sweetheart or mistress."
- *Rosinante*—the name of Don Quixote's steed—sometimes denotes "an old broken-down horse."
- The idiom *"tilting at windmills"* means "to joust or attack imaginary enemies."

During his 30-year writing career, Cervantes wrote a variety of poems and novels. None, however, turned out to be anywhere near as popular as *Don Quixote*. Many books, if well received by the book-reading public, are printed anew after those in the first edition sell out. If a book maintains its popularity, it will have several editions. It is unusual, however, for a book to have more than 20 editions. Amazingly, *Don Quixote* has had over 700 editions!

Boxed Cervantes quotation at top of previous page: Excerpt from page 53 of chapter XLII of Part II in Book III of Volume IV of the 1906 book *The History of the Ingenious Gentleman Don Quixote of la Mancha* (translated from Spanish to English by P. A. Motteau), Edinburgh, Scotland: John Grant.

Photo credit/attribution: Title: Photo of portrait engraving of Miguel de Cervantes; Artist: Frederick Mackenzie; Photographer: Unknown; Source: https://commons.wikimedia.org/wiki/File:Mackenzie,_Frederick_(1787-88_-_1854)_(engraver)_-_Miguel_de_Cervantes.jpg; Photo is in the public domain; Original photo has been cropped.

> *These strangers in a Foreign World—*
> *Protection asked of me*
> *Befriend them, lest Yourself in Heaven*
> *Be found a Refugee.*

Emily Dickinson, 1830-1886. Born in Massachusetts, Dickinson first attended school in a one-room schoolhouse, then at Amherst Academy for seven years, and finally one year at what has become Mount Holyoke College. After completing her formal education, she soon turned inward and  earned a reputation for being a recluse.

A psychological or physiological illness may have caused Dickinson's withdrawal from social life. Whatever the reason for her choice to be alone, Dickinson used her time to write poems. Lots and lots of poems.

Although only a few of Dickinson's poems were published while she was alive, she authored nearly 1,800 poems. Many of her poems used a "quatrain" structure—with an ABCB rhyming scheme—and involved the use of dashes and an unconventional system of capitalization. Those dashes and capitalized words were important to Dickinson; eliminating or neglecting them, she contended, would change the meaning of her poetry.

Immediately after Dickinson died and her poems were published, few people paid much attention to her work. In the 1920s and 1930s, however, scholars saw her poems as ingenious and artistic. By the 1950s, Dickinson was considered by some to have been the greatest woman poet in the English language. In 1994, Yale scholar Harold Bloom stated that Dickinson was as important as the great American poets Walt Whitman, T.S. Eliot, and Robert Frost.

The majority of Dickinson's poems dealt with four main themes: nature (especially sea and sun and stars, bees and birds); life, illness and death; religion; and places visited by one's mind and spirit. Representative of these four kinds of Dickinson poems are the following: "A sepal, petal, and a thorn," "I many times thought Peace had come," "Savior! I've no one else to tell—," and "There is a solitude of space."

When most people hear Emily Dickinson's name, they think of two words: female poet. However, another word describes this great poet: gardener. When young, Dickinson collected over 400 floral specimens and put them—pressed, labeled (with their Latin names), and classified—into a six-volume, well-organized, leather-bound set of books. This "herbarium" now sits in a library at Harvard University. Throughout the rest of her life, Dickinson maintained a garden of exotic flowers from which she sent samples (along with a poem) to each of her few friends.

Boxed Dickinson quotation at top of previous page: Poem 1096 on page 495 in the 1890 book edited by Thomas H. Johnson: *The Complete Poems of Emily Dickinson*, re-published in 1960 in Boston by Little, Brown and Company.

Comment about Dickinson from Harold Bloom: Excerpt from page 9 of the 1999 book he edited, *Emily Dickinson*, Broomall, Pennsylvania: Chelsea House Publishers.

Photo credit/attribution: Title: Circa 1859 photo of Emily Dickinson; Photographer: Unknown; Original tinted photo has been cropped and made black-and-white; Source #1: http://mit.zenfs.com/1103/2012/09/Limmagine-inedita-di-Emily-Dickinson-AP.jpg; Photo is in the public domain; Source #2: https://commons.wikimedia.org/wiki/File:Dickinson_and_Turner_1859.jpg.

> *Let certain things go.*
> *Not out of pride, inability,*
> *or arrogance, but simply because*
> *whatever it is no longer fits in your life....*
> *Stop being who you were and become who you are.*

Paulo Coelho, 1947-. Born in Brazil, Coelho is known worldwide as an inspirational author. His career path, however, was anything but easy. When in his teens, Coelho told his parents he wanted to be a writer. They said it was a bad idea. Undaunted, Coelho continued to talk about becoming a writer, prompting his  parents to put him in a mental institution for three years.

Once released from prison, Coelho started law school just to appease his parents. He soon dropped out and became a hippie. He wandered through Europe, Africa, and South America; he began using drugs. Back in Brazil, he became a songwriter and had other odd jobs to secure the needed income just to survive.

When 27, Coelho wrote his first book. It was not a success. Eight years later, his second book suffered the same fate. In 1987, Coelho achieved a more favorable outcome when he wrote a novel, *Pilgrimage*, based on his 500-mile walk in Spain on the Road of Santiago de Compostela. During his long trek, Coelho reported that he had had a spiritual awakening. He came to realize that the various jobs he had held (as a songwriter, actor, theater director, and journalist) were unfulfilling despite the salary he earned. As he stated in an interview, "I had money, but I was not achieving my dream: to be a writer."

A year later, Coelho finished his fourth book, *The Alchemist*. Initially, this book did not sell many copies. The publisher stopped printing it and returned the publishing rights to Coelho. Still believing in the book's potential, he found a new publisher. Coelho's perseverance paid off. That's because *The Alchemist* became an international bestseller with translations into 80 languages.

The central theme of Coelho's masterpiece is about taking risks, following one's dreams, and finding one's destiny. In the story, a Spanish shepherd boy named Santiago seeks a treasure that supposedly lies near the Egyptian pyramids. During his travels, he meets an alchemist who helps him understand his "true self" and the important insight that happiness, love, and truth are more valuable than any buried treasure.

Coelho has been quite prolific, producing a new book every two years. Over 250 million of these books have been sold, and his work has been published in more than 170 countries. Being other-centered, Coelho uses most of his books' royalties to help children, the elderly, and the poor.

Boxed Coelho quotation at top of previous page: Excerpt from page 177 of his 2005 book, *The Zahir* (translated from Portuguese into English by Margaret Jull Costa), New York: HarperCollins.

Comment from Coelho about his money versus his dreams: Excerpt from the article entitled "My Dream Was, and Still Is, to Be a Writer."*ZEENEWS,* July 6, 2009.

Photo credit/attribution: Title: 2007 photo of Coelho; Source: https://commons.wikimedia.org/wiki/File:Paulo_Coelho_2007-04-09_001_.jpg; Photo is used here under the Creative Commons Attribution 3.0 Unported license (https://creativecommons.org/licenses/by/3.0/deed.en) [CC BY 3.0]; Original color photo has been cropped and made black-and-white.

> *The pith* of conversation does not consist of exhibiting your own superior knowledge..., but in enlarging, improving, and correcting the information you possess by the authority of others.*
>
> [*"Pith" means "the essential quality or vital part."]

Sir Walter Scott, 1771-1832. Born in Scotland, Scott became one of his country's—and Europe's—most famous authors. Fortunately, Scott did not stick with his first career (law). His switch to writing gave others gifts galore.

Scott's writing career began when he penned extended poems, the most popular of which was *Lady of the Lake*. This 290-page poem inspired the literary "Highland Revival" in Scotland and was used as the basis of Rossini's opera, *La Donna del Lago*. It also had a connection to the American abolitionist Frederick Douglass. After escaping from slavery and beginning a new life, Frederick wanted a new last name. A friend who had been reading *Lady of the Lake* suggested "Douglas," the last name of two of the story's main characters. Frederick took the suggestion, adding an "s" to become Frederick Douglass. Another of Scott's poems, *Marmion*, contains the famous lines, "Oh, what a tangled web we weave, / When first we practice to deceive!"

When Scott turned 42, he devoted his full attention to writing novels, most of which are part of his set of books referred to as the "Waverley Novels." Over a span of 18 years, he produced 20 books in this series, the most well-known being *Ivanhoe*. The events of this historical novel take place in 12th-century England, with Scott describing castles, kings, knights, jousting tournaments, fair maidens, and the Saxon-Norman conflict. The main character's full name is Wilfred of Ivanhoe, a knight who represents moral goodness and eventually brings peace to opposing forces. Another important character in *Ivanhoe* is Locksley, who also went by the name "Robin Hood." According to the Scott-reinforced legend, Locksley and his "merry men" stole from the rich and gave to the poor.

There are two notable facts about Scott's childhood. First, he contracted polio and, for a period, was bedridden. However, he learned to walk again, though with a life-long limp.

The second interesting fact about Scott is that he was one of the youngest people ever to enter college. He did so at age 12 when he became a student at the University of Edinburgh. He didn't do well in his two years of Greek, and he acquired the not-too-endearing nickname: "the Greek Blockhead." Those who gave him that nickname were probably embarrassed upon learning that Scott was later knighted by Queen Victoria, that his poems were so well-liked that he was asked to be Scotland's "Poet Laureate," and that the Brontë sisters admired his work.

Significantly, a marble bust of Sir Walter Scott sits in the Poets' Corner of Westminster Abbey.

Boxed Scott quotation at top of previous page: Excerpt from page xxiii in the Introduction to Vol. I of his 1827 book *Quentin Durward*, Paris: A. and W. Galignani.C.

Photo credit/attribution: Title: Photo of 1822 portrait painting of Sir Walter Scott; Artist: Henry Raeburn; Photo is in the public domain; Source: https://commons.wikimedia.org/wiki/File:Sir_Walter_Scott_-_Raeburn.jpg. Location of painting: National Galleries of Scotland; Original color photo has been cropped and made black-and-white.

> *It is unwise to be too sure of one's own wisdom.*
> *It is healthy to be reminded that [you]*
> *and the wisest might err.*

Mahatma Gandhi, 1869-1948. Almost everyone knows that Gandhi was from the country of India. Most people also know that he led his country's effort—mainly through non-violent civil disobedience—to end British rule in India. However, there are a dozen other facts worth knowing about this charismatic figure who is revered worldwide.

- When in school, Gandhi was just an average student, both shy and tongue-tied.

- Gandhi's life-long concerns for the values of truth and love likely were formed when he read about two characters—Shravana and Harishchandra—who appear in Indian legends.

- Gandhi had a customary "arranged marriage" when he was 13 years old.

- Gandhi traveled to South Africa when he was 23 and stayed there for over two decades, trying to reduce racial discrimination.

- Gandhi lobbied not just for India's independence but also for equal rights for his country's women. He said: "I am uncompromising in the matter of woman's rights. In my opinion, she should labour under no legal disability not suffered by man."

- Gandhi demanded fair treatment for the so-called "untouchables." He undertook several fasts to support them, and he called these outcasts "the children of God."

- Gandhi was a prolific author. He wrote about religion, social reform, and vegetarianism.

- Gandhi never won the Nobel Peace Prize. In 2006, the Secretary of the Nobel Committee described this fact as "the greatest omission in our 106-year history."

- The majority of India's residents refer to Gandhi as "Bapu," the Indian term for "Father of the Nation."

- Albert Einstein once stated that

  Mahatma Gandhi's life achievement stands unique in political history.... We may all be happy and grateful that destiny gifted us with such an enlightened contemporary, a role model for the generations to come.

- "Mahatma"—a title meaning "Great Soul"—was used by others to honor Gandhi due to his achievements. Not surprisingly, he was embarrassed by that moniker.

- One of the many people influenced by Gandhi was Martin Luther King, Jr.

Boxed Gandhi quotation at top of previous page: Excerpt from page 2 of *Harijan*, Vol. VIII, No. 1, February 17, 1940.

Gandhi comment about women: Excerpt from page 31 of *The Collected Works of Mahatma Gandhi*, Vol. 14, Publications Division, Government of India.

Comment about Gandhi from 2006 Nobel selection committee: Excerpt from page 265 of V.K. Muthu's 2021 book, *Tales of Some Extraordinary Men and Women Who Shaped History*, Chandigarth, India: White Falcon Publishing.

Einstein comment about Gandhi: Excerpt from page 65 of Ravindra Kumar's 2008 book, *Gandhian Thought: New World, New Dimensions*, Delhi: Kalpaz.

Photo credit/attribution: Title: 1931 studio photo of Gandhi; Artist: Elliot & Fry; Source: http://philogalichet.fr/wp-content/uploads/2019/01/Gandhi_Photo-Alamy.jpg; Photo is in the public domain; Original photo has been cropped.

> *When you get into a tight place, and everything goes against you, till it seems as if you couldn't hold on a minute longer, **never give up then**, for that's just the place and time that the tide'll turn.*

Harriet Beecher Stowe, 1811-1896. Born in Connecticut, Harriet was the seventh of 13 children. Her formal education came mainly at the Hartford Female Seminary. The girls there studied topics (such as mathematics and languages) that were thought by many at the time to be appropriate just for boys.

When she was 21 years old, Harriet moved to Cincinnati, where she joined the Semi-Colon Club. This club was a literary organization made up of talented writers and great thinkers who met weekly to share ideas and critique each other's writing. The club's members included Cincinnati's first Superintendent of Schools, the city's most famous physician, the editor of a popular magazine, and a future Chief Justice of the U.S. Supreme Court.

Another member of the Semi-Colon Club was Calvin E. Stowe, a professor at Lane Theological Seminary. He, like Harriet, strongly opposed slavery. They fell in love and were married in 1836. Together, they supported the Underground Railroad by offering temporary housing to many fugitive slaves who crossed the Ohio River after a risky trek north.

Harriet Beecher Stowe was a prolific, versatile author. She published poems, dramas, novels, children's stories, biographies, and even a collection of letters she had sent to others while on a trip through Europe. Despite her literary

101

productivity, she is remembered most for just one of her works, her book that described the horrid living conditions of slaves.

In *Uncle Tom's Cabin*, Stowe unveiled the inherent immorality of slavery. Through a story focused on the noble slaves Tom and Eliza, the cruel slave owner Simon Legree, and the angelic young white girl Eva, Stowe argued that love can overcome evil. The complete novel, published in the spring of 1852, was an instant success. It sold 3,000 copies the first day it became available and nearly 300,000 copies during the next 12 months. Its content educated many in the north while angering countless southerners.

Uncle Tom's Cabin has been translated into more than 60 languages, and it was the best-selling novel of the 19th century. The book's popularity made Stowe an icon, and she used her fame to help abolish slavery. She went on speaking tours in America and Europe, using these events to drum up support for ending slavery, donating part of what she earned to assist the anti-slavery cause. In an 1862 meeting with Abraham Lincoln, the President supposedly said, in jest, "So you're the little woman who wrote the book that started this great war."

Boxed Stowe quotation at top of previous page: Excerpt from pages 457-458 of her 1869 book, *Oldtown Folks*, Montreal: Dawson Brothers.

Lincoln comment to Stowe: Excerpt from page xliii of the 2007 book *The Annotated Uncle Tom's Cabin* (edited by Henry Louis Gates and Hollis Robins), New York: W. W. Norton.

Photo credit/attribution: Title: Photo of Alanson Fisher's 1853 painting of Harriet Beecher Stowe; Photographer: Billy Hathorn; Source: https://commons.wikimedia.org/wiki/File:Harriet_Beecher_Stowe_at_National_Port rait_Gallery_IMG_4399.JPG; Photo is in the public domain; Original color photo has been flipped horizontally, cropped, and made black-and-white.

> *Nothing is a waste of time*
> *if you use the experience wisely.*

Auguste Rodin, 1840-1917. Born in Paris to a working-class family, Rodin was mainly self-educated. His interest in art appeared at age 10 when he began to draw. Between the ages of 14 and 17, Rodin attended a school specializing in art and mathematics. He then attempted (three times) to enter the famous Paris School  of Fine Arts. Even on his third try, he was not admitted.

Because of his inability to pursue art training at his preferred Paris school, Rodin joined a Catholic order. Soon, the school's founder recognized Rodin's artistic talent and encouraged him to leave so he could hone his artistic skills. For the next two decades, Rodin worked as a craftsman producing decorative objects and architectural embellishments.

When in his forties, Rodin began to win awards and commissions for his sculptures. During the rest of his life, Rodin created many famous works. His most well-known creation is *The Thinker*. It shows an unclothed man sitting (on a rock) and leaning forward with his chin resting on his bent right arm's fist. Commenting on this masterpiece, Rodin said:

> *What makes my Thinker think is that he thinks*
> *not only with his brain [and] his knitted brow,*
> *his distended nostrils and compressed lips, but*
> *with every muscle of his arms, back, and legs,*
> *with his clenched fist and gripping toes.*

Although most people worldwide are familiar with *The Thinker*, few realize that it was initially titled "The Poet."

Another of Rodin's noteworthy achievements was his sculpture, *The Burghers of Calais*. In this historical piece, six life-size figures represent a small group of male citizens from Calais who volunteered, in 1347, to be executed by England's King Edward III. England's army had besieged Calais, and Edward said he would change his mind and not kill everyone who lived in the city if six wealthy and prominent citizens came to him prepared to die. Rodin's sculpture "portrays the moment when the men, believing they are going to die, leave the city vulnerable yet heroic in the face of their likely fate." (The six were spared at the request of England's queen.)

Over his career, Rodin was both prolific and versatile. He produced thousands of sculptures, drawings, and paintings. Art historians consider Rodin to have been the greatest artist of his era, comparing him to Michelangelo. Not surprisingly, he was made a member of the French Légion d'honneur, and Oxford gave him an honorary doctoral degree.

Predictably, Rodin influenced other artists. One such artist was Pablo Picasso. Occasionally, works of these two legends are shown together in museums.

Boxed Rodin quotation at top of previous page: Excerpt from page 47 of Malvina Hoffman's 1936 book, *Heads and Tales*, New York: Charles Scribner's Sons.

Rodin comment about *The Thinker*: Page 456 of the article "A Michael Angelo of Modern Times" published in the January, 1918, issue of *The New Age Magazine*.

Comment about *The Burghers of Calais*: Excerpt from page 11 of Nelly Silagy Benedek's 2000 book, *August Rodin: The Burghers of Calais: A Resource for Teachers*, New York: Metropolitan Museum of Art.

Photo credit/attribution: Title: 1902 photo of Auguste Rodin; Photographer: George Charles Beresford; Photo is in the public domain; Source: https://commons.wikimedia.org/wiki/File:Auguste_Rodin_by_George_Charles_Ber esford_(NPG_x6573).jpg; Original photo has been cropped.

> *It all comes down to motivation.*
> *If you really want to do something,*
> *you will work hard for it.*

Edmund Hillary, 1919-2008. Born and raised in New Zealand, Hillary developed a high-level interest in the outdoors when he was a teenager. His two main loves were "tramping" (his country's term for hiking) and mountaineering.

When Hillary was 20 years old, he hiked to the top of New Zealand's Mt. Ollivier (elevation: 6,342 feet). After working as a beekeeper and participating in the health-oriented Radiant-Living movement, Hillary ascended Aoraki/Mt. Cook, his country's highest mountain (12,349 feet). This ascent was no easy task for the 29-year-old Hillary, for he knew that many climbers had died trying to reach the mountain's summit.

Following a stint as a navigator in World War II, Hillary continued to climb increasingly dangerous mountains. In 1953, a British team invited Hillary to join its effort to reach the top of Mt. Everest, the tallest mountain on Earth (29,028 feet). This "expedition" was well-planned and involved 20 Sherpa guides and over 300 porters who carried thousands of pounds of luggage.

Near the top of Everest, two other climbers in the group failed to reach the summit. The expedition's leader then directed Hillary and Tenzing Norgay to make the next try. (Norgay was a Nepali Sherpa mountaineer who once had saved Hillary's life during a joint climb.) Each carrying 30-pounds of equipment,

Hillary and Norgay reached Everest's summit—with Norgay graciously allowing Hillary to step first onto the ice-covered top.

Being the first person to conquer Everest, Hillary became a worldwide celebrity. In a variety of countries, he gave invited talks and received medals, honors, and awards. Most impressively, he was made a Knight in Britain's Most Noble Order of the Garter, a selected organization founded in 1348 that limits its membership to 26 living people (one of whom is the King or the Queen).

Hillary was a humble person who didn't enjoy being in the limelight. Despite that personality characteristic, he decided to use his fame to assist others. He set up the Himalayan Trust to help people living in Nepal, one of the poorest countries on Earth. Its workers built schools, airfields, and hospitals; they repaired monasteries, bridges, and water pipes. Hillary also established the Outdoor Pursuits Centre in New Zealand. That Centre provides outdoor activities for young people, aiming to have participants acquire desired traits such as integrity, perseverance, and courage.

Hillary wrote 10 books. One was titled *Nothing Venture, Nothing Win.* Another carried the title *High Adventure.* He wrote these books to encourage readers to confront and overcome the fears and obstacles in their lives.

Boxed Hillary quotation at top of previous page: Excerpt from *Newsletter 2010* published by the Himalayan Trust Nepal, P.O. Box 224, Kathmandu, Nepal.

Photo credit/attribution: Title: Circa 1953 photo of Edmund Hillary; Photographer: Unknown: Original photo was flipped horizontally and cropped; Source: https://commons.wikimedia.org/wiki/File:Edmund_Hillary,_c._1953,_autograph_re moved.jpg; Photo is in the public domain.

> *Fight for the things you care about, but do it in a way that will cause others to join you.*

Ruth Bader Ginsburg, 1933-2020. Born in New York, Ginsburg joined a family with European roots. Her father was from Ukraine; her mother's parents were from Poland. The Great Depression served as the backdrop of Ginsburg's youth.

Encouraged by her mother, Ginsburg became an excellent student and worker. After high school, she earned a B.A. degree (Phi Beta Kappa) at Cornell. She then garnered a law degree from Columbia, where she finished tied for first in her class. Ginsburg's initial jobs were faculty appointments, first at Rutgers, next at Columbia, and then at Stanford. In 1980, she was appointed to a judgeship on the District of Columbia Circuit Court, a position Ginsburg held for 13 years.

In 1993, President Clinton nominated Ginsburg for a spot on the U.S. Supreme Court. The Senate confirmed her in a landslide 96-3 vote. Ginsburg held this position until her death 27 years later. During her tenure on the High Court, she championed causes in which she sided with the disenfranchised, oppressed, powerless, and marginalized. Four cases in particular show this:

- Ginsburg advocated for gender equality and women's rights, writing the court's majority opinion that struck down the male-only admission policy at the Virginia Military Institute (VMI).

- Her dissenting opinion on a case prompted President Obama to endorse the Fair Pay Act, thereby giving employees a better chance to win salary discrimination claims.
- Ginsburg influenced her colleagues to rule that school officials were wrong to strip-search a 13-year-old girl.
- She wrote the majority opinion saying that mental illness should be covered by the Americans with Disability Act.

Ginsburg's success brought her prestigious awards and honors. She was inducted into the National Women's Hall of Fame, received a slew of honorary degrees, and was included in various lists of the most powerful and influential people. She also received the $1 million Berggruen Prize (and gave it all to charities).

Perhaps Ginsburg's most impressive accomplishment was unrelated to any legal matter. Instead, it concerned her friendship with Antonin Scalia, another member of the Supreme Court. He was conservative; she was liberal. Despite holding opposing views on many legal cases, they were close friends. They and their spouses often ate dinner with each other and frequently attended the opera. Together, Ginsburg and Scalia showed how people can embrace ideological differences without becoming hate-driven enemies.

Boxed Ginsburg quotation at top of previous page: Excerpt from Alanna Vagianos' article "Ruth Bader Ginsburg Tells Young Women: 'Fight for the Things You Care About,'" June 2, 2015, online newsletter of the Harvard/Radcliffe Institute.
Photo credit/attribution: Title: 2010 photo of Associate Justice R. B. Ginsburg; Source: https://commons.wikimedia.org/w/index.php?search=Ruth+Bader+Ginsburg&title=Special:MediaSearch&go=Go&type=image; Photographer: Unknown: Photo is in the public domain; Original color photo has been cropped and made black-and-white.

> *There can be no greater gift than that of giving one's time and energy to help others without expecting anything in return.*

Nelson Mandela, 1918-2013. Born in South Africa to poor and illiterate parents, Mandela stands as a powerful example of how a person can achieve greatness despite having had a disadvantaged childhood.

By the end of his life, Mandela was viewed as the leading force that ended apartheid in his home country. He had been elected president by his fellow citizens. Moreover, he was a respected, influential statesman in international affairs.

Along the way from his humble beginning—wherein one of his chores was tending a herd of cattle—to a position of fame and influence, Mandela remained committed to social justice, democracy, and education for all. Throughout his adult life, his dedication to these principles prompted him to challenge the status quo. He organized protest movements, spoke to crowds, defied existing laws, called for strikes, spent time in jail, served as a delegate to conventions, and traveled internationally to secure support for the anti-apartheid movement.

Although he was an activist, Mandela modeled the view that peace and reconciliation trump bitterness and retribution. Most impressively, he maintained an attitude of respect toward the men who guarded him during his 27-year imprisonment. (Mandela had been found guilty in 1964 of inciting workers' strikes over racial injustice and leaving the country without permission.)

After being released from his long stay in prison, Mandela was a world celebrity. He used this status to garner anti-apartheid support from presidents and prime ministers, kings and queens, religious leaders and everyday citizens. In 1994, Mandela's political party won South Africa's first non-white-only general election, and Mandela became the country's first black president. Apartheid was over.

Because of Mandela's life-long work to improve the plight of others, he received over 250 awards, honorary doctoral degrees, prestigious prizes, and accolades. Among these were the Nobel Peace Prize, the U.S Presidential Medal of Freedom, and the Lenin Peace Prize. Most likely, he was most touched by what South Africans called him: "Father of their country."

At Mandela's funeral, President Barack Obama spoke and said,

> *It took a man like Mandela to free not just the prisoner, but the jailer as well; to show that you must trust others so that they may trust you; to teach that reconciliation [necessitates] inclusion and generosity and truth.*

Boxed Mandela quotation at top of previous page: Excerpt from page 146 in Mandela's 2012 book *Notes to the Future: Words of Wisdom*, New York: Atria Books.

Comment about Mandela from Barack Obama: Excerpt from "Address at the public Memorial for Nelson Madela" located in the 2021 book entitled *Barack Obama: Selected Speeches*, San Diego: Canterbury Classics.

Photo credit/attribution: Title: 1994 photo of Mandela during his first trip to the U.S.; Source: https://commons.wikimedia.org/wiki/File:Nelson_Mandela_1994_(2).jpg; Artist: John Mathew Smith; Original color photo has been cropped and made black-and-white. Permission to use photo granted to Huck by Smith on April 27, 2022.

> *Teach me to feel another's Woe,*
> *To hide the Fault I see;*
> *That mercy I to others show,*
> *That Mercy show to me.*

Alexander Pope, 1688-1744. Born in London, Pope attended traditional school up to the age of 12. From that point on, he was self-educated. He learned French, Italian, Latin, and Greek, and he read works by authors such as Homer, Chaucer, and Shakespeare.

Pope loved poetry. And he was good at it. He is said to have produced "accomplished verse" when he was but a teenager. At age 21, a small collection of Pope's poems, called "Pastorals," appeared in a compendium of different authors' poems entitled *Poetical Miscellanies*.

Two years later, Pope had a work published by itself. Entitled *An Essay on Criticism*, this was a 740-line, 43-page poem composed of "heroic couplets" (two rhyming iambic pentameter lines). For example, lines 17-18 in Part I state: "Authors are partial to their wit, 'tis true / But are not critics to their judgment too?" This famous work contained three expressions that one occasionally hears today:

> *Fools rush in where angels fear to tread.*
> *To err is human, to forgive divine.*
> *A little learning is a dang'rous thing.*

Four of Pope's other main poetical works, each published as a book, were *The Rape of the Lock, The Dunciad,*

An Essay on Man, and *Moral Essays*. Through his poems, Pope took jabs at high society and commented on social mores.

In addition to creating his own poetry, Pope translated Homer's *Iliad* (and part of the *Odyssey*) from Greek to English. These were not direct translations; Pope rewrote each work as he believed Homer would have written it if he, Homer, had lived in 18th-century England rather than in ancient Greece. The eminent Dr. Samuel Johnson called Pope's *Iliad* "the noblest version of poetry which the world has ever seen" and "one of the great events in the annals of learning."

Because much of what he wrote was satirical and aimed at politicians, Pope was not universally liked. Yet, Pope's admirers nearly deified him and felt an enormous loss when he died. One artist's painting depicts an angel holding Pope as he died, with Chaucer, Milton, and Spenser bewailing the great poet's death.

According to the *Oxford Dictionary of Quotations*, Pope is and has been the second most quoted author in the world. Only Shakespeare's words appear more often. Why does Pope remain so popular? Dr. Johnson explained, saying, "a thousand years may elapse before there shall appear another man with a power of versification equal to that of Pope."

Boxed Pope quotation at top of previous page: Stanza X of his 1738 poem *The Universal Prayer* published in London by R. Dodsley.

Johnson's comment about Pope's *Iliad*: Excerpt from page 385 of Johnson's 1779 book, *Lives of the Most Eminent English Poets*, London: Frederick Warne and Co.

Johnson's "thousand years" comment: Excerpt from page 358 of James Boswell's 1791 book, *The Life of Samuel Johnson*, London: Hutchinson & Co.

Photo credit/attribution: Title: Engraving of Mr. Alexander Pope (Style: mezzotint print); Source: https://collections.britishart.yale.edu/catalog/tms:26192; Location: Yale Center for British Art; Artist: John Simon (after Michael Dahl); Photo is in the public domain; Original tinted photo has been cropped and made black-and-white.

Soichiro Honda, 1906-1991. Born in a tiny, rural Japanese village, Honda had a working-class upbringing. His father was a blacksmith, his mother a weaver. Out of this humble setting, Honda grew up to be one of the world's most prominent entrepreneurs, inventors,

and creators of a successful corporate philosophy.

Throughout his life, Honda tried to answer the simple question: How can motors be used to help transport people more effectively and efficiently? Honda's entrepreneurial skill showed through in 1945 when he needed money to produce motorized bicycles. He contacted about 18,000 bicycle shops in Japan and convinced a third of them to advance him the funds required to build a factory to produce his innovative product: motorbikes.

Indicative of his inventive talent was how he dealt with government rules designed to control automobile pollution. Other auto companies put a catalytic converter in a car's tailpipe to catch engine-created toxic fumes before being released into the atmosphere. Instead, Honda redesigned his car engines to reduce, at the outset, the number of pollutants the engines created.

Although Honda possessed entrepreneurial and inventive skills, it was his corporate philosophy that caused the

Honda Motor Company—manufacturer of motorcycles and cars—to be enormously successful. It had seven central tenets:

- Don't imitate other companies.
- Decrease hierarchy and bureaucracy.
- Recognize that workers on the assembly line have valuable knowledge not possessed by executives.
- Experiment and make mistakes, because problems and failures provide opportunities for improving process and product.
- Don't provide special perks to "bosses," such as reserved spots in the parking lot or fancy meals in a private dining room.
- Develop a spirit of teamwork and "togetherness."
- Give back to the communities that host Honda factories.

This corporate philosophy came to be known as "The Honda Way." It still exists, decades after Soichiro Honda died.

Considered to be "the Japanese Henry Ford," Honda received many honors and awards. Like Ford, he has been inducted into Detroit's Automotive Hall of Fame. And yearly, the American Society of Mechanical Engineers awards the Soichiro Honda Medal to someone who has Honda's traits.

Boxed Honda quotation at top of previous page: Excerpt from the October 26, 2018, issue of Honda's "Media Newsroom" from the American Honda Motor Co., Inc.

Tenets of "The Honda Way": Articulated in Susan Insley's article "The Honda Way: An Innovative Approach to Management and Production" located on pages 123-133 in the 1989 book *Managing Innovation and Change* (edited by S. B. Lundstedt and T. H. Moss), Dordrecht, Netherlands: Kluwer Academic Publishers.

Photo credit/attribution: Title: 1963 photo of Soichiro Honda; Source: https://commons.wikimedia.org/wiki/File:Soichiro_Honda_in_1963.jpg; Photo is used here under the Creative Commons 2.0 Generic license (https://creativecommons.org/licenses/by/2.0/deed.en) [CC BY 2.0]; Original photo has been cropped.

> *Great learning and superior abilities, should you ever possess them, will be of little value ... unless virtue, honor, truth and integrity are added to them.*

Abigail Adams, 1744-1818. Born in a small cabin in Massachusetts, Adams grew up to become the wife of one U.S. President and the mother of another. Educated by her mother and grandmother, she was taught well, for historians consider Adams to have been one of the most intellectually astute women ever to serve as First Lady.

Adams was an ardent supporter of women's rights and vehemently opposed slavery. She advised her husband, John, on many matters. However, her main legacy is the set of 1,160 letters she and John exchanged while he was away from home. Those letters reveal not only the love they shared and the intelligence each possessed but also the personal sacrifices they made for their emerging country. Moreover, the letters demonstrate Abigail's high-level understanding of world affairs, diplomacy, politics, and economics.

To all matters that came before her, Adams brought a profoundly positive outlook on life. Adams' grandson noted this aspect of his grandmother's character when he penned these impressive lines in an 1875 book he wrote:

> *In the midst of public or private troubles, the buoyant spirit of Mrs. Adams never forsook her. "I am a mortal enemy," she writes on one*

occasion to her husband, "to anything but a cheerful countenance and a merry heart, which, Solomon tells us, does good like medicine." ... The old age of Mrs. Adams was not one of grief and repining, of clouds and darkness. Her cheerfulness continued [on] to the last; and her sunny spirit enlivened the small circle around her, brightened the solitary hours of her husband, and spread the influence of her example over the town where she lived.

It is worth noting that Adams experienced more than her fair share of tragedy and disappointment. Of her six children, two died before turning two, and only two others outlived her. Her husband was absent from her life for extended periods. In her day, most men did not consider women their equals. She was frail with poor health. Her husband lost the bitter 1800 election to Jefferson.

The ordeals Adams suffered throughout her life might well cause others, if in her place, to become despondent and shrink into a shell. Not Abigail. With her joyful and upbeat demeanor, she remains a role model for handling life's "slings and arrows of outrageous fortune."

Boxed Adams quotation at top of previous page: Excerpt from a letter written by Abigail Adams to her son, John Quincy Adams, on June 10, 1780.

Quote from Adams' grandson: Found on pages xxvii-xxviii of the 1876 book by Charles F. Adams, *Familiar Letters of John Adams and His Wife Abigail Adams During the Revolution,* New York: Hurd and Houghton.

Photo credit/attribution: Title: Photo of portrait painting of Abigail Adams; Source: https://commons.wikimedia.org/wiki/File:Abigail_Smith_Adams_wife_of_John_Ad ams_-_photo_of_portrait_by_Gilbert_Stuart._LCCN2014648296.jpg; Artist/painter: Gilbert Stuart; Photographer: Chester A. Lawrence; Location of painting: National Gallery of Art, Washington, D.C.; Photo is in the public domain; Original color photo has been cropped and made black-and-white.

> *But shouldn't all of us on Earth give the best we have to others and offer whatever is in our power? ... You who are so richly gifted—what have you given to the world? What do you intend to give?*

Hans Christian Andersen, 1805-1875. Born into a low-income family living in Denmark, Andersen grew up to become one of the world's most beloved authors. Although he wrote novels, poetry, plays, and travel books, it was his set of 156 fairy tales that made him famous.

A few of Andersen's most popular tales are "The Emperor's New Clothes," "The Little Mermaid," "The Ugly Duckling," "Thumbelina," and "The Princess and the Pea." These and most of Andersen's other fairy tales have been translated into more than 120 languages. They are familiar to a worldwide audience.

Andersen's fairy tales became popular because they were not created solely for children. They were for adults, too. For example, "The Emperor's New Clothes" deals with the issues of peer pressure and conformity, and it begs both young *and* old readers to ponder three questions:

- Was I ever convinced that something was accurate when it wasn't?
- Do I ever blindly "follow the crowd"?
- Would I have the courage to do what the child did at the end of the story and challenge what most others say when, to me, what they say seems wrong?

Andersen often achieved his goal of having his readers think and reflect on such questions by having his tales' dialogue involve animals, plants, and inanimate objects. This effective literary technique likely influenced other authors such as Beatrix Potter, Lewis Carroll, and A. A. Milne.

Because of his life's work, Andersen has been honored in many ways. The Danish government declared that he was a "national treasure." The International Board on Books for Young People calls its most prestigious award in children's literature, given annually, the "Hans Christian Andersen Award." International Children's Book Day is celebrated yearly on April 2nd, Andersen's birthday.

New York's Central Park has a life-size statue of Andersen sitting on a park bench. He holds an open book on his lap, but his gaze points downward toward a separate, small figure of an animal on the ground. That animal? It's the Ugly Duckling!

It is worth noting that Andersen's literary success did not come easy. He suffered decades of toil, depression, and strife before he achieved global fame.

Boxed Andersen quotation on previous page: Excerpt from "The Snail and the Rosebush," located on page 314 of the 1948 book, *Hans Christian Andersen's Shorter Tales* (translated by Jean Hersholt), New York: Heritage Press.

Photo credit/attribution: Title: Photographic portrait of Hans Christian Andersen; Source: https://commons.wikimedia.org/wiki/File:(H._C._Andersen_portrait)_(3446741581). jpg; Photographer: Unknown; Original belongs to the Edvard Grieg Archives at the Bergen Public Library, Norway; Photo has no known restrictions on its use; Original photo has been flipped horizontally and cropped.

> *It's your life—but only if you make it so. The standards by which you live must be your own standards, your own values, your own convictions in regard to what is right and wrong, what is true and false, what is important and what is trivial. When you adopt the standards and the values of someone else or a community, you surrender your own integrity.*

Eleanor Roosevelt, 1884-1962. Though born into a wealthy family living in New York City, Roosevelt had a childhood permeated by significant loss and trauma. When just two years old, she was put in a lifeboat with her parents after their ocean  liner collided with another ship. Her mother and a younger brother died from diphtheria when she was eight. Her father, an alcoholic, committed suicide two years later.

Tutored privately when young and then formally educated in England, Eleanor Roosevelt learned to be an independent thinker. This trait, and other positive characteristics, allowed her to become a highly influential politician, diplomat, and activist. She accomplished these things in her own right, even though she was the niece of one U.S. president and married to another.

Eleanor Roosevelt was bright, talented, and concerned about others, especially those living on the margins of society. In her speeches, radio talks, and syndicated newspaper column ("My Day"), Roosevelt supported African-Americans, spoke out against prejudice toward the Japanese, and promoted government-sponsored daycare to help working women. She invited African-Americans to the White House, participated in starting a community for homeless coal miners in West Virginia, and helped begin a furniture-making company to employ poor people during the depression.

In addition to her efforts to help others, Roosevelt was a prolific author. She wrote 27 books, many of which dealt with critical, international issues. Five of her works were titled: *This Troubled World*, *The Moral Basis of Democracy*, *Growing Toward Peace*, *India and the Awakening East*, and *United Nations: What You Should Know About It*.

People noticed what Roosevelt had accomplished and what she stood for. President Harry Truman appointed her to be an official delegate to the United Nations (and in that role, she was the main force behind the creation of the UN's Declaration of Human Rights). Later, President John F. Kennedy tapped her to chair the Presidential Commission on the Status of Women. Roosevelt's work in those posts, combined with her other efforts to help people, brought her widespread admiration. Gallop listed her as one of the most widely admired people of the 20th century.

Interestingly, "Roosevelt" was not a name Eleanor acquired after marrying FDR. Even at birth, she was a Roosevelt. That's because her father's name was Elliott B. Roosevelt.

Boxed Roosevelt quotation at top of previous page: Excerpt from page 111 of her 1960 book, *You Learn by Living*, Louisville, Kentucky: Westminster John Knox Press.

Photo credit/attribution: Title: Photo of 1949 portrait painting of Eleanor Roosevelt: Artist: Douglas Chandor; Photo is in the public domain; Source: https://commons.wikimedia.org/wiki/File:Anna_Eleanor_Roosevelt.png; Photographer: Unnamed employee of the White House; Original color photo has been cropped and made black-and-white.

> *Do not counsel what is most pleasant, but what is best.*

Solon, 638-558 BCE. Born into a noble family on an island near Athens, Greece, Solon became an influential Greek statesman, lawmaker, and poet. He helped stop the economic and moral decline of ancient Greece, reduced regional disputes, and laid the foundation for democratic rule.

During his early adult life, Solon was a successful military leader. Primarily due to the fame he achieved by winning a war with the Megarians, Solon was chosen to be the "governor" of Athens. He established new laws and brought constitutional, economic, and moral reforms to his city:

- Solon's central constitutional reform was twofold: he gave ordinary people the power to elect officials, and he set up a court made up of citizens. These two changes eliminated the prior form of governance whereby the Athenian state was controlled only by those who had nobility and wealth.

- In the economic arena, Solon's main objective was an increase in foreign trade. To achieve this goal, he invited foreign merchants to settle in Athens while encouraging people in Athens to grow olives for exportation.

- Among Solon's moral reforms, he abolished extravagant dowries, allowed any citizen to take legal action on behalf of someone else who had been "wronged," and argued against the greed and arrogance of Athens' elite citizens. He also prohibited a practice—called "debt slavery"—by which the security for a loan was the person himself needing the loan.

In his 1907 book *The History of Freedom and Other Essays*, author Lord Action asserted that Solon was "not only the wisest man to be found in Athens, but the most profound political genius of antiquity." He said the leadership of Solon:

> *completely inverted the notion of human authority, for it inaugurated the reign of moral influence where all political power [up until then] had depended on moral force. Government by consent superseded government by compulsion, and the pyramid which had stood on a point was made to stand on its base. By making every citizen the guardian of his own interest, Solon admitted the element of Democracy into the State.*

Solon wrote many poems, one of which contrasts virtue with wealth:

> *Often the wicked prosper while the righteous starve;*
> *Yet I would never exchange my state for theirs,*
> *My virtue for their gold. For mine endures,*
> *While riches change their owners every day.*

Boxed Solon quotation at top of previous page: Excerpt from page 141 of "Apothegms of the Seven Sages" in *Early Greek Philosophy*, Vol. 2 (Loeb Classical Library), Vol. 525), Cambridge, Massachusetts: Harvard University Press.

Comments about Solon by Lord Action: Excerpt from pages 6-7 of his 1907 book *The History of Freedom and Other Essays*, London: Macmillan and Co.

Solon poem about virtue & wealth: Excerpt from the 1973 book by Plutarch (edited by Ian Scott-Kilvert) *The Rise and Fall of Athens: Nine Greek Lives*. London: Penguin Books.

Photo credit/attribution: Title: Solon: Son of Athens; Photographer: unknown; Source: https://commons.wikimedia.org/wiki/File:Solon_of_Athens.jpg; Image of Solon taken from page 103 of Guillaume Rouillé's 1553 iconography book *Prima Pars [et Secunda] Promptuarii Iconum Insigniorum*. Photo is in the public domain.

> *Look not mournfully into the Past.*
> *It comes not back again.*
> *Wisely improve the Present. It is thine.*

Henry Wadsworth Longfellow, 1807-1882. According to the Poetry Foundation, Longfellow "was one of the most widely known and best-loved American poets of the 19th century [who] achieved a level of national and international prominence previously unequaled in the literary history of the United States." He was  so popular in America that his 70th birthday was celebrated like a national holiday, with parades and speeches.

Longfellow was an icon not just in the U.S. but in England as well. He was awarded honorary degrees from Oxford and Cambridge. Queen Victoria invited him to have tea with her. And, a memorial bust of him was installed in the exclusive Poets' Corner of Westminster Abbey in London.

Longfellow published his first poem when he was just 13 years old, and he had almost 40 poems published while attending Bowdoin College. After graduating—when just 18 years old with a Phi Beta Kappa key—he became a faculty member (first at Bowdoin, then at Harvard). He taught courses in literature, but his passion was writing poems. After 20 years, Longfellow retired so he could devote all his time to poetry.

Longfellow was prolific, and his poetic creations were diverse in three main respects: length, form, and topic. In terms of length, certain of his poems contained fewer than 50 words, whereas others were composed of more than 10,000. Regarding form, Longfellow varied both rhyming scheme and meter. As for topic, his poems focused on slavery, Native Americans, famous people, nature, and many other subjects. Despite these differences in his creations, Longfellow's poems were similar in that they were easy to understand, focused on topics people cared about, and contained, as one literary scholar put it, a "sweet and settling mildness" and "serene reassurance."

Nine of Longfellow's most famous poems are:

Paul Revere's Rise   The Song of Hiawatha   Evangeline
The Courtship of Miles Standish   A Psalm of Life
Christmas Bells   The Day is Done   Children   Flowers

What did others think of Longfellow? Poe disliked him and his poetry. But Hawthorne praised Longfellow and wanted to collaborate on writing projects. And Emerson referred to him as "a sweet and beautiful soul."

What did the children who lived in Longfellow's hometown think of him? They adored him! As a gift to the poet on his 72nd birthday, they (and others) had a beautiful chair made for Longfellow. Its wood came from the local, recently cut-down "spreading chestnut tree" referred to in Longfellow's poem, "The Village Blacksmith."

Boxed Longfellow quotation at top of previous page: Excerpt from page 378 (in chapter VIII: "Foot-Prints of Angels") of Book IV of his 1839 novel *Hyperion: A Romance* published in Boston by Houghton, Mifflin and Company.

One scholar's comment about Longfellow's poetry: Excerpt from a 2002 online article entitled *America's Longfellow* written by Matthew Gartner for the U.S. National Park Service.

Emerson comment about Longfellow: Excerpt from Harriet Earhart Monroe's article "Statesman and Novelist," *Lippincott's Monthly Magazine*, January, 1887, 128-132.

Photo credit/attribution: Title: Photo of Longfellow; Photographer: unknown; Source: https://commons.wikimedia.org/wiki/File:HenryWadsworthLongfellowPhotographfr omBook.PNG; Photo from 1893 book *The Poems of Henry Wadsworth Longfellow*, New York: Thomas Y. Crowell Company; Photo is in the public domain. {{PD-US}}.

> *If the hills are high before, and the paths are hard to climb, keep a-pluggin' away. And remember that successes come to him who bides his time,— Keep a-pluggin' away. Delve away beneath the surface, There is treasure further down,— Keep a-pluggin' away.*

Paul Laurence Dunbar, 1872-1904. Born in Dayton, Ohio, to parents who had been slaves in Kentucky, Dunbar developed a love of poetry as a young child. He penned his first poem when he was six years old and only nine when he had a public recital. At 16, Dunbar had two of his poems published in Dayton's newspaper. In  his high school, where he was the only African American, he was elected president of the literary society, chosen to be editor of the school's newspaper, and tapped to be the class poet.

Financially unable to attend college, Dunbar worked as an elevator operator, using his salary to publish his first book of poems, *Oak and Ivy*. Recognizing Dunbar's talent, two benefactors provided the funds needed to get his second book, *Majors and Minors*, published. A positive review of that work appeared in *Harper's Weekly*, thus making Dunbar the first African-American writer to gain an international reputation.

Dunbar wrote some of his poems in standard English. His most famous poetic creations, however, were expressed in African American dialect. Perhaps the most beautiful of these latter works—"When Malindy Sings"—was read in San Francisco in the mid-1990s by the prominent author and poet Maya Angelou. Her stirring, melodic presentation prompted those in attendance to clap in time to the poem's rhythm.

Before tuberculosis sadly ended Dunbar's short life at age 33, he had authored several books of poetry, short stories, novels, and a play. He was, in the minds of many, one of America's best poets. The famous writer Langston Hughes listed Dunbar first when he wrote that "my chief literary influences have been Paul Laurence Dunbar, Carl Sandburg, and Walt Whitman," and the great orator, abolitionist, and statesmen, Frederick Douglass, referred to Dunbar as "one of the sweetest songsters his race has produced."

It is interesting to note that two of Dunbar's high school classmates were Orville and Wilbur Wright. Orville was Dunbar's close friend, and they tutored each other. Dunbar helped Orville with writing and literature; Orville assisted Dunbar with math and Science. Dunbar once wrote a clever little poem about his friend who had designed a new kind of printing press: "Orville Wright is out of sight / In the printing business. / No other mind is half so bright / As his'n is."

Another interesting fact is that Dunbar wrote the words for *The Tuskegee Song*, the school's alma mater. He did so at the request of the university's founder, Booker T. Washington.

Boxed Dunbar quotation at top of previous page: Excerpt from page 46 of the 1922 book by W. D. Howells, *The Complete Poems of Paul Laurence Dunbar*, New York: Dodd, Mead and Company.

Douglass comment about Dunbar: Excerpt from the description of Dunbar accompanying the painting of him, (by William McKnight Farrow) at the Smithsonian's National Portrait Gallery in Washington, D.C.

Dunbar poem about Orville Wright: Excerpt from the testimony on August 1, 1991 of Tom D. Crouch before the U.S. House of Representatives' Subcommittee on National Parks and Public Lands, Washington D.C.: U.S. Government Printing Office.

Photo credit/attribution: Title: Portrait of Paul Lawrence Dunbar; Photographer: unknown; Original tinted photo has been made black-and-white; Source #1: https://commons.wikimedia.org/wiki/File:Paul_Laurence_Dunbar_portrait.jpg; Source #2: Page 12 of C. Richardson's 1919 book, *The National Cyclopedia of the Colored Race*, Montgomery, National Publishing Co.; Photo is in the public domain.

> *Do not be afraid of spending quality time by yourself. Find meaning or don't find meaning, but "steal" some time and give it freely and exclusively to your own self.*

Albert Camus, 1913-1960. Born in a small, working-class Algerian town near the Mediterranean Sea, Camus became a famous journalist, philosopher, playwright, and author. At the young age of 44, he earned the Nobel Prize in Literature. In choosing Camus for this prestigious award, the selection committee  pointed to "his important literary production, which with clear-sighted earnestness illuminates the problems of human consciousness in our times."

At age 11, Camus earned a scholarship to attend a prestigious high school near his country's capital, Algiers. Soon after graduating, Camus contracted tuberculosis and had to delay further education. When he was 20, he entered the University of Algiers, where, three years later, he earned his B.A. degree after writing his required thesis. His chosen topic: the Greek philosopher Plotinus.

After completing his formal education, Camus worked for newspapers both in Algeria and Paris. He then turned his attention to penning novels, short stories, essays, non-fiction books, and plays. His most famous works are his books *The Stranger* and *The Plague*, his essays *The Rebel* and *The Crisis of Man*, and his play *Caligula*. Through these vehicles, Camus raised philosophical questions concerning the meaning of life.

In addition to posing esoteric philosophical questions of interest mainly to other philosophers, Camus concerned himself with many issues that the non-philosopher layperson could easily understand. For example, Camus

- argued that people have a right to revolt against oppression and injustice.
- supported political tolerance and dialogue.
- took the position that suicide is not a justifiable response to the "absurdity" of life.
- opposed the death penalty.
- did not believe, as many French people did at the time, that the Arab and Berber inhabitants of Algeria were inferior human beings.

Scholar David Simpson paid Camus an enormous compliment, saying that Camus "lived his philosophy." Simpson believed that Camus' words and actions displayed "tolerance, justice, liberty, open-mindedness, respect for personhood, condemnation of violence, and resistance to tyranny." Camus' work, Simpson stated, was in service to both truth and liberty.

Boxed Camus quotation at top of previous page: Excerpt from his 1962 book, *Notebooks*, 1951-1959 (translated into English in 2008 by Ryan Bloom), Chicago: Ivan R. Dee, Publisher.

Comments about Camus from Professor David Simpson: Excerpt from Section 8 ("Significance and Legacy") of his entry, "Albert Camus (1913-1960)," in the *Internet Encyclopedia of Philosophy*.

Photo credit/attribution: Title: 1957 photo of Camus; Photographer: Unnamed employee of United Press International (UPI); Source: http://loc.gov/pictures/resource/cph. 3c08028/; Photo is in the public domain; Original photo has been cropped

> *There are seasons when things go wrong,
> and they just have to be lived through.*

Beatrix Potter, 1866-1943. Born to wealthy parents who lived in an affluent section of London, Potter had  limited contact with other children when she was young. She was educated at home by a governess who exerted tight control over her. For the most part, her friends were her pets: frogs, snails, caterpillars, mice, rabbits, and a hedgehog.

In light of young Potter's pet animals, it is not surprising that she, as an adult, wrote 23 children's books about animals. Her most famous work was *The Tale of Peter Rabbit*, a heartwarming book that was an instant success. It has been translated into more than 35 languages and sold more than 45 million copies.

Although many people know that Potter was the author of children's stories, few are aware that she was an accomplished botanist with a particular interest in mycology (the study of fungi). She conducted research and wrote scientific papers. One of her papers—entitled "On the Germination of the Spores of Agaricineae"—was presented to the Linnean Society of London, a scholarly group intent on advancing the field of natural history.

Potter was also interested in art. As a young girl, she drew detailed pictures of her pets and other animals. Moreover, she visited art museums where she examined (and even critiqued!) paintings by masters such as Turner, Gainsborough, and Rubens. Motivated by her interest in mycology, Potter produced 350 detailed images of fungi; some of these works were so advanced that instructors used them to teach fungal taxonomy. The works of art for which Potter is most well-known, however, are the beautiful illustrations in her children's books, especially those in *Peter Rabbit.*

Besides being a writer, scientist, and artist, Potter had two other loves: farming and conservation. When she was 50, she and her husband began raising sheep, pigs, chickens, and cows. Potter's sheep won awards, and she was elected president of the Herdwick Sheep-Breeders' Association. A life-long lover of flora and fauna, Potter wanted to help protect nature's beauty against development. Thus, she specified in her will that 4,000 acres of land be given to UK's National Trust, an organization that safeguards landscapes, homes, and gardens.

One final activity of Potter's life is worth noting. Beginning when she was 14, she wrote a private diary for 16 years. In it, she shared, among other things, her innermost thoughts regarding her parents (whom she resented), her depression, and her bouts with poor health. What's so amazing about this diary is that Potter wrote it in secret code. It wasn't until 23 years after her death that a passionate fan of Potter's broke the code so it could be read.

Boxed Potter quotation at top of previous page: Excerpt from a letter Potter wrote to Henry P. Coolidge on June 28, 1928; located on page 16 in the 1982 book (edited by Jane Crowell Morse), *Beatrix Potter's Americans: Selected Letters*, Boston: The Horn Book.

Photo credit/attribution: Title: 1912 photo of Beatrix Potter; Photographer: her father, Rupert; Original black-and-white photo has been cropped; Source https://commons.wikimedia.org/w/index.php?search=beatrix+potter&title=Special: MediaSearch&go=Go&type=image; Photo is in the public domain {{PD-US}}.

> *Friendship is a priceless gift...So when you ask God for a gift, be thankful if He sends not diamonds, pearls, or riches, but the love of real, true friends.*

Muhammad Ali, 1942-2016. When he was in his early 20s, the boxer Ali was a highly controversial figure, even though he had won a gold medal in the 1960 Olympics. For many, he was a legitimate target of condemnation because he seemed to be ultra-conceited, because he switched religions from Christianity to Islam  (and discarded his original name, Cassius Clay), and because he refused to be inducted into the U.S. Army to fight in the Vietnam War.

Over time, more and more people came to respect Ali. Support for him grew as the Vietnam War came to be seen as unjust and as support for religious plurality in the U.S. increased. Also, Ali—when allowed to box again— demonstrated in the ring that perhaps he was "the greatest," just as he had boasted.

Ali had worldwide name recognition. An estimated billion people watched the TV broadcast of his 1974 fight in Africa. *Sports Illustrated* named him the greatest athlete of the 20th century. Some even claimed that Ali was the most famous and documented human being of that period. Notably, Ali was chosen to light the flame at the 1996 Summer Olympics, even though he was noticeably affected by Parkinson's Disease.

People who know only a little about Ali consider him to have been just a boxer. He was, however, far more than that. Ali was a philanthropist, a humanitarian, and an activist. He donated large sums of money to help feed disadvantaged people of all religious backgrounds. He spoke to children about the importance of education. He visited and supported Palestinian refugees, Sudanese victims of famine, and Native Americans. He spoke out against the discrimination of blacks.

For his efforts to make the world a better place, Ali received several awards, including the Presidential Medal of Freedom from George W. Bush (because "his deep commitment to equal justice and peace touched people around the world"), the Presidential Citizens Medal from Bill Clinton (because of "his advocacy for peace, tolerance, and compassion"), and the Arthur Ashe Courage Award (because "he stood up for racial pride, spoke of peace, and was willing to fight for what one believes and for what is right no matter what the cost."). Ali also received an honorary doctoral degree from Princeton.

Perhaps the most meaningful honor Ali received came in the form of eight words from Coretta Scott King, wife of Martin Luther King, Jr. She referred to Ali as "a champion of justice and peace and unity."

Boxed Ali quotation on previous page: Excerpt from 1974 videotaped Ali interview with Harold Bell (https://www.youtube.com/watch?v=InSFYdFaS3E).

George W. Bush comment about Ali: Citation for 2005 Presidential Medal of Freedom.

Bill Clinton comment about Ali: Citation for 2001 Presidential Citizens Medal.

Arthur Ashe Courage Award citation for Ali: Read by Sydney Portier at ESPYS award ceremony, December 13, 1997.

Coretta Scott King comment about Ali: Located on page 150 of Michael Ezra's 2009 book, *Muhammad Ali: The Making of an Icon*, Philadelphia: Temple University Press.

Photo credit/attribution: Title: Muhammad Ali in 1967; Photographer: Ira Rosenberg; Source #1: http://loc.gov/pictures/resource/cph.3c15435/; Source #2: https:// commons.wikimedia.org/wiki/File:Muhammad_Ali_NYWTS.jpg; Photo is in the public domain. Original photo has been flipped horizontally, rotated slightly, and cropped.

> *As to the money-getting life, that is no life at all.... Wealth is valuable only for the things it can procure you; and these are pleasure to the extent of your capacity for enjoyment and honour—from fools. It will not procure you the higher goods of wisdom and virtue.*

Aristotle, 384-322 BC. Considered to be the "Father of Western Philosophy," Aristotle developed many of his ideas during the two decades he spent as one of Plato's students. About the time Plato died, Aristotle left Plato's Academy and became the head of the Royal Academy of Macedonia. There, he tutored two future kings as well as Alexander the Great, then just a boy.

After returning to Athens at age 49, Aristotle established his school called the Lyceum. He taught there for 12 years. During this period, Aristotle wrote authoritative treatises on various subjects, including astronomy, ethics, geology, political theory, mathematics, agriculture, physics, economics, dance, and psychology.

Aristotle made essential contributions to many sub-fields of philosophy, one of which was logic. A well-known part of Aristotelian logic was the three-part syllogism comprised of a major premise, a minor premise, and a deduced conclusion. Here's an example: (1) All fish live in the water; (2) A trout is a fish; (3) Therefore, a trout lives in the water.

Because of Aristotle's lasting contributions to so many areas of knowledge (from art to zoology), many view him as one of the most influential people who ever lived. The author Dante referred to Aristotle as "the Master of those who know." Medieval Arabic scholars referred to him as "The first teacher."

Perhaps the most impressive compliment to Aristotle came from the famous painter Raphael, over 1,800 years after Aristotle died. Raphael's artistic masterpiece, "The School of Athens," contains images of over 50 people. Many are famous philosophers, mathematicians, and scientists from antiquity (such as Socrates, Diogenes, Euclid, and Pythagoras) who, in the painting, seem to be sharing their ideas with interested learners. In the painting's center are two intellectual giants, one of whom is Aristotle.

In 2020, an article about Aristotle appeared in the *Stanford Encyclopedia of Philosophy*. This article presented a contemporary opinion of Aristotle. The opening sentence asserted that he "numbers among the greatest philosophers of all time." The article ended with this bold statement:

> *Today, philosophers of various stripes continue to look to Aristotle for guidance and inspiration in many different areas [and] it seems safe at this stage to predict that Aristotle's stature is unlikely to diminish anytime in the foreseeable future.*

Boxed Aristotle quotation at top of previous page: Excerpt from page 13 of the 1987 book (edited by St. George Stock), *Lessons in the Lyceum*, London: Longmans, Green, and Co.

Dante's characterization of Aristotle: Located on line 131 of Canto IV of the Inferno portion of *The Devine Comedy*. (Found in James R. Sibbald's 1884 translation of Dante Alighieri's masterpiece.)

Excerpt from the *Stanford Encyclopedia of Philosophy*: article written by Christpher Shields, George N. Shuster Professor of Philosophy at the University of Notre Dame.

Photo credit/attribution: Title: Marble bust of Aristotle; Photographer: Sergey Sosnovskiy; Source: https://commons.wikimedia.org/wiki/File:Head_of Aristotle.jpg; Location: Museum of Art History, Vienna; Photo is used here under the Creative Commons Attribution-Share Alike 2.0 Generic license (https://creativecommons.org/licenses/by-sa/2.0/deed.en) [CC-BY-SA-2.0]; Original color photo has been cropped and made black-and-white.

> *If you feel unhappy, rise above it and act so that*
> *your happiness may be independent*
> *of all outside events.*

Catherine the Great, 1729-1796. Born in the Prussian town of
Szczecin (in what now is Poland), Catherine
joined a regal, influential family. Her father
was a prince, a general in the army, and the
governor of his city. Her mother's relatives
were wealthy with royal connections. Two
of her first cousins became Swedish kings.

Private tutors and a French governess provided Princess
Catherine with her education. Among other things, she learned
etiquette, French, and theology. When she was 15, Catherine
and her politically ambitious aunt moved to Russia.

In an arranged marriage in St. Petersburg, Catherine, at
age 16, wed Peter III, grandson of Peter the Great and nephew
of the ruling Empress, Elizabeth. Following the death of
Elizabeth, Peter III became Emperor, and Catherine acquired
the title of "Empress Consort." Six months later, Peter III, who
had sided with Prussia against Russia in the Seven Years' War,
was murdered in a coup d'état. This elevated Catherine to
Empress, leader of the country.

Catherine came to love her adopted country, and she
reigned from 1762 until she died in 1796. Under her leadership,
Russia prospered. It won wars against the Ottoman Empire and
Persia, thereby increasing its territory. Just as important as her
military victories, Catherine improved Russia's agriculture and
farming efforts, modernized its monetary system, and created a

new government structure. Significantly, Catherine revamped her country's educational system, adopting many procedures, goals, and rules from other—mainly European—countries.

In the opinion of many historians, Catherine's most notable achievements involved arts and culture. Among other undertakings in this arena, Catherine

- built the now-famous Hermitage Museum, filling it with her books, paintings, sculptures, and gems.
- supported the opera (which she loved).
- studied Western philosophy and corresponded with Voltaire.
- brought accomplished scientists and writers to Russia.
- updated Russia's educational system with higher academic and moral goals.

Initiatives such as these caused most Russians to view Catherine as one of the most cultured people in their country. The masses greatly admired her.

Catherine the Great sometimes is referred to as Catherine II (because Peter the Great's second wife was Catherine I). She became Catherine at age 15. Few people know that her name at birth was Sophia Friederike Auguste von Anhalt-Serbst!

Boxed Catherine quotation at top of previous page: Excerpt from page 212 of Robert K. Massie's 2012 book, *Catherine the Great: Portrait of a Woman*, New York: Random House.

Photo credit/attribution: Title: Photo of portrait painting (circa 1870) of Catherine the Great; Artist: Johann Baptist von Lampi the Elder; Source: https://commons.wikimedia.org/wiki/File:Levitzky_Catherine_the_Great.jpg; Location of painting: Vienna's Kunsthistorisches Museum; Photo is in the public domain{{PD-US}}; Original color photo has been cropped and made black-and-white.

> *He drew a circle that shut me out—*
> *Heretic, rebel, a thing to flout.*
> *But Love and I had the wit to win:*
> *We drew a circle that took him in!*

Edwin Markham, 1852-1940. Born in the American West, Markham spent much of his childhood working on the family farm. Initially, his single-parent mother would not buy books for him; however, she eventually supported his education. Markham graduated from the California State Normal School when 21.

Markham's first career was in schools, where he held positions, over time, as a classroom teacher, principal, and superintendent. When he was about 43 years old, he chose to be called Edwin (a variation of his actual middle name, Edward) and gave up using his first name, Charles. He also made a change in his career, becoming a full-time poet.

Literary critics consider Markham's early poem, *The Man with the Hoe*, to be his best work. It was inspired by Jean-François Millet's painting of an exhausted field worker leaning on his hoe. This poem touched the hearts of many, for it illuminated inhumane labor practices that exploited the poor. Soon, this poem appeared in newspapers across the country, prompting discussions of social reform. This single poem made Markham a national celebrity.

In 1922, a formal ceremony took place to dedicate the new Lincoln Memorial in Washington, D.C. For this special event, President Taft invited Markham to read his poem,

Lincoln, the Man of the People. Henry Van Dyke, professor of English at Princeton, stated that this poem was "the greatest poem ever written on the immortal martyr, and the greatest that will ever be written."

Markham did more than write poetry. He founded the Poetry Society of America. He served as Oregon's Poet Laureate for eight years. He also was a popular speaker, giving lectures about poetry and societal issues. Markham was the lead author of *Children in Bondage*, an exposé of the abuses of child labor.

In 1929, Markham commented on the importance of poetry. He wrote:

> *Poetry writing is as practical as bread-making; and, from a high ground, it is just as necessary to the life of man. Poetry is bread for the spirit: it is the bread that is made of earthly wheat and yet is mixed with some mystic tincture of the skies. It nourishes all the higher hopes and aspirations of man.*

Boxed Markham quotation at top of previous page: The entirety of his poem, "Outwitted." Located on page 765 in the 1927 book (edited by Leonidas Warren Payne) *Selections from American Literature*, Chicago: Rand McNally & Co.

Comment from Henry Van Dyke: Excerpt from page 65 of the 1965 book (edited by William Wilson Belts) *Lincoln and the Poets*, Pittsburgh: University of Pittsburgh Press.

Markham's comment on the importance of poetry: Excerpt from his article "Old Friendship Between Poets Inspiring" that appeared March 22, 1929, in the *State College Times.*

Photo credit/attribution: Title: Photo of Edwin Markham; Photographer: McMichael & Gro, New York; Source #1: unnumbered page (after p. 144) in Volume 35, 1905, of *The Arena* (edited by B. O. Flower), Trenton, N.J.: Albert Brandt Publisher; Source #2: https://commons.wikimedia.org/wiki/File:Portrait_of_Edwin_Markham.jpg; Photo is in the public domain {{PD-US}}. Original photo has been flipped horizontally and cropped.

> *Endeavor to conquer yourself rather than fortune,*
> *and to change your desires rather than*
> *the order of the world.*

René Descartes, 1596-1650. Born in central France, Descartes survived a rough childhood. He then became one of the foremost intellectuals of his time. Scholars refer to him as the "father of modern philosophy" and the "father of analytic geometry." He also possessed an advanced talent for physics, and he  contributed to the 17th-century scientific revolution.

After Descartes earned a college degree in law, he spent four years in the military. He was not involved in combat, however. Instead, he studied military engineering and worked to link mathematics and physics. While still wearing a uniform, his career interest switched from becoming a "military man" to pursuing intellectual ideas. After his military commitment ended, he began to write essays and books on philosophy.

Though Descartes became known throughout Europe for his mathematical genius, his contributions to philosophy are even more impressive. Many people are familiar with his famous Latin saying, *Cogito, ergo sum*, which, when translated, says, "I think, therefore I am." However, Descartes contributed far more to the field of philosophy than just that short phrase. For one thing, he articulated criteria for ascertaining what qualifies as "truth."

Descartes believed that everyone could tell what is true or false by "the natural light of reason." He chose to write his influential books in French rather than Latin so common people could read his work and learn to think for themselves. Perhaps his most crucial philosophical doctrine was his dualism of body and mind. Descartes believed that the body and mind are physical and non-physical, respectively. The mind and body, according to Descartes, are separate and distinct but connected because they interact. Descartes also wrote about religion, and he is famous for his philosophical proof that God exists.

Descartes established four "rules" (i.e., steps) for addressing problems in math, science, and other fields: One should proceed, he said, by (1) accepting nothing as true that is not self-evident; (2) dividing problems into their simplest parts; (3) solving problems by proceeding from simple to complex; (4) rechecking one's reasoning. These rules may well be helpful to most (or all) people today!

Although Descartes was a brilliant thinker, he also was "normal" in many ways. While in Paris, he gambled, went to the theater, and participated in fencing events. He also could grieve like any other human being, for he openly cried when his five-year-old daughter died of scarlet fever. Like many people today, Descartes had a sleep disorder and often slept until late in the morning.

Boxed Descartes quotation at top of previous page: Excerpt from page 605 of Charles A. Dubray's 1912 book *Introductory Philosophy: A Textbook for Colleges and High Schools*, New York: Longmans, Green, and Co. (Original source: Descartes, *Discours de la méthode, P. III, 3rd maxim.*)

Photo credit/attribution: Title: Photo of portrait painting of Réne Descartes (circa 1670); Artist: Frans Hals; Location: Louvre Museum, Paris; Photographer: André Hatala; Source: https://commons.wikimedia.org/wiki/File:Frans_Hals_-_Portret_van_Ren%C3%A9_Descartes_(cropped).jpg; Photo is in the public domain; Original color photo has been flipped horizontally, cropped, and made black-and-white.

> *Whether you succeed or not is irrelevant....*
> *Making your unknown known is the important thing.*

Georgia O'Keeffe, 1887-1986. Born to dairy farmers in a small Wisconsin town, O'Keeffe grew up to become one of the 20th-century's best-known artists.

Even as a child, O'Keeffe loved art and wanted to have a career as an artist. After graduating from high school, she worked as an art instructor while continuing her studies at the Art Institute of Chicago, the University of Virginia, and Columbia University. When 31 years old, O'Keeffe moved to New York City. There, she began to paint the city's skyscrapers and its skyline. She also created the first of her "magnified" renditions of flowers.

When she was 58 years old, O'Keeffe moved to Abiquiú, New Mexico, a small town north of Santa Fe. Her renovated hacienda became her Southwestern summertime home and studio. Three years later, O'Keeffe moved permanently into her hacienda (that now is a National Historic Landmark). She continued painting—even after her eyesight began to fail—until she was 96 years old.

Unfortunately, many people have only two things come to mind when they hear the name Georgia O'Keeffe: painted pictures of enlarged flowers and New Mexico. However, O'Keeffe deserves to be remembered for many other notable accomplishments. For example:

- O'Keeffe was among the early American artists to achieve international recognition for producing abstract paintings. These include her works "Ladder to the Moon" and "Blue and Green Music."

- O'Keeffe's urban paintings depicting New York City are as valuable as some of her flower paintings.
- She is known as the "Mother of American Modernism," a movement characterized mainly by abstraction, innovation, and emotion.
- The painting called "Jimson Weed/White Flower No. 1" by O'Keeffe sold in 2014 for over 44 million dollars.
- O'Keeffe's love of nature was not confined to her paintings; she ventured out into it in dramatic ways, as evidenced by her many rafting trips down the Colorado River.

In recognition of her life's work, O'Keeffe received several impressive awards and honors, including a Medal of Freedom (presented by President Gerald Ford), a National Medal of Arts (presented by President Ronald Reagan), honorary degrees from Harvard and the College of William & Mary, and memberships in both the National Women's Hall of Fame and the American Academy of Arts and Letters. Even an extinct bird species has been named in her honor: *Effigia okeeffeae* ("O'Keeffe's ghost").

Boxed O'Keeffe quotation at top of previous page: Excerpt from page 240 of Hunter Drohojowska-Philp's 2004 book, *Full Bloom: The Art and Life of George O'Keeffe*, New York: W. W. Norton & Company.

Photo credit/attribution: Title: 1915 photographic portrait of Georgia O'Keeffe; Photographer: Rufus W. Holsinger; Photo is in the public domain; Source https://commons.wikimedia.org/wiki/File:Georgia_O%27Keeffe_UVa.jpg Original tinted photo has been cropped.

J. M. Barrie, 1860-1937. Born in, raised in, and a lifetime resident of Scotland, James Matthew Barrie grew up to become one of his country's (and the world's) most beloved playwrights and novelists. That reputation is attributable to his series of plays and books about "the boy who never grows up," Peter Pan.

As a child, Barrie enjoyed reading and story-telling. When he attended high school at Dumfries Academy, he and his friends formed a drama club and often assumed the role of pirates. After graduating from Dumfries, Barrie went to the University of Edinburgh, where he studied literature and wrote drama reviews. After graduating, Barrie took a job as a newspaper journalist, writing stories he later expanded into novels.

In addition to writing novels, Barrie created plays. In 1904, his *Peter Pan* debuted on stage. He continued to be a successful playwright, but in 1911 he transformed his play about Peter, Tinker Bell, the Darling children, Captain Hook, and the crocodile into a novel. In the story, Peter takes Wendy and John from their London home to Neverland, a far-away place where they have adventurous encounters with pirates and Indians and the Lost Boys.

Although Barrie wrote a host of plays and books throughout his adult life, they all were overshadowed by the enormous success of his works focused on Peter Pan. On the surface, these books and plays were aimed at children. However, several literary scholars believe that these creations of Barrie truly are stories *about* children intended *for* adults. According to these scholars, parents and teachers can better understand the thinking and actions of children by noting that Wendy and John leave their boring home, that Peter doesn't want to grow up, and that Neverland is filled with adventure.

In 1929, Barrie gave the copyright for *Peter Pan* to the Great Ormand Street Hospital in London. This children's hospital is the largest center for child heart surgery in the UK and one of the world's largest centers for heart transplants. Still today, it receives royalties for plays, films, and novels based on Barrie's most well-known character, Peter Pan.

Not surprisingly, Barrie received several prestigious honors for his accomplishments. He was appointed a "baronet" by King George V, tapped to be a member of the British Commonwealth's Order of Merit, had a London school named after him, and gave the 1922 Rectorial Address at the University of St. Andrews. Notably, a 14-foot sculpture of Peter Pan stands in London's Kensington Park.

Boxed Barrie quotation at top of previous page: Excerpt from Barrie's Rectorial Address (entitled "Courage") delivered at St. Andrew's University in Scotland on May 3, 1922.
Photo credit/attribution: Title: 1902 photo of Barrie; Photographer: George Beresford; Source: https://commons.wikimedia.org/wiki/File:J._M._Barrie_in_1902.jpg; Location: National Portrait Gallery, London; Photo is in the public domain; Original tinted photo has been cropped and made black-and-white.

> *Be true and honest in all you say, and seriously earnest in all you do. ... When you are afoot, let these two counsels be two companions preceding you, yourself viewing them from behind.*

Confucius, 551-479 BCE. Born in Lu, a state in northeast China, Confucius grew up to become his country's most revered teacher, philosopher, and political theorist.

Confucius was raised by his mother, as his father died when Confucius was just three years old. After being educated at schools for commoners, he initially held a series of modest positions in government. However, his work in those jobs allowed others to notice his intelligence, insight into human character, political commonsense, and concern for integrity and virtue. As pointed out by scholar Matt Stefon, "He always made sure that the ruler and his mission were well prepared [and] he also knew how to advise them to bring a difficult negotiation to a successful conclusion."

Disillusioned by the selfishness and squabbling of government leaders, Confucius left Lu and embarked on a 14-year journey through neighboring states. His goal was to find a ruler who ran a virtuous government. Accompanying him on this journey were his students, young men who wished to learn from Confucius. Over time, the number of his followers increased, and when his journey ended, he took back to Lu both admirers and the reputation of being a wise elder from whom others (including government leaders) should seek advice.

Today, "Confucianism" comes mainly from the *Analects*, a book of sayings and short dialogues attributed to Confucius and assembled, after his death, by his students. The nearly 500 elements of the *Analects* deal with three main topics: social interactions, education, and political philosophy. Regarding the social domain, Confucius argued that people should strive to be tolerant, trustworthy, respectful, and kind. As for education, Confucius believed that the masses should be educated, that people should strive to achieve "skilled judgment" rather than memorizing lots of rules, and that teaching should be a respected vocation. Concerning politics, Confucius believed leaders should be self-disciplined, guided in their actions by virtue, and quick to manage citizens with love and respect rather than punishment and coercion.

One mark of how much people still admire Confucius is genealogical in nature. Over two million people claim to be his direct descendant! Interestingly, Confucius may have coined the Golden Rule. However, he stated it negatively: "What you do not want done to yourself, do not do to others."

Boxed Confucius quotation at top of previous page: Excerpt from page 84 of the 1900 book, *The Wisdom of Confucius* (translated into English by William Jennings), New York: The Colonial Press.

Matt Stefon's characterization of Confucius: Excerpt from his online article "Confucius: Chinese Philosopher," *Britannica.com*.

Confucius version of the Golden Rule: Excerpt from Chapter 23 of Book 15 of James Legge's 1861 book, *The Chinese Classics—Volume I: Confucian Analects,* London: Trubner & Co.

Photo credit/attribution: Title: Statue of Confucius, Beijing; Photographer: D. Morrow; Source: https://commons.wikimedia.org/wiki/File:Confucius_statue_in_beijing.jpg; Photo is in the public domain [CC0-1.0 Universal Public Domain]; Original color photo has been cropped and made black-and-white.

> *Live your life while you have it.*
> *Life is a splendid gift. There is nothing small in it.*

Florence Nightingale, 1820-1910. Born into an affluent British family living in Italy, Nightingale had a privileged upbringing. Her parents made sure she received a classical education that included studies in math, German, French, and Italian. Her wealthy family lived in two homes, one for use in summer, the other in winter.

When young, Nightingale helped poor and sick people who lived in a village near her parents' estate. Later, in her teenage years, she felt "called" to serve others as a nurse. Her family, however, disapproved, thinking that a woman's role was to be a wife and mother. Undaunted, Nightingale became a nurse when 24.

To a degree, Nightingale became self-educated in the art of nursing. (She had paid close attention—during family trips to Greece, Egypt, and Germany—to the way others cared for the sick.) Her formal training in nursing took place in a Lutheran hospital in Germany. After returning to London, Nightingale was hired as a nurse and quickly found herself promoted to Superintendent of Nursing.

During the Crimean War, Nightingale took a group of volunteer nurses she had trained to care for wounded soldiers in what is now Istanbul. Her work is said to have reduced the death rate there from 42% to 2%. One reason for Nightingale's success was the fact that she first amassed data about people, sanitary conditions, and disease; she then used statistical tools—some of which she invented—to analyze her data. Nightingale also showed her "soft" side while there. She came to be called "The Lady with the Lamp," a nickname she earned because of her solitary rounds late at night to check on wounded soldiers.

Using a monetary gift from Queen Victoria and funds raised on her behalf, Nightingale, in 1860, founded the Nightingale Home and Training School for Nursing. Each student's curriculum was based on Nightingale's helpful book, *Notes on Nursing*. The initial graduates were called "Nightingales." This famous nurse-training facility, now called the Florence Nightingale School of Nursing and Midwifery, operates today as part of King's College London.

Considered to be the person who founded modern nursing, Nightingale received several honors. Many hospitals bear her name. The International Red Cross awards the Florence Nightingale Medal. International Nurses Day is celebrated on her birthday. After their training, nurses recite the Nightingale Pledge (a modification of the Hippocratic Oath). Nightingale most likely would be pleased with none of those or other forms of recognition. Instead, she probably would take greatest pride in knowing that nursing is now a respected profession.

Boxed Nightingale quotation at top of previous page: Excerpt from page 434 in the 1913 book by Sir Edward Cook *The Life of Florence Nightingale* (Vol. 2), London: Macmillan and Co., Ltd.

Photo credit/attribution: Title: Photo of Florence Nightingale (circa 1860); Photographer: Henry Hering; Location: National Portrait Gallery, London; Source: https://commons.wikimedia.org/wiki/File:Florence_Nightingale_(H_Hering_NPG_x 82368).jpg. Photo is in the public domain; Original photo has been cropped.

> *Find the good. It's all around you.*

Jesse Owens, 1913-1980. Born in Alabama to a sharecropper, Owens was the grandson of enslaved people. As a young boy, he helped his family earn money by picking cotton. He was nine years old when he and his family moved to Cleveland, Ohio. They and many others moved north to avoid the South's blatant racism.

In junior high school, Owens worked in a shoe-repair shop, loaded train cars, and delivered groceries. When not working, he loved to run. He was amazingly fast in the short sprints. His long jump achievements were equally impressive. When he reached high school, Owens tied the world record for the 100-yard dash and set state records in three other events.

In the 1935 Big Ten Conference track meet, Owens set three world records and tied a fourth. He did all this within three-fourths of an hour (and with an injured back), a feat considered by some to be "the greatest 45 minutes in sports history." A few weeks later, he won the same four events in the NCAA track competition. The following year: same result.

Naturally, Owens was selected to compete in the 1936 Olympics held in Berlin, Germany. Before any of the track events had taken place, Adolf Hitler bragged about how Germany's superior, Aryan-race athletes would dominate the competition. The Nazi leader received his comeuppance from Owens, who won gold medals in each of the four events he entered: 100m dash, long jump, 200m sprint, and 4x100m sprint relay. After returning to the U.S., Owens was honored in New York City with a ticker-tape parade.

Although Owens had achieved international fame, his legendary status did not open doors to prestigious jobs, endorsement contracts, or even an invitation to visit the White House. Because of his skin color, he remained a target of racial discrimination. His post-Olympic jobs found him working as a gas station attendant, a janitor, and a manager of a dry-cleaning firm. Eventually, his life improved. He became Assistant Personnel Director with the Ford Motor Company, a Goodwill Ambassador for the U.S., and a coach for the New York Mets.

Both before and after he died, Owens received many awards and honors. Not surprisingly, Owens was among the first group of athletes inducted into the U.S. Olympic Hall of Fame. He received the Presidential Medal of Freedom (from Gerald Ford), the Living Legend Award (from Jimmy Carter), and the Congressional Gold Medal (from George H. W. Bush). The most meaningful tribute to Owens may have been these words uttered by President Carter after Owens died:

> *Perhaps no athlete better symbolized the human struggle against tyranny, poverty, and racial bigotry. His personal triumphs as a world-class athlete and record-holder were the prelude to a career devoted to helping others.*

Boxed Owens quotation at top of previous page: Excerpt from page 166 of his 1970 book (written with Paul G. Niemark), *Blackthink: My Life as Black Man and White Man*, New York: William Morrow and Company.

President Carter comment about Owens: Excerpt from page 26 of G. Wiener's 2020 book, *Athlete Activism*, New York: Greenhaven Publishing.

Photo credit/attribution: Title: 1935 photo of Jesse Owens (with Ercole Gallegati); Photographer: unknown: Photo is in the public domain. Source: https://commons.wikimedia.org/wiki/File:Jesse_Owens_e_Ercole_Gallegati_1935.jpg; Original photo has been flipped horizontally, rotated slightly, and cropped.

> *To live is to choose. But to choose well, you must know who you are and what you stand for, where you want to go, and why you want to get there.*

Kofi Annan, 1938-2018. Born in Africa in what now is Ghana, Annan had three relatives—two grandfathers and an uncle—who were tribal chiefs. When of high school age, Annan attended a Methodist boarding school. He began college in his home country but transferred to and graduated from Macalester College in  Minnesota. Annan then earned DEA (Diplôma d'éstudes approfondies) and Master's degrees, the latter from MIT.

When 24, Annan began working for the United Nations, holding various essential posts for 34 years. Then, in 1996, he was elected to the UN's top position: Secretary-General. Following his five-year term of office, Annan was elected, unopposed, for a second term.

Annan was anything but a figurehead. Among other accomplishments, he:

- reformed the way the UN worked.
- refocused the UN's primary goal to one of "enabling men, women, and children, in cities and villages around the world, to make their lives better."
- established the Global AIDS and Health Fund.
- clarified that the UN had an obligation to prevent conflict and civilian suffering.
- prompted the UN to help nations transition from military to civilian rule.

After leaving office at the UN in 2006, Annan established a not-for-profit organization: the Kofi Annan Foundation. It works to promote fairer governance and strengthen the ability of individuals and countries to enjoy a more equitable and peaceful world. To accomplish this overall objective, the Foundation works to achieve four goals: gender equality, diversity, inclusion, and sustainability.

Besides being involved with his Foundation, Annan worked on several projects during the last 12 years of his life. He was the University of Ghana's Chancellor. He chaired the Global Commission on Elections, Democracy and Security. With others, he sought to end armed conflict in Syria and Kenya.

Not surprisingly, many honors and awards came to Annan. They included a Nobel Peace Prize, honorary doctorates from 25 universities located around the world, and a John F. Kennedy Profile-in-Courage Award. Impressively, three entities bear his name: the Kofi Annan International Peacekeeping Centre, the Ghana-India Kofi Annan Centre of Excellence, and the Kofi Annan University of Ghana.

People sometimes ask about Annan's first name. In Akan, the native language of Ghana, "Kofi" is the given name for a male baby born on a Friday!

Boxed Annan quotation at top of previous page: Excerpt from Annan's June 6, 1997 commencement address at MIT in Cambridge, Massachusetts.

Annan's refocused UN goal: Page 7 of the UN document *We, the Peoples: The Role of the United Nations in the 21st Century*, New York: United Nations Department of Public Information, 2000.

Photo credit/attribution: Title: Kofi Annan...Nobel Peace Prize Winner; Source: https://commons.wikimedia.org/wiki/File:Kofi_Annan_in_Washington_D.C.jpg; Photo is used here under the Creative Commons Attribution-Share Alike 2.0 Generic license: (https://creativecommons.org/licenses/by-sa/2.0/deed.en) [CC BY-SA 2.0]; Original color photo has been flipped horizontally, cropped, and made black-and-white. Photographer: John Mathew Smith.

> *Let us all unite to fight injustice and oppression.*
> *Let us raise our voices together and say:*
> *no to violence, yes to peace;*
> *no to slavery, yes to freedom;*
> *no to racial discrimination,*
> *yes to equality and to human rights for all.*

Nadia Murad, 1993-. It is shocking that certain groups of people subject others to hateful, perverse, and tortuous acts. Can a single victim of this kind of brutal injustice speak out with such force and authenticity that others worldwide become aware of the evil group's crimes against humanity? Yes, and a prime example  of such an individual is the Iraqi woman, Nadia Murad.

Born in a small farming village in northern Iraq, Murad became part of a community-wide religious/cultural group, or sect, called the Yazidis. In 2014, the terrorist group ISIS invaded and took control of Murad's defenseless village. Most Yazidi men were beheaded or shot, the invaders brainwashed children into joining their ranks, older women were sold in a market, and younger women were raped and turned into sex slaves.

During the ISIS-perpetrated genocide, six of Murad's brothers were killed. So were her parents. Murad was taken captive, tortured, and repeatedly raped. After months of horrific abuse, she escaped. Once free, she spoke out about what ISIS was doing (despite the recurring death threats she received). Murad first told a Belgian newspaper of what had happened to the Yazidi people. Six months later, she related her story to the Security Council at the United Nations.

As a result of her report to the United Nations, Murad became the UN's first Goodwill Ambassador for the Dignity of Survivors of Human Trafficking. Although that UN position gave her a platform for alerting others to the horrific crime of human trafficking, Murad also used other means to achieve her goals. She founded "Nadia's Initiative," a non-profit organization designed to help survivors of sexual violence and those who witness genocide. She met with Pope Francis and sought help for religious minorities. Murad wrote an autobiography, *The Last Girl: My Story of Captivity,* and another book, *My Fight Against the Islamic State.* She also penned various articles intended to expose ISIS atrocities.

Murad's efforts to speak out on behalf of others has not gone unnoticed. Among other kinds of recognition, she has received a Nobel Peace Prize, the Sakharov Prize for Freedom of Thought, the Václav Havel Human Rights Prize, the Clinton Global Citizen Award, and the Golden Plate Award of the American Academy of Achievement. She also was the focus of an award-winning movie, *On Her Shoulders.* In 2022, she gave the commencement address at Chapman University in California.

Notably, Murad has given the money from her awards to Nadia's Initiative and the other organizations she supports. She has kept none of that money for herself.

Boxed Murad quotation at top of previous page: Excerpt from Murad's Nobel Lecture on December 10, 2018, in the Oslo City Hall, Norway.

Photo credit/attribution: Title: 2015 photo of Murad in New York; Source: https//commons.wikimedia.org/wiki/File:Nadia_Murad,_2015_(cropped).jpg; Photog-rapher: Unnamed U.S. Dept. of State Employee; Photo is in the public domain; Original color photo has been cropped and made black-and-white.

> *Travel is fatal to prejudice,*
> *bigotry, and narrow-mindedness.*
> *Broad, wholesome, charitable views*
> *cannot be acquired by [staying] in one*
> *little corner of the earth all one's lifetime.*

Mark Twain, 1835-1910. Most people know three facts about Mark Twain: that he wrote books about Tom Sawyer and Huckleberry Finn, that his real name was Samuel Clemons, and that he was a famous humorist responsible for pithy statements that poked fun at what people do or think. (One of his humorous comments: "We ought never do wrong when people are looking.")

Beyond the three facts about Twain that are common knowledge, six additional aspects of his life are worth noting:

- Twain's formal education in Hannibal, Missouri, ended when he was 12. He then took a job at a local newspaper. By setting the type for the paper's stories, he kept abreast of both domestic and international events.

- In his early 20s, Twain earned a license to be a steamboat pilot on the Mississippi and Missouri rivers. Among other things, he learned that the phrase "mark twain" was used to indicate that a river's depth was at least two fathoms (12 feet), deep enough for safe passage.

- After moving to Nevada in 1861, Twain worked as a miner, then as a writer for the Virginia City newspaper. There, for the first time, he wrote an article under his pen name, "Mark Twain."

- Twain was quite interested in science. He obtained patents for three of his inventions, and he once hosted Thomas Edison at his home.
- Twain was an abolitionist and a supporter of women's rights. He paid for two black students to attend college, and in his famous speech "Votes for Women," he called for women's full enfranchisement in elections.
- Twain wrote far more than just his stories about Tom and Huck. He penned other novels, short stories, travel books, essays, a play, poems, and an autobiography.

Twain's accomplishments earned him high praise from several literary giants. William Faulkner claimed that Twain was "the first truly American writer," Ernest Hemingway said *Huckleberry Finn* was superb, Eugene O'Neill called Twain the "father of American literature," and George Bernard Shaw (in a letter to Twain) said:

> *I am persuaded that the future historian of America will find your works as indispensable to him as a French historian finds the political tracts of Voltaire.*

Boxed Twain quotation at top of previous page: Excerpt from page 650 in his 1901 book, *The Innocents Abroad, or The New Pilgrims Progress*, Hartford, Connecticut: The American Publishing Company.

George Bernard Shaw's comment about Twain: Excerpt from page 1398 in Volume IV of Albert Bigelow Paine's 1923 book *Mark Twain: A Biography*, New York: Gabriel Wells Publisher.

Photo credit/attribution: Title: 1907 photo of Mark Twain; Source: https://commons.wikimedia.org/wiki/File:MarkTwain.LOC.jpg; Photographer: Unknown; Photo is in the public domain; Original photo has been flipped horizontally and cropped.

> *We are all formed of frailty and error;*
> *let us pardon reciprocally each others' folly.*

Voltaire, 1694-1778. Born into an aristocratic Parisian family, François-Marie d'Arouet—the future Voltaire—became a famous French historian, philosopher, poet, and social critic. He was admired by Jean-Jacques Rousseau, Victor Hugo, Goethe, Napoléon, Frederick the Great, and many more. The  Russian Empress Catherine the Great was so impressed with him that she bought his library (after he died) and had it moved, intact, to the Hermitage Museum in St. Petersburg.

Once old enough, d'Arouet received a first-rate education at a Jesuit college in Paris. After graduating, he followed his parents' wishes and worked at a series of jobs designed to propel him into a prestigious bureaucratic position like that his father held. However, d'Arouet wanted, from his youth, to become an author and playwright. Following his heart, he stopped trying to be someone he wasn't; he joined literary groups and began to write. And write he did! He wrote an enormous number of items, and his written products spanned a wide range of topics.

When he was 24, d'Arouet decided to become known as Voltaire. He did this following his release from the Bastille, where he had been imprisoned for writing a verse that made fun of a member of France's royal family. Not dissuaded from his opinions, Voltaire continued to be an outspoken critic of intolerance, religious dogma, the French aristocracy, and slavery. Moreover, he became a "voice of the Enlightenment" as he argued for religious tolerance and freedom of speech.

Of Voltaire's numerous written works, his novel *Candide* is the most famous. It is a satire that poked fun at theologians, government, armies, philosophers, and religion. Initially, the book was banned because its content was hostile to both church and state. Now, most consider it to be a masterpiece. Literary critic Martin Seymour-Smith labeled it as "one of the 100 most influential books ever written."

To say that Voltaire was a prolific writer does not give him adequate credit for what he accomplished. He wrote over 50 plays, 28 novels, seven books of history, science books, non-fiction items (such as *Dictionnaire Philosophique*), essays, and pamphlets. He also penned more than 20,000 letters!

Voltaire's work is looked upon by many—including the National Assembly of France—as having helped to bring about the French Revolution. As Otis E. Fellows (a scholar of 18th-Century French literature) put it, Voltaire's name "symbolizes freedom of thought, and hatred of prejudice, superstition, and injustice." Clearly, Voltaire made his mark by what he did.

Boxed Voltaire quotation at top of previous page: Excerpt from page 142 in the 1946 book *The Living Thoughts of Voltaire*, London: Cassell and Co.

Candide's status: Martin Seymour Smith's 2001 book *The 100 Most Influential Books Ever Written*, New York: Citadel Press.

Fellows' comment about Voltaire: Excerpt from page 64 of Brian Nelson's 2015 book *The Cambridge Introduction to French Literature*, Cambridge: Cambridge University Press.

Photo credit/attribution: Title: Photo of 1736 painting of François-Marie d'Arouet; Artist: Maurice Quentin de la Tour; Location: Palace of Versailles; Photographer: Gérard Blot; Photo is in the public domain; Source: https://commons.wikimedia.org/wiki/File:D'_Maurice_Quentin_de_La_Tour,_Fran çoisMarie_Arouet,_dit_Voltaire_(chateau_de_ Versailles).jpg; Original color photo has been flipped horizontally, cropped, and made black and white.

> *Knowledge is the food of the soul; and we must take care, my friend, that the Sophist does not deceive us when he praises what he sells, like the dealers wholesale or retail who sell the food of the body; for they praise indiscriminately all their goods, without knowing what are really beneficial or hurtful.*

Plato, 427-348BC. Born into a wealthy and politically active family in Greece, Plato was educated by distinguished teachers who taught him grammar, music, mathematics, wrestling, and gymnastics. They also taught him philosophy, the subject area for which Plato is most famous. One of his eminent teachers was  Socrates. Another notable and significant influence on Plato was Pythagoras.

Plato founded the Academy, the earliest form of a "university." It was an outdoor garden-like setting in which Plato posed problems for others to solve. One such problem involved geometry, and it asked what one should do to double the area of any square. (Double each side's length? Nope. Make each side 50 percent longer than it was initially? No. So, dear reader, what is the solution?)

Plato's problems for the Academy's students dealt with math, science, and, of course, philosophy. Plato's Academy is depicted in Raphael's artistic masterpiece, "The School of Athens," which is housed in the Vatican in Rome. In this famous painting, one of the two central figures is Plato; the other is the Academy's most famous student, Aristotle.

Plato did not simply sit around and think and talk about esoteric topics. He also wrote. He authored several famous books, including *The Republic*, *Dialogues*, and *The Symposium*. Centuries after they were written, these works often appear on required reading lists in college courses in philosophy.

Plato was the first philosopher to utilize dialogue and dialectic forms in his written work. They show up, for example, in the *Republic,* when the character Socrates discusses with others the meaning of justice, education, and politics. This book also contains Plato's well-known "allegory of the cave," in which he argues that it's wrong to equate our mental images of the objects we see with the actual external objects that create those mental images. Plato also wrote about love, and the contemporary phrase "platonic relationship" honors the latter of two kinds of love he said people can have: "Eros" or "Divine."

Ironically, nearly everyone knows at least a little about Plato, yet few know that "Plato" comes from his nickname, "Platon." In the ancient Greek language, "Platon" meant "broad." Why he acquired this name—which has been shortened to "Plato"—is unknown. Some believe that it was given to him by his wrestling coach because of his broad shoulders; others think it derives from his incredible breadth of knowledge.

Boxed Plato quotation at top of previous page: Excerpt from page 147 of the 1927 book, *The Dialogues of Plato: Selections from the Translation of Benjamin Jowett* (edited by William C. Greene), New York: Liveright Publishing.

Photo credit/attribution: Title: Photo of marble bust of Plato (copy of Greek 4th-century original); Location: The Museo Pio-Clementino, Rome; Artist: Unknown; Photographer: Marie-Lan Nguyen; Photo is in the public domain; Source: https://commons.wikimedia.org/wiki/File:Plato_Pio-Clemetino_Inv305.jpg; Original color photo has been cropped and made black and white.

> *Don't follow fashion—make it!*

Martha Graham, 1894-1991. Born in Pittsburgh, Graham moved with her family to California when she was 14. Two years later, she began studying dance in Los Angeles. At age 32, Graham left the West Coast, moved to New York City, and founded the Martha Graham Center of Contemporary Dance.

Graham's dance company—the oldest in America—had a rocky start because it used new techniques. Quickly, however, it became highly successful. In 1942 Graham and a colleague commissioned Aaron Copland to write the music for a ballet choreographed by Graham. Copland referred to his musical piece as the "Ballet for Martha" until Graham suggested, just before its premiere, that it be called *Appalachian Spring*. Graham was its lead dancer.

Graham's modern dance style was in sharp contrast to classical ballet. For example, she used innovative movement techniques called "contraction and release" and "spiraling." She also investigated how dancers could use weight, gravity, and falls in novel ways.

Because she was so highly respected, Graham received coveted awards and was chosen to show how dance could be a form of art. For instance, Graham was:

- the first dancer to perform at the White House.
- inducted into the National Women's Hall of Fame.
- elected a Fellow of the American Academy of Arts and Sciences.

- the first dancer to travel abroad as a U.S. Cultural Ambassador.
- given the highest U.S. award for civilians, the Presidential Medal of Freedom.
- called "a national treasure" by President Gerald Ford.
- named, in 1999, as "Dancer of the Century" by *Time* magazine.

Despite these and other accolades, Graham would likely be most proud that instructors worldwide teach her modern dance technique today.

Graham is known as a dancer and choreographer. However, she deserves praise for her willingness to stand up to Nazi Germany. Hitler's aide, Joseph Goebbels, invited Graham to dance at a festival in Berlin during the 1936 Olympic games. In a letter declining that invitation, Graham said:

> *I would find it impossible to dance in Germany at the present time [because] so many artists whom I respect and admire have been persecuted.... I should consider it impossible to identify myself, by accepting the invitation, with the regime that has made such things possible.*

Boxed Graham quotation at top of previous page: Excerpt from page 64 of Helen McGehee's article "Working for Martha Graham" that appeared in the scholarly journal *Dance Research: The Journal of the Society for Dance Research*, Vol. 3, No. 2 (Summer 1985), pages 56-64.

Graham's comment about the 1936 Olympics: Excerpt from Angelica Gibbs' article "The Absolute Frontier" published in *The New Yorker* on December 27, 1947.

Photo credit/attribution: Title: 1976 photo of Graham receiving the Medal of Freedom; Photographer: Unknown; Photo is in the public domain; Source: https://commons.wikimedia.org/wiki/File:President_Gerald_R._Ford_Presents_Mart ha_Graham_with_the_Presidential_Medal_of_Freedom_-_NARA_-_6829647.jpg; Original color photo has been flipped horizontally, cropped, and made black-and-white.

> *It is good sometimes to feel the power of Nature*
> *You bend in silence and accept the beauty,*
> *without words. Thou Wondrous Earth!*

Knud Rasmussen, 1879-1933. "The name Knud Rasmussen might not be on most people's list of most famous explorers of all time. But it should be. What Rasmussen accomplished in the early 20th Century should be held in similar regard to names as notable as Captain Cook, Lewis & Clark, Roald Amundsen, and  Ernest Shackleton. He was a legend." Thus wrote Daven Hafey, a professional guide on more than 40 polar expeditions.

Born in Greenland, Rasmussen grew up among its indigenous people, the Arctic Inuit. In his youth, he learned to hunt, fish, and drive dog sleds in extreme weather conditions. Commenting on that period of his life, Rasmussen wrote that "my playmates were native Greenlanders. From the earliest boyhood I played and worked with the hunters, so even the hardships of the most strenuous sledge-trips became pleasant routine for me."

In his adult years, Rasmussen explored his country's northernmost, inaccessible fjords and coastlines. Though it is proper, in one sense, to say that Rasmussen was an explorer, this famous Greenlander is even more widely considered to have been a world-class ethnographer, a type of cultural anthropologist. Like Margaret Mead, Rasmussen traveled to a distant and unfamiliar setting to observe a primitive group of people. In Rasmussen's case, he was interested in the "Polar

Eskimos" who lived north of the Arctic Circle. His goal was to learn about and document the Eskimos' "intellectual culture," as revealed in their beliefs, songs, fables, and customs. He also wanted to know how they survived in some of the most austere environmental conditions on Earth.

To achieve his ethnographic goals, Rasmussen did not simply swoop in for a few days to ask questions in English and take photos. Instead, he lived with the Eskimos, learned their unique language, gained their trust, and participated in their hunts, celebrations, and funerals. Later, he wrote several acclaimed books that drew international attention to the Inuit, especially their storytelling traditions. Two of these books were *The People of the Polar North* and *Eskimo Folk Tales.*

For what Rasmussen achieved, the University of Copenhagen and the University of St. Andrews awarded him honorary doctorates. He also received several medals, including the Royal Geographical Society's Gold Medal. Moreover, a string of mountains in western Greenland is called "The Knud Rasmussen Range."

Decades after he died, Rasmussen remains a hero in the eyes of Greenlanders.

Boxed Rasmussen quotation at top of previous page: Excerpt from page 91 of his 1908 book, *The People of the Polar North: A Record*, London: K. Paul, Trench, Trübner and Company.

Hafey comment about Rasmussen: Excerpt from his April 19, 2018, article: "A Northwest Passage Legend: Knud Rasmussen and His Fifth Thule Expedition" published by Quark Expeditions

Rasmussen's comment about his youth: Excerpt from page xxxi of his 1927 book, *Across Artic America*, New York: G.P. Putnam's Sons.

Photo credit/attribution: Title: Undated Photo of Danish/Greenland Explorer Knud Rasmussen; Location: George Grantham Bain Collection, U.S. Library of Congress; Source: https://commons.wikimedia.org/wiki/File:Knud_Rasmussen_01.jpg; Photo is in the public domain {{PD-US}}; Photographer: Unknown; Original photo has been flipped horizontally and cropped.

> *Inspiration exists, but it has to find you working.*

Pablo Picasso, 1881-1973. Born and raised in southern Spain but a resident of France most of his life, Picasso was one of the most influential artists of the 20th century. One art critic affiliated with New York's Metropolitan Museum of Art asserted that Picasso "impacted the development of modern and contemporary  art with unparalleled magnitude." Sotheby's, the world's largest and most trusted marketplace for art for over 250 years, reports that Picasso's works "are enormously desirable and continue to be highly sought after."

Most people know two things about Picasso: that many of his paintings are abstract—or "cubist"— in nature, and that he had many mistresses. However, here are four lesser-known, but noteworthy, aspects of this great artist's life:

- Picasso refused to accept $100,000 for designing the 50-foot-high public sculpture that sits outside in Chicago's Daley Plaza.
- He served for three years as Director of Madrid's famous art museum, the Museo del Prado.
- The phrase "ultra-prolific" aptly describes Picasso. According to one source, he produced 1,885 paintings, 1,228 sculptures, 2,880 ceramics, and 12,000 drawings.
- Picasso was not just an artist but also a poet, a playwright, and a novelist.

One interesting facet of Picasso's life was his relationship with the great post-impressionist painter Henri Matisse. Matisse was 11 years older than Picasso, and although they didn't get along at first, they became good friends. They spurred each other on with their innovative ideas of what art can be.

Near the end of his life, Picasso is reported to have said: "It took me four years to paint like Raphael, but a lifetime to paint like a child." His late-in-life masterpieces, such as his crayon picture *Self Portrait Facing Death* or his simple drawings of cows or bulls, appear at first glance to resemble what a child might produce. However, they are almost priceless, having come from Pablo Picasso!

If asked to name the person who painted *Guernica* or *The Old Guitarist*, most people would say, "Picasso." If asked to give the painter's full name, many would quickly say, "Pablo Picasso." That two-word name is grossly inadequate! Picasso, when baptized, was given the name: Pablo Diego José Francisco de Paula Juan Nepomuceno Cipriano de la Santísima Trinidad María de los Remedios Alarcón y Herrera Ruiz y Picasso.

Boxed Picasso quotation at top of previous page: Excerpt from page 264 of Tomás R. Villasante's 1994 book, *Las Ciudades Hablan: Identidades y Movimientos Sociales en Sies Metrópolis Latinoamericanas*, Caracus: Nueva Sociedad.

Art critic comment about Picasso: Excerpt from page 1 of James Voorhies' article "Pablo Picasso" located in *Heilbruun Timeline of Art History*, New York: The Metropolitan Museum of Art.

Sotheby comment about Picasso: Online document located at https://www.sothebys.com/en/artists/pablo-picasso.

Picasso comment about painting like a child: Excerpt from page 134 of Daniel A. Siedell's 2015 book, *Who's Afraid of Modern Art*, Eugene, Oregon: Cascade Books.

Photo credit/attribution: Title: 1962 photo of Pablo Picasso; Source: https://commons.wikimedia.org/wiki/File:Pablo_picasso_1.jpg; Photographer: Unknown; Photo is in the public domain.

> *In spite of illness, in spite*
> *even of the archenemy sorrow,*
> *one can remain alive long past the usual*
> *date of disintegration if one is unafraid of change,*
> *insatiable in intellectual curiosity*
> *interested in big things, and*
> *happy in small ways.*

Edith Wharton, 1862-1937. Born into a wealthy family living in New York City during the American Civil War, Wharton grew up to become an award-winning author, a famous designer, and a caring-for-others worker and philanthropist.

Part of Wharton's education came from her travels through Europe with her affluent family. While abroad, she was taught by tutors and governesses, and she became fluent in French, Italian, and German. Impressively, she desired to learn more than just what she was in her lessons. On her own, she read many of her father's books (written by the likes of Milton, Hugo, and Wordsworth).

As an author herself, Wharton was a child prodigy. At first, she wrote poetry. Then, at age 11, she penned her first novel. When 15, Wharton authored a 30,000-word novella. At 18, five of her poems appeared in the *Atlantic Monthly*. Despite those achievements, Wharton is known mainly for the 85 short stories she wrote as well as her award-winning full-length novel, *The Age of Innocence*. That novel made her the first woman to win a Pulitzer Prize.

In addition to being a professional writer, Wharton had architectural and artistic interests in Italian villas and gardens. In 1902, she designed her expansive, 128-acre Massachusetts estate: The Mount. It includes a large home modeled after Italian and French chateaus, stables, a greenhouse, and several exquisite gardens. There, she entertained "the cream of the American literary society." Today, Wharton's Mount is on the list of America's Gilded-Age Mansions and has been declared a National Historic Landmark.

Despite her advantaged upbringing, Wharton had a caring heart for the less fortunate. She demonstrated this when living in Paris during World War I. Wharton started a sewing business that provided work, money, and self-esteem to unemployed women. She also collected more than $100,000 to help feed, clothe, and house nearly 1,000 refugees who fled Belgium after their homes were bombed. According to one description, "she worked tirelessly in charitable efforts for refugees, the injured, the unemployed, and the displaced."

In recognition of her accomplishments, Wharton was inducted into the National Women's Hall of Fame, she was a three-time nominee for the Nobel Prize in Literature, and she received Yale University's first honorary doctoral degree given to a woman.

Boxed Wharton quotation at top of previous page: Excerpt from page 46 in her 1934 book *A Backward Glance*, New York: D. Appleton-Century Company.

Comment about Wharton's volunteer work in France: Excerpt from page 454 of Hermione Lee's 2007 book *Edith Wharton*, London: Chatto & Windus.

Photo credit/attribution: Title: 1889 photo of Edith Wharton; Source: https://commons.wikimedia.org/wiki/File:Edith_Newbold_Jones_Wharton_(cropped).jpg; Location: Beinecke Rare Book and Manuscript Library, Yale University; Photographer: E. F. Cooper; Photo is in the public domain. Photo has been cropped.

> *What is the use of living, if it not be*
> *to strive for noble causes and to make*
> *this muddled world a better place for*
> *those who will live in it after we are gone?*

Winston Churchill, 1874-1965. Most people know that Churchill was a political leader from Great Britain who, during World War II, famously said: "Never in the field of human conflict was so much owed by so many to so few." From photos and news films from Churchill's era, people today also know that he was a big  man who liked to smoke cigars, often with two fingers from his right hand extended upwards to form a "V," his symbol for Victory. Churchill is widely remembered, too, for saying, "I have nothing to offer but blood, toil, tears, and sweat."

In addition to these well-known facts about Churchill, there are 10 other things worth knowing about him:

- In a 2002 BBC poll designed to identify the 100 greatest Britons of all time, Churchill came in first place. He received more votes than Charles Darwin, William Shakespeare, Isaac Newton, Queen Elizabeth I, Jane Austen, Henry VIII, and Queen Victoria.

- Churchill won the Nobel Prize in Literature "for his mastery of historical and biographical description as well as for brilliant oratory in defending exalted human values."

- As a youngster in school, he often misbehaved and was not a good student. Later, however, he recognized his deficiencies and began a project of self-education, reading Plato, Darwin, and other well-known writers.

- In the military, he once gave skin from his chest as a graft for an injured officer.

- In his late 20s, Churchill went on a lecture tour that took him to several foreign countries. In the United States, Mark Twain once introduced him.

- In the role of Home Secretary, he engaged in prison reform by establishing libraries and concerts for prisoners, by creating a distinction between criminal and political prisoners, and by abolishing almost entirely the imprisonment of people under the age of 21.

- In 1911, Churchill supported women's suffrage.

- Churchill had an excellent relationship with FDR during WWII. Between 1939 and 1945, they exchanged around 1,700 letters and telegrams.

- In 1945, Churchill surprisingly was not re-elected Prime Minister, but then, in 1951, he was.

- Churchill took up painting when he was in his 40s. Over the rest of his life, he created more than 500 works, many of which are judged to be exceedingly good.

Boxed Churchill quotation at top of previous page: Excerpt from a speech entitled "Unemployment" that Churchill made at Kinnaird Hall, Dundee, Scotland on October 10, 1908. (Printed on page 210 in Churchill's 1909 book, *Liberalism and the Social Problem*, 2nd ed., London: Hodder and Stoughton.)

Results of BBC's 'Greatest Briton" poll: Page 1 of *BBC News: World Edition*, Sunday, November 24, 2002.

Photo credit/attribution: Title: 1941 photo of Churchill, "The Roaring Lion"; Source: https://commons.wikimedia.org/wiki/File:Sir_Winston_Churchill_-_19086236948. jpg; Photographer: Yousuf Karsh; Location: National Portrait Gallery, London; Photo is in the public domain {{PD-1996}}; Photo has been cropped.

> *The world we are living in today is quite complex.*
> *To succeed, you will need to remain vigilant,*
> *focused, ethical, and disciplined.*

Sam Nujoma, 1929 -. The country of Namibia sits next to the
Atlantic Ocean in southern Africa. Its
surrounding neighbors are Angola, Botswana,
Zambia, and South Africa. In the opinion of
most Namibians, Sam Nujoma is a true hero.
His reputation, however, extends far beyond
Namibia's borders.

In Africa, Nujoma has received awards in Kenya,
Tunisia, Ghana, Zimbabwe, the Republic of Congo, Nigeria,
Malawi, Zambia, and South Africa. Nujoma has also been
honored, on other continents, in the countries of Portugal, India,
Italy, Vietnam, Cuba, Romania, Brazil, China, Russia, and the
United States. "Why," one might ask, "has Nujoma been so
widely recognized?"

There are two reasons why Nujoma is known and
respected by so many people. First, he was the lead activist who
helped Namibia become an independent nation. His life was
threatened as he fought, both figuratively and literally, for
Namibia to be free from outside control. Then, once
independence came about, Nujoma worked to unite disparate
factions within the new country.

To understand Nujoma's importance to Namibia, one
needs to consider a critical aspect of the country's history. In
1920, the League of Nations allowed South Africa to annex the
then colony of Namibia (which at that time was called South

West Africa). This arrangement did not work primarily because the rules of apartheid, already operational in South Africa, were imposed, in 1948, on the Namibian people. When that occurred, Nujoma became a political activist opposed to South Africa's control of Namibia. In 1960, Nujoma was elected president of an organization—the South West Africa People's Organization (SWAPO)—that opposed any outside entity ruling its country. Six years later, Namibians began a war of independence, a 24-year-long conflict that eventually achieved its objective.

In 1990, Nujoma was elected Namibia's first president. He served in that capacity for three consecutive five-year terms, guiding his new country into the 21st century. As one report put it, Nujoma "successfully united all Namibians into a peaceful, tolerant, and democratic society." Not surprisingly, Namibia's Parliament has officially designated Nujoma as the "Father of the Nation."

Nujoma's accomplishments and reputation are all the more impressive when one considers his early life. He was born into a peasant family. His main childhood chore involved tending the family's cattle and goats. Later, he worked as a store clerk and as a low-paid steward in the dining car of a train.

Boxed Nujoma quotation at top of previous page: Excerpt from page 3 of his commencement address on September 29, 2017, to the graduates of Namibia's International University of Management.

Comment about Nujoma's impact on Namidian society: Excerpt from H. Melber's paper, "Implications of the Namidian Elections," presented at the 2010 Conference on Election Processes, Liberal Movements, and Democratic Change in Africa.

Photo credit/attribution: Title: 2003 photo of President San Nujoma; Source: https://commons.wikimedia.org/wiki/File:Namibia.SamNujoma.01.jpg; Photographer: Marcello Casal, Jr., of Agência Brasil, a public Brazilian news agency; Photo is used here under the Creative Commons Attribution 3.0 Brazil license (https://creativecommons.org/licenses/by/3.0/br/deed.en) [CC BY 3.0 BR]; Original color photo has been cropped and made black-and-white.

> *Experiment! Meet new people. ... You will find the unexpected everywhere as you go through life. By adventuring about, you become accustomed to the unexpected.*

Amelia Earhart, 1897-1937. Born in Kansas, Earhart grew up to become an aviation pioneer, a successful author, and an early supporter of equal rights for women. She was a risk-taker, a non-conformist, and a trendsetter.

After working as a nurse's aide caring for soldiers returning from World War I, two events caused Earhart to become interested in aviation. First, when in her early 20s, she saw a flying exhibition put on by a WWI ace. Second, her father paid a small fee so she could take a plane ride with a pilot who later became an air racer. After that flight, she was hooked!

Earhart had her first flying lesson at age 24, and two years later, she became just the 16th woman in the United States to be issued a pilot's license. In 1928, she and two male pilots flew across the Atlantic Ocean, bringing her fame and the nickname "Queen of the Air." During an interview after landing in Europe, she said: "Maybe someday I'll try it alone." Four years later, Earhart became the first woman to fly that route by herself. Soon after that, she became the first person to make other solo flights. These and other accomplishments increased Earhart's stardom. They brought her awards and gave her the chance to meet world leaders.

After going on a lecture tour and writing a book, Earhart made plans to fly around the world. Although a few others had done this previously, Earhart's planned flight was to be the longest, as it was going to be at the Earth's "waistline," the equator. Her first attempt to do this failed. In her second attempt, Earhart and her one-person crew (Fred Noonan) got three-fourths of the way around the world when their aircraft disappeared in the Pacific near Howland Island. The plane and its passengers were never found with absolute certainty.

One of the many people saddened by Earhart's tragic death was Eleanor Roosevelt. That's because these two women had become friends, with both sharing a concern for promoting women's causes. Moreover, Mrs. Roosevelt had once flown with Earhart and contemplated getting a pilot's license. After Earhart's plane could not be found, Roosevelt stated in her popular newspaper column:

> *I only hope that it [Earhart's last, tragic flight] will spur us on to do something in her memory which will carry on the influence which her personality and spirit brought to everyone with whom she came in contact.*

Today, decades after her final flight, Earhart is an inspiration to many, especially young girls and women.

Boxed Earhart quotation at top of previous page: Excerpt from page 49 of Kathleen C. Winters' 2010 book, *Amelia Earhart: The Troubled Life of an American Icon*, New York: Palgrave Macmillan.

Roosevelt comment about Earhart: Excerpt from her daily newspaper column entitled "My Day" that appeared on July 14, 1937.

Photo credit/attribution: Title: 1935 photo of Amelia Earhart; Source: https://commons.wikimedia.org/wiki/File:Amelia_Earhart_1935.jpg; Photographer: Unnamed member of NBC Radio; Photo is in the public domain; Original photo has been cropped.

> *Life is a difficult game. You can win it only by retaining your birthright to be a person. And to retain this right, you will have to be willing to take the social or external risks involved in ignoring pressures to do things the way others say they should be done.*

A.P.J. Abdul Kalam, 1931-2015. Born to poverty-stricken parents living in southern India, Kalam was a hard worker even when young. At age eight, he would arise at 4:00 am to get tutored in math and Arabic; then, he would deliver newspapers before spending a full day in school. Not surprisingly, his teachers considered him to be bright with a strong desire to learn.

Kalam's formal education led to a bachelor's degree in physics and a postgraduate degree in aerospace engineering. For several years, he worked as a space and nuclear scientist. During Kalam's time at the Indian Space Research Organization, he served as project director for the program that launched India's first successful satellite into orbit around the Earth. Because of his involvement in several other aerospace endeavors, Kalam (at age 61) was chosen to be Chief Scientific Advisor to India's Prime Minister.

When 71, Kalam was nominated to be his country's president. He ran and won easily. He served in that post for five years, quickly acquiring the nickname "The People's President." Kalam's integrity and simple lifestyle earned him this affectionate label. He never owned a TV, and he had few personal possessions. Moreover, Kalam was unpretentious. He once attended a gathering and noted that his chair was larger than the others; he refused to be seated until that chair was replaced with one just like the rest. Kalam was also admired because he respected his country's varied religions and cultural traditions.

After leaving office, Kalam taught at several research and academic institutions. He also wrote books, worked to reduce crime and corruption, and interacted with thousands of students. In 2012, he started the "What Can I Give Movement," designed to create an other-centered, "giving" attitude among India's youth.

Because of his many accomplishments, Kalam earned India's highest civilian award, the Bharat Ratna. He also received honorary doctorates from 40 universities. And, in a 2012 survey of over 20 million people to identify "The Greatest Indian," Kalam came in 2nd place, three spots ahead of Mother Teresa!

This great man's initials, A.P.J., do not stand for a title or any honor he received due to his sterling accomplishments. Instead, they are simply the initials of the first three-fifths of his birth name: Avul Pakir Jainulabdeen Abdul Kalam.

Boxed Kalam quotation at top of previous page: Excerpt from page 176 of his 1999 book *Wings of Fire: An Autobiography*, Hyderguda, India: University Press.

Results of poll to identify the greatest Indian: Excerpt from S. M. Khan's 2016 book *The People's President: Dr. A.P.J. Abdul Kalam*, New Delhi, India: Bloomsbury.

Photo credit/attribution: Title: 2005 photo of A. P. J. Abdul Kalam; Source: https://commons.wikimedia.org/wiki/File:The_President_Shri_A.P.J._Abdul_Kalam addressing_the_Nation_on_the_eve_of_the_Republic_Day,_in_New_Delhi_on_Jan uary_25,_2005.jpg; Photographer: Government of India; Under India's Government Open Data License (GODL) and India's National Data Sharing and Accessibility Policy (NDSAP), permission is granted to use this photo as if it is in the public domain; Original color photo was cropped and made black-and-white.

> *It is possible to be both bright and kind.*

Nicholas Hobbs, 1915-1983. Born in South Carolina, Hobbs was an outstanding student. He completed his undergraduate studies at The Citadel, then earned Master's and Ph.D. degrees at Ohio State. After completing his formal education, Hobbs had a career that, over time, cast him into positions of greater and greater importance and influence. Time and  time again, others noted the talents of this gifted psychologist, educator, and child advocate.

During World War II, Hobbs was chosen to direct the Aviation Psychology Program. After leading the clinical psychology program at Columbia University, he became head of the psychology department at LSU. He then moved to Vanderbilt, where he initially chaired the Division of Human Development and then was made the university's provost. On the national level, Hobbs was appointed, by President John F. Kennedy, to be the 1st Director of Selection for the Peace Corps. He also served on the National Advisory Mental Health Council, a group that advised the Secretary of Health and Human Services, the National Institutes of Health, and the National Institute of Mental Health.

Despite his many high-level positions, Hobbs is remembered most for his concern for emotionally disturbed children. He started a program (funded by the National Institutes of Health) called "Project Re-ED." That program de-emphasized therapy and instead encouraged children and their caregivers to learn constructive ways to address and overcome problem situations. Five of Re-ED's foundational "12 Principles" are relevant to all people regardless of age:

- Life is to be lived now, not in the past.
- Trust is essential.
- Feelings should be nurtured.
- Communities are important.
- Know joy each day.

Hobbs described the impact of Project Re-ED in his book, *The Troubled and Troubling Child.* This work had a positive impact across the United States.

During his career, Hobbs held coveted positions and received a host of awards. Many others in his shoes would have become pompous and elitist. Not Hobbs. He was humble and gracious to everyone. While serving as the academic leader at Vanderbilt, he prodded professors—even the super-smart ones—to realize that "it is possible to be both bright and kind." He modeled the essence of those nine words, for Hobbs rarely sought out and talked with other luminaries at special events. Instead, he would go talk with those who seemed to be ill at ease and who stood or sat apart from the rest of the group with likely thoughts that they were "outsiders." Hobbs tried his best to make them feel as much a part of the group as anyone.

Boxed Hobbs quotation at top of previous page: Excerpt from page 219 of John Carl Habel's 1989 Ph.D. dissertation *Precipitating Himself into Just Manageable Difficulties: An Intellectual Portrait of Nicholas Hobbs*, University of Tennessee.

Photo credit/attribution: Title: Photo of a 1968 painting of Nicholas Hobbs; Source: https://www.sbbh.pitt.edu/sites/default/files/hobbs_nicholas_wikipedia.pdf; Artist: Louise LeQuire; Photographer: Unknown; Location of painting: Nicholas Hobbs Laboratory of Human Development at Vanderbilt University; Original color photo was cropped and made black-and-white. Photo is in the public domain.

Queen Elizabeth I of England, 1533-1603. Born to King Henry VIII and Anne Boleyn, Elizabeth's childhood was tragic. When she was just two years old, her mother's marriage to Henry was annulled, and Anne was beheaded. That caused Elizabeth to be declared illegitimate. Next, she lost her  right to succeed Henry on the throne when Henry's next wife, Jane Seymour, gave birth to a son, Edward.

Elizabeth was well-educated via a string of private tutors. She learned history, theology, and philosophy. She could converse in four languages and write in three others. In addition to those skills, Elizabeth possessed key traits that she probably inherited from her parents; she was ambitious, astute, and shrewd.

When Elizabeth was 14, her half-brother, Edward, became king. After six years, he died. Lady Jane Grey (Elizabeth's cousin), queen for just nine days, was unseated by Elizabeth's half-sister, Mary, daughter of Henry and Catherine of Aragon. Mary ruled for five years before dying. Then, in 1559, Elizabeth (at age 25) became queen.

Elizabeth reigned for 45 years—a period often referred to as the Elizabethan Era. Those years are considered by many to have been the Golden Age of England. That romanticized term is misleading, for it overlooks both the domestic and the foreign problems that Elizabeth confronted. She worked to unify a country with two strong and opposed religious groups

(Protestant and Catholic); dealt with Spain, a country that wanted to invade England; tried to manage the Nine Years War in Ireland; and grappled with internal economic problems.

Despite the difficulties she faced, Elizabeth's reign involved several impressive successes. The exploratory voyages of Frances Drake and Walter Raleigh were productive; England defeated the Spanish Armada in 1588; the arts flourished (especially theater, but also music and painting); and most of the country's subjects supported their queen. One such supporter was William Shakespeare. Elizabeth saw at least two of his plays, *The Merry Wives of Windsor* and *Love's Labour's Lost*.

Though she had many suitors, Elizabeth never had a husband or children. Consequently, people referred to her as "the Virgin Queen." Her other, more-kindly nicknames were "the Good Queen Bess" and "Gloriana." Being husbandless did not seem to disturb Elizabeth. That's because she considered herself to be "married" to England.

Looking back in time from today's perspective, do historians consider Elizabeth I to have been a good queen? Yes! The online site *Britannica*, for example, asserts that Elizabeth I was "one of England's most illustrious monarchs."

Boxed Elizabeth quotation at top of previous page: Excerpt from a letter Princess Elizabeth wrote on July 31, 1548, to her mother, Queen Dowager Catherine Parr (the last of Henry VIII's six wives). Located on page 8 in the 1968 book (edited by George B. Harrison) *The Letters of Queen Elizabeth I*, London: Funk & Wagnalls.

Photo credit/attribution: Title: Photo of 1592 engraving of Queen Elizabeth I; Source: https://commons.wikimedia.org/wiki/File:Queen_Elizabeth_I_Met_DP-18112-001.jpg; Artist: Crispijn de Passe the Elder; Photographer: Unknown; Location: Metropolitan Museum of Art, New York City; Original tinted photo has been cropped and made black-and-white. Photo is used here under the Creative Commons CC0 1.0 Universal Public Domain Dedication (https://creativecommons.org/publicdomain/zero/1.0/deed.en) [CC0 1.0].

> *Be more concerned with your character than your reputation, because your character is what you really are, while your reputation is merely what others think you are.*

John Wooden, 1910-2010. Born in a small town in central Indiana, Wooden once scored both a double-eagle and a hole-in-one during the same round of golf! His sport of passion, however, was not golf. It was basketball.

Wooden was a highly talented basketball player. He was selected to the All-State team three times in high school. While at Purdue University, he became the first player recognized as a three-time All-American. As a pro, he was a star in the National Basketball League.

In his work as a basketball coach, Wooden was even more talented than he was as a player. At the high school and collegiate levels, his teams won an astounding 81% of their games. While a coach at UCLA, his teams won 10 NCAA championships during a 12-year stretch. During those dozen years, Wooden's teams once won 88-games in a row, and four of his teams recorded perfect 30-0 seasons.

Although Wooden was known most for his legendary accomplishments as a basketball player and coach, he did other things that are worth noting. He was a popular lecturer, and his talks often focused on how to live life successfully, whether or not one is an athlete. Wooden also was an author, writing books about leadership. In them, he shared his "pyramid of success," a delineation of the needed beliefs and behaviors of those who aspire to lead others, whether in sports, business, education, the military, or elsewhere.

In Wooden's coaching, lectures, and books, he seldom talked or wrote about winning. Instead, he emphasized "being successful"—defined by him as being the best one can be. He created and shared many pearls of wisdom, such as:

- *Don't let yesterday take up too much of today.*
- *Things turn out best for the people who make the best of the way things turn out.*
- *You have to be what you are. Don't try to be somebody else.*
- *Seek opportunities to show you care. The smallest gestures often make the biggest difference.*

Wooden received a host of honors, including a Presidential Medal of Freedom (given by George W. Bush), the Lombardi Award of Excellence, and the American Academy of Achievement's Golden Plate Award. Despite these and countless other awards, Wooden was a humble man, always wanting to share his success with others. He even asked that his wife's name appear ahead of his when UCLA renamed its basketball court in his honor.

Boxed Wooden quotation at top of previous page: Excerpt from page 38 of Brian D. Biro's 2001 book *Beyond Success: The 15 Secrets to Effective Leadership and Life Based on Legendary Coach John Wooden's Pyramid of Success*, New York: Berkley Publishing Group.

Photo credit/attribution: Title: 2006 photo of John Wooden; Source: https://commons.wikimedia.org/wiki/File:Johnwooden.jpg; Photographer: Unnamed member of congressman Brad Sherman's office; Photo is in the public domain; Original color photo has been cropped and made black-and-white.

> *Family connections are always worth preserving, good company always worth seeking.*

Jane Austen, 1775-1817. Most people know that Jane Austen was a famous British author who wrote extremely popular novels such as *Pride and Prejudice, Sense and Sensibility,* and *Mansfield Park.* However, many individuals who can match Austen's name to her book titles—or who also know of her  novels' characters and plots—are oblivious to several noteworthy aspects of Austen's life and legacy.

Many of the lesser-known facts about Austen are worth knowing. Here are 10 such facts:

- When she was eight years old, Austen came down with typhoid fever and almost died.
- Austen was mainly educated by her father and through her access to his extensive home library.
- Austen began writing poems, stories, and plays when she was not yet a teenager; by age 23, she had completed the first drafts of three of her six novels.
- During Austen's lifetime, her novels were published anonymously. Her first book, *Sense and Sensibility,* was said to be authored "By a Lady," with her subsequent books saying that they were written "by the author of *Sense and Sensibility.*"
- *First Impressions* was the initial title of Austen's famous novel, *Pride and Prejudice.*

- Although Austen never married, she came close to "tying the knot" with three different men. (She accepted a proposal from one of her suitors but backed out the next day because she realized her love for him was not authentic.)
- Austen was paid far less for her well-liked and fast-selling books than the amount of money male authors received for their second-rate works.
- During World War II, Winston Churchill asked his daughter, Sarah, to read *Pride and Prejudice* to him while he was recovering from the flu. He did this because he earlier had read and liked *Sense and Sensibility*.
- In 2017, the Bank of England issued a new £10 banknote featuring a picture of Austen; her image replaced earlier versions of that banknote that had featured portraits of Florence Nightingale, Charles Dickens, and Charles Darwin.
- Austen's novels have not gone out of print in over 200 years, and they have been translated into 40 different languages.

Boxed Austen quotation at top of previous page: Excerpt from Chapter 16 of Austen's 1818 book, *Persuasion*, London: John Murray Publishing Company.

Photo credit/attribution: Title: 1871 image of Jane Austen; Source #1: https://commons.wikimedia.org/wiki/File:Jane_Austen.jpg; Source #2: Cover image on James Edward Austen-Leigh's 1871 book *A Memoir of Jane Austen*, 2nd edition (London: Richard Bentley and Son), from a watercolor by James Andrews of Maidenhead based on an unfinished work by Cassandra Austen, engraving by Lizars; Photo is in the public domain {{PD-US}}; Original image has been rotated slightly and cropped.

> *Be strong in body, clean in mind, and lofty in ideals.*

James Naismith, 1861-1939. Born and raised in Canada, the young Naismith loved sports and games.  While attending college at McGill University, he joined the school's football, soccer, rugby, gymnastics, and lacrosse teams. After graduating with degrees in physical education and theology, Naismith taught P.E. courses at his alma mater. Within a year, he was chosen to be McGill's first director of athletics.

When Naismith was 30, he took a job at the YMCA International Training School in Massachusetts (now Springfield College). One of his first duties was to create an indoor game to help athletes stay in shape during winter when few outdoor sports could be played. For the new game he devised, Naismith attached two peach baskets to the opposite ends of a gym balcony. The new game's objective was for each team to get the ball—then a soccer ball—into the basket that the other team defended. If the ball went in, a helper in the balcony retrieved it and tossed it down to the game's referee. (Before long, the peach baskets were replaced by metal rims, with nets, attached to backboards.)

In 1892, Naismith created 13 rules for his new game. These rules specified, among other things, the game's length, how a team could move the ball toward its basket, how points could be earned, penalties for rough behavior, and the referee's duties. (The original copy of these 13 rules is nearly priceless.

When it last sold, the buyers paid more in time-adjusted dollars than a 1787 letter from George Washington to his nephew, more than Einstein's manuscript *On the Theory of Relativity*, and more than Lewis Carroll's copy of *Alice's Adventures in Wonderland*.)

In the mid-1890s, people began playing Naismith's new game across the United States, especially in YMCA facilities. During that period, Naismith moved to Denver to study medicine. After earning his medical degree, the University of Kansas hired him as a P.E. instructor and Chapel Director. Once there, Naismith founded KU's basketball program and served as the team's head coach for nine years. Surprisingly, Naismith coached teams that collectively lost more games than they won. That fact likely did not bother Naismith because his main interest was improving physical conditioning, not winning games.

Naismith was a humble man. He never sought personal fame, a patent, or riches from the game he invented. His reward, no doubt, was seeing basketball become popular and having it introduced, in 1936, as an Olympic sport. How proud he would be today to know that each spring's NCAA basketball tournament has a passionate international following and that over 300 million people play basketball worldwide.

Boxed Naismith quotation at top of previous page: Excerpt from page 41 of Carlotta Hacker's 1931 book, *Great Canadian Inventors*, Calgary: Weigl Publishers.

Photo credit/attribution: Title: Circa 1920 photo of Dr. James Naismith; Source: https://commons.wikimedia.org/wiki/File:James_Naismith_at_Springfield_College_circa_1920.jpg; Photographer: Unknown; Original photo has been cropped; Photo is used here under the Creative Commons Universal Public Domain Dedication (https://creativecommons.org/publicdomain/zero/1.0/deed.en) [CC0 1.0].

> *The future of the planet concerns all of us, and all of us should do what we can to protect it.... You don't need a diploma to plant a tree.*

Wangarĩ Muta Maathai, 1940-2011. Born and raised in rural Kenya, Maathai was an outstanding student. She earned a bachelor's degree from Mount St. Scholastica College in Kansas and a Master's degree in biology from the University of Pittsburgh. Then, after further study in Germany, Maathai obtained a Ph.D.  in veterinary anatomy from the University of Nairobi.

Maathai's accomplishments after her schooling were even more impressive than her educational achievements. She was a leader, an activist, and a person who tried to solve environmental and social problems. Maathai became the director of Kenya's Red Cross Society, chair of Kenya's National Council of Women, and head of the Environmental Liaison Centre International.

Perhaps Maathai's greatest success was the Green Belt Movement that she founded. This organization encourages poor women to plant tree seedlings and create nurseries, with a small stipend given to participants via funds secured from the United Nations. Over time, millions of trees have been planted via the GB Movement. Maathai's long-standing dedication to this project generated three complimentary nicknames for her: "Tree Woman," "Green Militant," and "Eco Warrior."

Maathai was a pro-democracy and environmental activist who was harassed and jailed because she opposed deforestation. Maathai was not deterred. She was later elected to Kenya's parliament, winning 98 percent of the votes. Her high-level governmental position was in the Ministry for Environmental, Natural Resources, and Wildlife.

Maathai received many high honors and awards for her life's work (that included the four books she authored). Among these accolades were the Indira Gandhi Prize, the Conservation Scientist Award, the Africa Prize for Leadership, and the Nobel Peace Prize. She also became the first female African Nobel Laureate, with the Nobel selection committee describing her as "a source of inspiration for everyone in Africa fighting for sustainable development, democracy, and peace."

In her autobiography, *Unbowed*, Maathai described her efforts to help Africa's women, forests, and democracy. After reading this book, Former President Bill Clinton said:

> *Wangari Maathai's memoir is direct, honest, and beautifully written—a gripping account of modern Africa's trials and triumphs, a universal story of courage, persistence, and success against great odds in a noble cause.*

Boxed Maathai quotation at top of previous page: Excerpt from page 138 of her 2007 book *Unbowed: A Memoir*, New York: Anchor Books.

Comment about Maathai from the Nobel Selection Committee: *The Nobel Peace Prize Press Release*, Oslo, October 8, 2004.

Comment about Maathai from Bill Clinton: Statement printed on the front cover of the 2007 edition of Maathai's book *Unbowed*.

Photo credit/attribution: Title: 2005 photo of Wangarĩ Maathai; Source: https://commons.wikimedia.org/w/index.php?search=Wangari+Maathai&title=Speci al:MediaSearch&type=image; Photographer: James Mathew Smith; Photo is used here under the Creative Commons Attribution-Share-Alike 2.0 license (https://creativecommons.org/licenses/by-sa/2.0/deed.en) [CC BY-SA 2.0]; Original color photo has been cropped and made black-and-white.

Pope Francis, 1936 -. Born in a middle-class section of Buenos Aires, Argentina, the future Pope was named Jorge Mario Bergoglio. His father was an Italian immigrant; his mother was a native of Buenos Aires with Italian ancestors. Bergoglio's early education included time at a school that trained boys to be priests. After  graduating from college, he continued his theological studies in Ireland and Germany.

When 33 years old, Bergoglio was ordained as a Jesuit priest. As time passed, he moved up the Catholic hierarchy, becoming bishop, then archbishop, then cardinal. As his career unfolded, Bergoglio became highly respected among his peers. In 2005, he reportedly received the second most votes at the Papal Conclave held after the death of John Paul II. Getting the most votes was Joseph Ratzinger, who became Pope Benedict XVI. Six years later, Benedict resigned because of health issues. The ensuing Papal Conclave ended—with white smoke rising from a chimney atop the Sistine Chapel—when the cloistered cardinals chose Bergoglio to be the new Pope. He chose the name Francis in honor of Saint Francis of Assisi.

Soon after Bergoglio became Pope, reports of his unexpected humility endeared him to both Catholics and non-Catholics worldwide. Two examples of his selflessness are compelling:

- Instead of sending an assistant to pay his remaining bill at the boarding house where he stayed before becoming Pope, Francis performed this errand himself.
- Francis chose to live in a simple, two-bedroom apartment rather than move into the glamourous papal residence in the Vatican.

In addition to showing authentic humility upon becoming Pope, Francis has taken positions on various matters that signal his caring and merciful (rather than unbending) outlook on controversial issues. In 2019, for example, Pope Francis signed the *Document on Human Fraternity for World Peace and Living Together*. So did Sheikh Ahmed el-Tayeb, who represented Muslims of the Sunni Islamic Faith. This document contained the following passage that likely alarms anyone who thinks that only one religion is "right" while all others are defective:

> *Freedom is a right of every person: each individual enjoys the freedom of belief, thought, expression and action. The pluralism and the diversity of religions [have been] willed by God in His wisdom.... Therefore, the fact that people are forced to adhere to a certain religion or culture must be rejected, as too the imposition of a cultural way of life that others don't accept.*

Boxed Francis quotation at top of previous page: Excerpt from an interview Pope Francis had with Eugenio Scalfali (summarized on October 1, 2013, by Michael S. Winters in the *National Catholic Reporter*).

Photo credit/attribution: Title: 2013 photo of Pope Francis; Source: https://commons.wikimedia.org/wiki/File:Pope_Francis_in_March_2013.jpg; Photographer: Unnamed worker at Casa Rosada, office of Argentina's president; Photo is used here under the Creative Commons Attribution-Share-Alike 2.0 Generic license (https://creativecommons.org/licenses/by-sa/2.0/deed.en) [CC BY-SA 2.0]; Original color photo has been cropped and made black-and-white.

> *Change happens by listening
> and then starting a dialogue with the people
> who are doing something you don't believe is right.*

Jane Goodall, 1934-. Soon after Jane was born in London, Goodall's father gave her a stuffed chimpanzee. She loved it dearly. That gift foreshadowed Goodall's enormously successful and influential career.

Goodall had always been interested in African animals, and she left school at 18 to earn the money needed to make her dream of studying them come true. When 23, Goodall went to Kenya for a short time before ending up in Tanzania. She worked there under her mentor, the famous archeologist and paleontologist Louis Leakey. He was so impressed with her work that he sent her to Cambridge University to study. Her Ph.D. dissertation detailed what she had learned about how chimpanzees lived in the wild within Tanzania's Gombe Stream National Park.

After leaving Cambridge, Goodall returned to Tanzania, where she continued to observe chimpanzees. Over time, the chimpanzees overcame their fear of Goodall and allowed her to come close and even "mingle" with them. What she reported exposed many misconceptions about chimpanzees. For instance, she discovered that they could make and use simple tools and were not "dumb chimps," as previously believed. Such reports made Goodall the world's leading expert on chimpanzees.

Goodall is a dedicated advocate for *all* animals. She is opposed to using animals in zoos, medical research, farming, and sports. In addition to her concern for animals, she is an outspoken environmentalist. In an article she wrote for *Time* magazine, Goodall said,

> *I feel deep shame when I look into the eyes of my grandchildren and think how much damage has been done to Planet Earth since I was their age. Each of us must work as hard as we can now to heal the hurts and save what is left.*

In recognition of her life's work, Goodall has received numerous awards and honors. These include being named a United Nations Messenger of Peace, being listed in 2019 (by *Time* magazine) as one of the world's most influential people, and being inducted into the French Légion d'honneur. She has received several prestigious awards from afar, including Japan's Kyoto Prize, the Gandhi/King Award for Nonviolence, the Medal of Tanzania, the Champion Award from the Rainforest Alliance, and the Benjamin Franklin Medal in Life Science. Not surprisingly, Goodall has also been awarded honorary doctoral degrees from universities worldwide.

Boxed Goodall quotation at top of previous page: Excerpt from page 23 of Yolanda Brooks' 2008 book *Do Animals Have Rights*, Paris, France: Hatchet.

Goodall comment about saving Planet Earth: Excerpt from her article entitled "The Power of One" that appeared in *Time* magazine on Monday, August 26, 2002.

Photo credit/attribution: Title: 2015 photo of Jane Goodall; Source: https://commons.wikimedia.org/wiki/File:Jane_Goodall_2015.jpg; Photo is in the public domain. Photographer: Unnamed member of the United States Department of State; Original color photo has been flipped horizontally, cropped, and made black-and-white.

> *Do not expect the world to look bright*
> *if you habitually wear gray-brown glasses.*

Charles W. Eliot, 1834-1926. Born into a wealthy New England family, Eliot graduated from Boston Latin School and then from Harvard University. He stayed at Harvard, teaching math and chemistry, for 13 years. He next spent two years in Europe investigating the educational systems of several countries.

Upon returning to the United States, Eliot became a professor of analytical chemistry at the newly established Massachusetts Institute of Technology (MIT). Four years later, Eliot—at age 35—was selected to be Harvard's President. He served as Harvard's leader for 40 years, a longevity record he still holds. Eliot was not just Harvard's longest-serving chief administrator; he was one of its greatest presidents.

Eliot transformed Harvard from a regional college into one of the world's preeminent universities. Under Eliot's leadership, Harvard reorganized its faculty into schools and departments, began to emphasize research, significantly expanded its facilities, and sought donations from the wealthy. While Eliot was at its helm, Harvard made several improvements in its graduate programs. The "case method" of instruction was introduced in its law school, lab work became standard for students in medical school, and doctoral degrees became available to students in the arts and sciences.

Eliot also brought about a reform in the goals and methods of Harvard's undergraduate curriculum. He opposed vocational education and wanted Harvard's students to think wisely and make intelligent choices in their careers and personal lives. To make this possible, Eliot believed in, and argued for, offering a "liberal" college education. To clarify what he meant by this, Eliot edited the Harvard Classics, a collection of 51 items of world literature. Eliot helped decide which books to include in what became known as the "5-foot shelf."

Another critical part of Eliot's educational reform was the introduction of "electives." This set of curricular options allowed undergraduate students to determine many of the courses they took. Having control over part of their curriculum allowed these Harvard students to follow and pursue what Eliot felt were their "natural bents." Needed specialization was reserved for graduate and professional schools.

Eliot received many awards and honors. These included honorary LLD degrees from Brown, Dartmouth, Harvard, Johns Hopkins, Princeton, Williams, and Yale. He was awarded the Roosevelt Medal for Distinguished Service and a Gold Medal from the American Academy of Arts and Letters. Despite these and other forms of recognition, Eliot likely was most proud of his impact on improving the education offered at American high schools, colleges, and universities.

Boxed Eliot quotation at top of previous page: Excerpt from page 5359h of the 1917 book, *The World's Best Literature, Volume 9* (edited by John Cunliffe and Ashley H. Thorndike), Toronto: The Warner Library Company.

Photo credit/attribution: Title: C. W. Eliot profile portrait; Source #1: Library of Congress, Division of Prints & Photographs; Source #2: https://commons.wikimedia.org/wiki/File:C.W._Eliot,_profile_portrait_LCCN20146 80569.jpg; Photographer: Unnamed member of the Bain News Service; Photo is in the public domain; Original photo has been cropped.

> *Many of the faults you see in others, dear reader, are your own nature reflected in them.*

Rūmī, 1207-1273. If you have ever heard, seen, or used the term "whirling dervish," you ought to know a few things about a man named Rūmī. He was a 13th-century Persian poet, scholar, and spiritual leader.

Born in what now is Afghanistan, Rūmī was a young teenager when he and his family moved westward. They emigrated because Genghis Khan's ruthless Mongolian army invaded from the east. Rūmī and his family traveled through areas currently called Iran, Iraq, and Saudi Arabia, eventually settling in Turkey. There, Rūmī's father worked as the head of an Islamic school. Upon his father's death, Rūmī inherited that position of influence.

At age 37, Rūmī's life changed direction when he met a charismatic mystic. For four years, Rūmī exchanged ideas with and learned from this persuasive friend and mentor. That association caused Rūmī to adopt an ascetic lifestyle, and he, too, became a religious mystic. He spent the rest of his life talking about the path one must take to reach Allah.

To move in the direction of Allah, Rūmī said a person must have certain beliefs and live a life characterized by proper behavior. Central among these concerns (articulated in poems, sermons, and letters), Rūmī said a person should:

- see the beauty of a loving heart.
- become other-centered in deeds.

- resist negative thoughts toward other races, classes, or nations.

Rūmī and his followers—a group referred to as the Mevlevi Order of Sufism—also believed that meditation is important, especially when combined with music and dance. Thus, they created a religious ceremony that involved people seeming to be in a trance as they whirl around in white robes and cone-like headdresses. Participants did not do this dance to entertain onlookers. Nor did they do it for their own merriment. Instead, the costumed whirling was a form of Muslim prayer, with the spinning designed to clear one's mind and cleanse the heart so the dancer might receive spiritual advice from Heaven.

Rūmī created a sect that was considered to be quite strange by many in his Turkish hometown of Konya. Nevertheless, leaders of various other faiths participated in a ceremony to honor Rūmī after he died. He was respected, even by those who disagreed with his notions about religion.

Surprisingly, the term "whirling dervish" is often used today to describe someone who is hyperactive and who creates disorder. Those traits were not at all possessed by Rūmī's whirling dervishes!

Boxed Rūmī quotation at top of previous page: Excerpt from page 18 of the 2000 book, *The Rumi Collection* (selected and edited by Kabir Helminski), Boston: Shambhala Publications, Inc.

Photo credit/attribution: Title: Rūmī's Imaginary on a Tiling Art; Source: https://commons.wikimedia.org/wiki/File:Rumi_Vignette_by_User_Chyah.jpg; Photographer: Yeni Qapi, Istanbul; Artist: Unknown; Photo is in the public domain; Original color photo has been flipped horizontally, cropped, and made black-and-white.

> *Winning is great, sure,*
> *but if you are really going to do something in life,*
> *the secret is learning how to lose.*

Wilma Rudolph, 1940-1994. Born into a large family living in Tennessee, Rudolph easily could have remained "in the shadows" as a child and adult. For one thing, she had 19 older siblings. For another, she suffered from major illnesses as a youngster: polio (requiring her to wear a leg brace from age five to 11), scarlet fever, and double pneumonia.

With grit and determination, Rudolph overcame her debilitating childhood physical problems. She played basketball in 8ᵗʰ grade and high school, with her teammates and coach calling her "skeeter" (for mosquito) because she quickly darted around the court. No opposing player could keep up with her.

Rudolph also ran track in high school. And run, she did! A college track coach noticed her speed and became her trainer. While still a high school student, Rudolph qualified for the 1956 Olympics. There, she was in the 400-meter relay race that won a bronze medal. However, she did not run fast enough to be in the finals of her premier event, the 200-meter race. That loss caused her to train even harder once she returned home.

Four years later, Rudolph again qualified for the Olympics. This time, she was unbeatable in the events she entered. She set a record, becoming the first woman in a single Olympics to win three Gold Medals; Rudolph did this in the 100- and 200-meter races and the 400-meter relay. She broke three world records in the process! She was dubbed the fastest woman sprinter in the world and nicknamed "The Tornado," "The Black Gazelle," and "The Black Pearl."

Rudolph's athletic feats made her world-famous and led to her receiving several prestigious honors. She earned the Sullivan Award and the Helm World Trophy, was inducted into four different Halls of Fame, worked in Africa as a U.S. Goodwill Ambassador, and was the first person to receive President Clinton's National Sports Award. Impressively, Rudolph used her fame to promote racial integration and to teach others. (Of interest to some, Rudolph was a faculty member at DePauw University and Tennessee State University).

Each year, the Women's Sports Foundation gives the Wilma Rudolph Courage Award to someone who

> *exhibits extraordinary courage in her athletic performance, demonstrates the ability to overcome adversity, makes significant contributions to sports and serves as an inspiration and role model to those who face challenges, overcomes them, and strives for success at all levels.*

Boxed Rudolph quotation at top of previous page: Excerpt from page 65 of her 1977 book, *Wilma*, New York: New American Library.

Recipient criteria for the Wilma Rudolph Courage Award: Excerpt from page 401 in Alan Tomlinson's 2010 book, *The Oxford Dictionary of Sports Studies*, Oxford, England: Oxford University Press.

Photo credit/attribution: Title: 1960 photo of Wilma Rudolph; Source: https://commons.wikimedia.org/wiki/File:Aankomst_Amerikaanse_Olympische_atl eten_op_Schiphol,_vlnr_Otis_Davis_,_Wilma,_Bestanddeelnr_911-6067.jpg; Photographer: Henk Lindeboom; This image is used here under the Creative Commons Attribution-Share Alike 3.0 Netherlands license (https://creativecommons.org/ licenses/by-sa/3.0/nl/deed.en) [CC BY-SA 3.0 NL]; Original photo has been cropped and rotated slightly.

> *We must train young people*
> *to get another vision of nature.*
> *We call it "wilderness," and we think*
> *it is progress to get further and further*
> *away from it. How crazy!*

Thor Heyerdahl, 1914-2002. Born in Norway, Heyerdahl attended college at the University of Oslo. He focused his studies there on zoology, geography, botany, and ethnography. On his own, he studied a privately-owned collection of books and papers on Polynesian history and culture.

When 22 years old, Heyerdahl traveled to the Marquesas Islands in French Polynesia. Eleven years later, he became famous for his journey on a raft (made of balsa logs) called *Kon Tiki.* He and five other adventurers sailed for 101 days, covering 4,300 miles—in a westwardly direction—across the Pacific Ocean. They did this to demonstrate that earlier, primitive humans could have migrated from South America to Polynesia.

Later in his life, Heyerdahl and fellow adventurers sailed a new raft—*Ra II*—across the Atlantic from Morocco to Barbados. Again, he showed that people could have used rafts to migrate. There is a difference, however, between the notions "could have migrated" and "did migrate," and Heyerdahl's theories about how people ended up where they did were controversial.

Heyerdahl made other voyages during his life, and he also was in charge of archeological excavations on Easter

Island, the Galapagos Islands, and Peru's north coast. However, he was far more than just an explorer and anthropologist. Heyerdahl was an environmentalist, an artist, an activist who lobbied world leaders to work for world peace, and a scholar who gave talks and wrote books. Despite Heyerdahl's varied accomplishments and skills, he is remembered most for his Kon Tiki and Ra II adventures.

For his life's work, Heyerdahl received prestigious awards, medals, honors, and memberships in exclusive organizations. Universities in six different countries gave him honorary doctorates. A museum in Oslo houses the Kon Tiki raft. Impressively, four documentary movies were made about Heyerdahl's adventures: *Kon Tiki*, *The Ra Expeditions*, *Galapagos*, and *Aku-Aku*.

It is important to note that Heyerdahl deliberately chose to have heterogenous crews on his expeditions. He wanted his crews to represent different races, religions, nationalities, and political viewpoints. He did this to show that cooperation, respect, and peaceful living not only *can* occur in the presence of diversity but also are more achievable *because of* different kinds of people working together.

Boxed Heyerdahl quotation at top of previous page: Excerpt from Drew Snider's March 13, 2000, article "Heyerdahl: Morals, Not Money, Will Save the Planet" published by the Environmental News Service (ENS).

Photo credit/attribution: Title: Photo of mural on an outside wall of the Kon Tiki Museum in Oslo, Norway; Photographer: Unknown; Source: https://commons.wikimedia.org/wiki/File:KonTikiQuote.jpg; Image is used here under the Creative Commons Attribution-Share Alike 3.0 Unported license (https://creativecommons.org/licenses/by-sa/3.0/deed.en) [CC BY-SA 3.0]; Original tinted photo has been cropped and made black-and-white.

> *'Tis much better to do a little [explaining] with certainty, ... than to explain all things by conjecture without making sure of any thing.*

Isaac Newton, 1643-1727. Choose people at random and ask them to explain why Isaac Newton is famous. In response to your request, many of your selected "examinees" will likely say: "Oh, he's the guy who was sitting under an apple tree and discovered gravity after a falling apple hit him in the head."

Although it may be a myth that an apple actually hit Newton on the head, there is evidence that there was, in fact, a falling apple. William Stukeley (1687-1765), who was with Newton on the day in question, gave this account:

> *We went into the garden...only he and myself. Amidst other discourse, he told me: "Why should that apple always descend perpendicularly to the ground; why should it not go sideways or upwards? but constantly to the Earth's center? assuredly, the reason is, that the earth draws it. there must be a drawing power in matter [and] if matter thus draws matter, it must be in proportion of its quantity."*

While Newton legitimately is credited with "discovering" gravity, there is far more worth knowing about this remarkable scientist. For example:

- Regarding his education, Newton was the top-ranked student in high school. He continued his studies at Cambridge, where he focused his studies on philosophy, astronomy, and mathematics.

- After graduating from college, Newton joined the faculty at Cambridge. There he developed calculus, built the first reflecting telescope, calculated the speed of sound, and proposed his three laws of motion. One of those laws said: "For every action, there is an equal and opposite reaction."

- Many scholars assert that Newton's *Principia* is the greatest scientific book ever written.

- Due to his reputation as an intellectual leader in mathematics, physics, classical mechanics, optics, gravitation, and theology, Newton was knighted by Queen Anne. Moreover, he was made president of the prestigious Royal Society, and he served for 28 years as Master of the Mint.

- Despite the many honors he received, Newton was a humble person. In a letter he wrote to a contemporary rival (the scientist Robert Hooke), Newton famously acknowledged others' work, saying: "If I have seen further, it is by standing on the shoulders of giants."

Boxed Newton quotation at top of previous page: Excerpt from page 643 of Richard S. Westfall's 1983 book *Never at Rest: A Biography of Isaac Newton*, New York: Cambridge University Press.

William Stukeley quote: excerpt from page 13 of his 1752 book, *Memoirs of Sir Isaac Newton's Life*, London: The Roral Society.

Comment about Newton's *Principia*: Excerpt from page 81 of Michael Ravitch and Diane Ravitch's 2006 book, *The English Reader: What Every Literate Person Needs to Know*, New York: Oxford University Press.

Newton's "shoulder-of-giants" comment: Excerpt from page 142 of Sir David Brewster's 1855 book, *Memoirs of the Life, Writings, and Discoveries of Sir Isaac Newton* (Vol. 1), Edinburgh, Scotland: Thomas Constable and Co.

Photo credit/attribution: Title: Photo of circa 1720 portrait of Sir Isaac Newton; Photo is in the public domain {{PD-US}}. Source: https://commons.wikimedia.org/wiki/File:Isaac_Newton,_English_School,_1715-20.jpg; Original color photo has been flipped horizontally, cropped, and made black-and-white.

> *Have regular hours for work and play;*
> *make each day both useful and pleasant,*
> *and prove that you understand the worth of time*
> *by employing it well.*

Louisa May Alcott, 1832-1888. Born in Philadelphia, Alcott and her family moved to Massachusetts when she was two years old. Her father was an educator, and he and his friends provided much of her informal schooling. This informal group of her "teachers" included Henry David Thoreau, Ralph Waldo Emerson, and Nathaniel Hawthorne!

As a young adult, Alcott worked at various jobs to help earn money for her struggling family. At the same time, she devoted energy toward her true passion, writing. She published—under pen names—poems, short stories, and a play. In 1860, she began to write articles—now under her own name—published in the *Atlantic Monthly* and *Lady's Companion*. In 1863, Alcott published a book entitled *Hospital Sketches*; in it, she described her six-week job as a volunteer nurse in a Union hospital.

In 1868, Alcott penned her most successful work: *Little Women*. In this work, Alcott described the lives of the four March sisters—Meg, Jo, Amy, and Beth—as they grow from teenagers into adult women. When Alcott's father and her publisher read drafts of the initial chapters, they thought it was dull. However, the publisher's niece and other girls loved what Alcott had written. The opinion of those young "reviewers" matched what others thought once the book was published. *Little Women* was an immediate success, bringing Alcott instant fame. This book, her *magnum opus*, has stood the test of time. Moreover, it has been adapted into a play, movies, a television musical, and even an opera.

Many literary scholars and historians believe that *Little Women* promoted women's rights. That's because the four March sisters are talented, independent characters who do not consider being married a necessary condition for living a happy and productive life. (To illustrate, Jo one day says to her sisters, "I want to do something splendid before I'm dead. I don't know what, but I'm on the watch for it.... I think I shall write books, and get rich and famous; that would suit me.") The book also argues for resistance to society's effort to reduce or eliminate individuality.

Most people know that Louisa May Alcott wrote *Little Women*. However, two other interesting facts about Alcott are not so well known. First, her family moved 22 times in 30 years. Second, her family served as station masters on the Underground Railroad, and they housed a fugitive slave for a week.

Boxed Alcott quotation at top of previous page: Excerpt from page 173 of Louisa M. Alcott's 1880 book, *Little Women*, Boston: Roberts Brothers.

Photo credit/attribution: Title: 1870 photographic portrait of Louisa May Alcott, writer, abolitionist, and Civil War nurse; Photo is in the public domain {{PD-US}};Source #1: http://loc.gov/pictures/resource/ppmsca.53264/; Source #2: https://commons.wikimedia.org/wiki/File:Louisa_May_Alcott,_c._1870_-_Warren%27s_Portraits,_Boston.jpg; Photographer: George Kendall Warren (restored by Adam Cuerden); Original tinted photo has been cropped and made black-and-white.

> *Your relationships that you have are not entirely yours;
> you share those relationships with other people [and]
> you have a responsibility to protect those people.*

Wole Soyinka, 1934 -. Born in southwestern Nigeria, Soyinka grew up to become an Oxford-trained university professor and his country's most famous literary figure. Highly versatile, Soyinka has written plays, novels, short stories, poetry collections, essays, and memoirs. He directed films and released an  album of his music. Soyinka edited a literary journal. He translated (from Yorùbá into English) mystery novels written by fellow Nigerian Daniel Fágúnwà.

Of his many impressive achievements, Soyinka is known mainly for his plays and for founding the Drama Association of Nigeria. In 1986, Soyinka won the Nobel Prize in Literature. (Previously, no Black person nor any African had been so honored.) The press release announcing this prestigious award stated that Soyinka was "one of the finest poetical playwrights that have written in English."

Soyinka is not just a literary artist; he is also a political and humanitarian activist. He strongly objected to his country being a colonial outpost in the British Empire, and he celebrated when Nigeria became an independent republic in 1963. In 1964, he protested a fraudulent election and found himself jailed for two months. In 1966, a coup d'état put a corrupt military-run government in control. Soyinka protested, was again imprisoned, and spent nearly two years in solitary confinement.

After his release, Soyinka continued to denounce dictators who ruled African countries. He did this in many ways, including within two of his satirical plays: *Requiem for a Futurologist* and *A Play of Giants*. Those and other Soyinka plays dealt with two main themes: tyranny and hypocrisy.

Soyinka's passionate concern about human rights and the abuse of power did not fade as he has aged. In 2007, at age 73, he fearlessly charged that ballot fraud had tainted Nigeria's presidential election. Twelve years later, he spoke out again—this time in advance of the presidential election—and encouraged women and young people to vote. Soyinka did this because he wanted Nigeria's government to represent all people, including those who earlier had been disenfranchised from politics.

In addition to being a Nobel Laureate, Soyinka has been widely recognized for his literary talent and social justice advocacy. He received the Europe Theater Prize, the International Humanist Award, the Academy of Achievement Golden Plate Award, and honorary doctoral degrees from Harvard, Princeton, and the University of Leeds. Impressively, Soyinka was named a United Nations Goodwill Ambassador. Not surprisingly, he has given invited talks worldwide.

Boxed Soyinka quotation at top of previous page: Excerpt from Soyinka's videotaped talk on April 27, 2006 (hosted by the Harvard Book Store) at the First Parish Church in Cambridge, Massachusetts.

Photo credit/attribution: Title: 2018 photo of Wole Soyinka during a lecture at the Stockholm Public Library; Photographer: Frankie Fouganthin; Source: https://commons.wikimedia.org/wiki/File:Wole_Soyinka_in_2018_in_Stockholm.jpg; This image is used here under the Creative Commons Attribution-Share Alike 4.0 International license (https://creativecommons.org/licenses/by-sa/4.0/deed.en) [CC BY-SA 4.0]; Original color photo has been flipped horizontally, cropped, and made black-and-white.

> *Resolve to edge in a little reading every day, if it is but a single sentence. If you gain fifteen minutes a day, it will make itself felt at the end of the year.*

Horace Mann, 1796-1859. Born to farming parents living in central Massachusetts, Mann did not attend school much while he was young. Nevertheless, he became highly self-educated by going to, and using, his town's public library, the first such library in America. At age 20, Mann entered Brown  University. He excelled there, graduating (in just three years) as valedictorian of his class.

After completing his undergraduate education, Mann worked as a tutor and in a library. He then earned a law degree. At age 31, he became a Massachusetts legislator. Voters later sent him to the U.S. Congress. In those two elected posts, Mann was quite active. He argued for public charities and state support of the mentally ill; he lobbied against lotteries and slavery. Despite those and other interests, Mann's central and overriding concern was educational reform.

In 1837, Mann was appointed secretary of his state's newly-formed Board of Education. From that point forward, Mann withdrew from law and politics and devoted all his time and energy to improving educational goals, personnel, and procedures. Mann visited every school in his state. He also took a self-funded trip to Prussia to find out the status of their public schools and why some worked better than others. What Mann learned from his school visits at home and abroad resulted in his six main principles about public education:

- Education should be provided by trained teachers.
- Schools should be non-sectarian.
- Children from families of different socio-economic levels should be taught together.
- Education must embrace the spirit, methods, and discipline of a free society.
- Education should be paid for and controlled by an interested public.
- The public should not be ignorant.

Beyond the borders of Massachusetts, many other states became engaged in educational reform during the mid-1800s. Most adopted some or all of Mann's six principles. In addition to articulating those principles, Mann helped Massachusetts establish America's first "normal school" to train teachers.

Mann's work has not gone unnoticed. He is called "the Father of American Public Education." Over 50 schools across the U.S. carry his name. In 1940, the U.S. Post Office issued a stamp honoring Mann as a part of its "Famous Americans Series," putting him on par with Emerson, Sousa, and Twain.

Boxed Mann quotation at top of previous page: Excerpt from page 252 in Charles W. Currier's article "Education by Reading" located in *The Ohio Educational Monthly*, Vol. XXXIV, No. 6, June, 1885.

Photo credit/attribution: Title: 1859 lithograph portrait of Horace Mann; Source: https://commons.wikimedia.org/wiki/File:Horace_Mann_by_Francis_D%27Avigno n,_1859,_lithograph_with_tintstone_on_paper,_from_the_National_Portrait_Gallery_-_NPG-NPG_77_224Mann-000002.jpg; Artist: Francis D'Avignon; This image is used here under the Creative Commons CC0 1.0 Universal Public Domain license (https://creativecommons.org/publicdomain/zero/1.0/deed.en) [CC0 1.0]; Original tinted image has been cropped and made black-and-white.

> *When thou art offended with any man's transgression, presently reflect upon thyself; and consider what thou thyself art guilty of in the same kind.*

Marcus Aurelius, 121-180. Born in Rome to wealthy parents, Aurelius received his education from private tutors. They trained him in oratory and taught him philosophy, law, and other subjects deemed appropriate for the elite.

After his training ended, the 19-year-old Aurelius served as an apprentice to the Roman emperor, Antoninus. In that role, he learned the business of government and assumed a variety of public positions. Following his marriage to the emperor's daughter, Aurelius became a "junior emperor" and heir apparent.

In the year 161, the older Antoninus died, and the Roman Senate wanted Aurelius to be the next emperor. However, Aurelius refused the post unless another leader, Lucius Verus, was appointed co-emperor. Impressively, Aurelius chose to share power rather than grab it for himself. This act, and his emerging leadership style, exemplified the practice of a "Stoic philosophy," a way of thinking that valued self-restraint, duty, and respect for others.

As emperor, Aurelius was well-liked by the citizens of Rome. He acquired the reputation of a "Philosopher King," the kind of ruler Plato earlier had described as being in charge of the utopian city of Kallipolis. Although Aurelius may have had admirable personal characteristics, Rome (and its vast empire) was anything but a serene paradise. Wars with Parthia and Germanic tribes were taking place, there was corruption among the army's officers, and a devastating 15-year plague killed more than five million people. To help deal with these problems, Aurelius named his son, Commodus, to be his co-ruler. Three years later, Aurelius died.

The legacy of Aurelius is not limited to his being an unselfish leader. He also gave future generations a 12-volume book, *Meditations*. This massive work included a set of personal insights Aurelius gained during his life, such as how one can be "good" in the face of obstacles. *Meditations* contained hundreds of maxims such as "Do nothing against thy will…" and "Never esteem anything as profitable [if it] requireth the secret of walls or veils." Aurelius considered his maxims to be helpful to people living in his time. They are useful yet today.

In 1863, scholar Matthew Arnold paid Aurelius a high compliment. He wrote that Aurelius was

> *one of the best of men [and] one of those consoling and hope-inspiring marks, which stand forever to remind our weak and easily discouraged race how high human goodness and perseverance have once been carried.*

Boxed Aurelius quotation at top of previous page: Excerpt from Section 30 of Book 10 of Aurelius' *Meditations* (translated by Meric Casaubon in 1634).

Arnold's characterization of Aurelius: Located on page 262 of Arnold's 1873 book *Essays in Criticism* (5th ed.), Boston: James R. Osgood and Company. (Arnold's words first appeared 10 years earlier in *The Victoria Magazine*.)

Photo credit/attribution: Title: Photo of marble bust of Marcus Aurelius; Source: https://commons.wikimedia.org/wiki/File:Marcus_Aurelius_Glyptothek_München.j pg; Location: The Glyptothek Museum, Munich, Germany; Photographer: Bibi Saint-Pol; Photo is in the public domain; Original tinted image has been cropped and made black-and-white.

> *Haste, unlock the hoarded store;*
> *Feed the hungry, clothe the poor;*
> *Aid the injured, nor the sigh*
> *Of sorrow, pass unheeded by.*

Sarah J. Hale, 1788-1879. Ironically, most individuals know little or nothing about Sarah Hale, yet almost everyone in the world can recite (or sing) the  first stanza of her most popular poetic creation. That poem is "Mary Had a Little Lamb." It is unfortunate that Hale's many other accomplishments are not widely known—or that she erroneously is thought to be a "children's author"—because she was incredibly successful and had several spheres of influence.

Hale was a prolific author, writing nearly 50 books. These works included novels, her original poetry, anthologies of others' poetry, cookbooks, and guides for personal improvement. In addition to being an author, Hale was the first editor of an American magazine. Titled *Godey's Lady Book*, this monthly periodical was the most widely read magazine of the 19th century. It contained works by Nathaniel Hawthorne, Edgar Allan Poe, Oliver Wendell Holmes, Harriet Beecher Stowe, and Washington Irving. Hale was its editor for 40 years.

Hale was outspoken on various societal issues. She was an early advocate for women's rights, especially in education. She helped create Vassar College and worked to get women on its faculty. More generally, she promoted higher education for women and physical education for younger-aged girls. Hale also spoke out against slavery. She did this in several ways, one of which was through her book, *Northwood*. In this novel, she argued that slavery dehumanizes not just the slave but the slaveowner as well.

Hale spent several decades working to have Thanksgiving established as a national holiday. Her effort to accomplish this goal was, for her, a crusade and a near obsession. Hale published editorials about the need for a Day of Thanksgiving, petitioned governors, and over time wrote letters to five U.S. presidents (Taylor, Fillmore, Pierce, Buchanan, and Lincoln). In 1863, President Lincoln issued a proclamation that did what Hale had requested.

One feature of Hale's most famous children's poem is worth noting. The original version of this poem (entitled "Mary's Lamb") had a final eight-line stanza that doesn't appear in "Mary Had a Little Lamb." In it, Mary's classmates ask why the lamb loves Mary. The teacher responds:

> *And you each gentle animal*
> *In confidence may bind,*
> *And make them follow at your call,*
> *If you are always kind.*

Boxed Hale quotation at top of previous page: Excerpt from Hale's poem "Happiness." Located on page 103 of her 1823 book *Genius of Oblivion and Other Original Poems*, Concord, New Hampshire: Jacob B. Moore. (When first published, this book's author was said to be "a Lady of New Hampshire.")

Final stanza of Hale's poem "Mary's Lamb": Located on page 5 of the 1851 book *Poetical Recreations for the Home and the Family for All Ages and All Seasons*, London: White & Pike Publishers.

Photo credit/attribution: Title: 1850 photo of Sara Hale in *Godey's Lady's Book;* Source: https://commons.wikimedia.org/wiki/File:Sarah_Hale_in_Godeys_Cropped.jpg; Photographer: Chambers; Photo is in the public domain {{PD-US}}; Original tinted image has been cropped and made black-and-white.

> *The most important person is the one you are with in this moment.*

Leo Tolstoy, 1828-1910. Born into a wealthy and prominent family of Russian nobility living south of Moscow, Tolstoy grew up to become one of the world's greatest authors. His most famous books are *War and Peace, Anna Karenina,* and *The Death of Ivan Ilich.* Besides these and other novels, the prolific Tolstoy wrote plays, short stories, religious  and philosophical essays, commentaries on art and literature, pedagogical articles, and an autobiography.

Tolstoy's talent as a writer did not go unnoticed. Ultra-flattering comments about him have been made by a multitude of respected individuals, including fellow Russian writer Anton Chekhov, former South African president Nelson Mandela, Tolstoy biographer and historian Alexander Fodor, India's iconic leader Mahatma Gandhi, and the acclaimed 20th-century novelist Virginia Woolf. While alive, Tolstoy was nominated five times for the Nobel Prize in Literature.

Although it is a well-known fact that Tolstoy was a great novelist, other interesting attributes of this famous man are often overlooked. These concern Tolstoy's opinions of how men and women should think and act:

- Tolstoy advocated non-violent resistance to oppression, tyranny, and other forms of evil.
- Tolstoy developed a passionate dislike for organized government. He wrote: "the State is a conspiracy

designed not only to exploit, but above all to corrupt its citizens."

- In 1859, Tolstoy founded a school for peasant children. His main pedagogical idea of "minimal structure" foreshadowed that of Maria Montessori.

- In Tolstoy's opinion, patriotism can never be good or useful because it is, at its very core, antithetical to human equality.

- "Forgiveness," in Tolstoy's opinion, is a highly important human characteristic. Putting his belief into action, he wrote a letter recommending clemency for the assassins who, in 1881, blew up the royal carriage in which the Russian Tsar was riding.

- Tolstoy became a vegetarian (and advised others to follow his example), believing it was immoral to take an animal's life.

Surprisingly, the great Tolstoy was not always thought to be great. When he was at Kazan University, a teacher of his wrote that Tolstoy was "both unable and unwilling to learn."

Boxed Tolstoy quotation at top of previous page: Excerpt from page 206 in the 2002 book, *The Path of Life* by Lev Tolstoy (translated by Maureen Cote), New York: Novinks Books.

Tolstoy comment about government: Excerpt from page 146 in A. N. Wilson's 1988 book *Tolstoy*, New York: W. W. Norton & Company.

Teacher comment about Tolstoy: Excerpt from page 215 in Michael Marcovici's 2014 book *The 50 Most Influential People in History*, Books on Demand.

Photo credit/attribution: Title: 1908 photo of Leo N. Tolstoy; Source: https://commons.wikimedia.org/wiki/File:Tolstoy_portrait_tolstoy.ru.jpg; Photographer: Unknown; Photo is in the public domain {{PD-US}}; Original tinted image has been cropped, and made black-and-white.

> *Never miss an opportunity to teach.*
> *When you teach others, you teach yourself.*

Itzhak Perlman, 1945-. Born in Tel Aviv, Israel, to parents who had immigrated from Poland, Perlman developed an interest in classical music when he was just three years old. Fascinated with the violin sounds he heard on the radio, he  wanted to make those sounds himself. So, he initially practiced on a toy fiddle.

When Perlman was four, he contracted polio. This disease permanently paralyzed his legs, and doctors were skeptical about him continuing to play music. Nevertheless, Perlman persevered. He had regular violin lessons and gave his first recital when he was 10. Soon after that, Perlman's family moved to New York, where he studied at the exclusive and famous Juilliard School.

Perlman performed in Carnegie Hall when he was just 18. The following year, he won the prestigious Leventritt Competition. Over time, he became well-known worldwide for his live violin performances and recordings. Perlman has played during several events at the White House—including a dinner in 2007 honoring Queen Elizabeth II—as well as at concerts in Moscow, Warsaw, and Budapest.

Many people heard Perlman's violin music when they saw the highly acclaimed 1993 film *Schindler's List*. The memorable melodies in this movie accompanied, on the one hand, the horrific scenes of Nazi extermination camps, as well as those of Oscar Schindler's courageous effort to save people from being murdered, on the other. This film won the Academy Award for the best original musical score.

It is worth noting that Perlman is not just a violinist. He also is a conductor and a teacher. Perlman has conducted the Detroit Symphony Orchestra and New York's Westchester Philharmonic. Regarding Perlman's role as a teacher, he has long helped hone the skills of both talented and beginning students. As one might expect, he teaches in the Perlman Music Program, which was founded in 1995 by his wife.

Perlman's sterling career has brought him a host of awards and honors. These include the Presidential Medal of Freedom (given by Barack Obama), the National Medal of Arts (presented by Bill Clinton), the Medal of Liberty (conferred by Ronald Reagan), Israel's coveted Genesis Prize, the Golden Plate Award (bestowed by Elie Wiesel), 16 Grammy Awards, and four Emmy Awards.

One interesting fact about Perlman is that he does not use a modern musical instrument. Instead, his beautiful music comes from a Stradivarius violin that is over 300 years old. It is said to be the most expensive violin in the world!

> *Hold on to your dreams,*
> *believe in yourself,*
> *and live life to the full.*

Maria Mutola, 1972-. Raised in the slums near Mozambique's capital city, and being the youngest of seven siblings, Mutola easily could have been stifled by her life circumstances. Instead, she grew up to become one of her country's most beloved citizens. Mutola gained this stature due to her incredible  athletic talent and unwavering concern for her country's underprivileged.

A track coach saw how fast Mutola could run while she was playing soccer. He enticed her to run the 800-meter race in track events. At age 15, she made her country's Olympic team. Mutola didn't win a medal in the 1988 Olympic Games, but she went home determined to do better in the future. And improve she did!

Mutola was an Olympian six times during a 20-year span (1988-2008), becoming only the second female sprinter in Olympic history to achieve this record number of appearances. During this time interval, Mutola won a gold medal in the 2000 Olympics, she won an amazing 42 international 800-meter races in a row, and in 2003 she won a prize of $1,000,000 (from the International Association of Athletics Federations) for remaining undefeated in six international races. Understandably, Mutola was chosen to carry her country's flag in the Opening Ceremony of one of her Olympics appearances.

Mutola was not just a great athlete. She was also a dedicated humanitarian. After becoming an Honorary Youth Ambassador for the United Nations, Mutola spent time raising awareness of the AIDS disease in Africa. Moreover, she took the bulk of her prize money and established the Lurdes Mutola Foundation. This organization's mission is to "promote and facilitate the empowerment and development of youth through education and sport." However, it does other things, too, such as working with UNICEF to immunize Mozambiquans against measles and polio.

In 2019, Pope Francis visited Mozambique. Using Mutola as an example in a talk, the Pope said: "Our best dreams are only attained through hope, patience, and commitment [and] we must never fall into the trap of giving up because things did not go well at first." He continued his praise for Mutola, pointing out that

> *her success did not make her self-absorbed; her nine world titles did not let her forget her people, her roots—she continued to look out for the needy children of Mozambique.*

Boxed Mutola quotation at top of previous page: Excerpt from Kamleesh Seeruttan and Reynolds Quirin's October 27, 2000, article in *World Athletics*.

Comments about Mutola from Pope Francis: Excerpts from pages 3-4 of the Pope's "Interreligious Meeting with Youth" at Maxaquene Stadium in Maputo, Mozambique on Thursday, September 5, 2019.

Photo credit/attribution: Title: 2008 photo of Maria Mutola during the IAAF World Championships in Valencia, Spain; Photographer: Erik van Leeuwen Source: https://commons.wikimedia.org/wiki/File:Maria_Mutola_Valence_2008_cropped.jpg ; Image is used here under the GNU Free Documentation License (https://en.wikipedia.org/wiki/GNU_Free_Documentation_License) [GNU FDL]; Original color image has been rotated slightly, cropped, and made black-and-white.

> *It is better to suffer wrong than to do it, and happier to be sometimes cheated than not to trust.*

Samuel Johnson, 1709-1784. As a child growing up in England, Johnson was highly precocious. He memorized passages from *The Book of Common Prayer* at age 3. He entered school at age 4. Not surprisingly, he attended college at Oxford.

After unsuccessful attempts at being a teacher and a school headmaster, Johnson turned his attention to writing. His initial efforts were a 263-line poem and a biography of his friend, poet Richard Savage. These early works were quickly overshadowed by what has been referred to as one of the greatest single achievements in scholarship: Johnson's *Dictionary of the English Language.* It took Johnson nine years to complete his *Dictionary.* The finished product was so impressive that King George III gave Johnson an annual pension in appreciation of his work. It also earned Johnson a Master of Arts degree from Oxford. Johnson's *Dictionary* was so complete that it remained the authoritative resource on word meaning and etymology for 150 years.

After completing his *Dictionary,* Johnson wrote hundreds of essays, poems, and even sermons. However, none of these items was as noteworthy as his next large-scale project: an eight-volume, edited version of the dramas written by the "Bard of Avon." Entitled *The Plays of Shakespeare,* Johnson's volumes were helpful in two major ways. First, they corrected the plays' words and phrases that either had been corrupted over the years during the reprinting process or had become obsolete. Second, Johnson provided his and others' explanatory notes to provide insight into the difficult-to-understand passages written by Shakespeare.

It should be noted that Johnson was the subject of Boswell's famous biography, *The Life of Samuel Johnson.* Several other biographies of Johnson have been written, but literary scholars consider Boswell's to be the best. One reason for this is that Boswell did not focus on the dates of events, Johnson's achievements, and the names of places where events took place. Instead, Boswell described the "inner man" of Johnson: his thoughts and feelings. Boswell could do this because he and Johnson were friends. Boswell's biography of Johnson was admired immediately after it was first published. Centuries later, it's included in lists of the best 100 books ever written.

Many scholars consider Johnson to have been the most distinguished "man of letters" in English history. Accordingly, it is no surprise that he received an honorary doctorate from Oxford and was buried in Westminster Abbey. Impressively, the Church of England lists December 13 in its Calendar of Saints. It does that to commemorate the day Johnson died.

Boxed Johnson quotation at top of previous page: Excerpt from Johnson's article published in *The Rambler* on Tuesday, December 18, 1750.

Current status of Boswell's biography of Johnson: Robert McCrum's 2018 book *The Best 100 Best Nonfiction Books of All Time*, Cambridge, UK: Galileo Publishers.

Photo credit/attribution: Title: Photo of 1833 engraving of Samuel Johnson; Source: https://commons.wikimedia.org/wiki/File:Dr-Johnson.jpg; Artist: William Holl; Photo is in the public domain; Original image has been cropped.

> *You should endeavor
> not only to be learned
> but virtuous.*

George Washington, 1732-1799. Most people know that Washington was a general in America's Revolutionary War, that he crossed the Delaware River, and that he was his country's first president. It is also well known that Washington, as a young boy, supposedly began his confession to his  father—after cutting down a prized cherry tree on the family's farm—by saying, "I cannot tell a lie." Beyond these four items, there are 10 other facts worth knowing about George Washington:

- Washington's full name was George Washington, as his parents chose not to give him a middle name.
- The famous 1851 painting, *Washington Crossing the Delaware*, was not the work of an American; instead, it was painted by the German artist Emanuel Gottlieb Leutze. (Painted 75 years after the event, the work contains several inaccuracies, such as the American flag that did not yet exist in 1776.)
- Washington was his wife's second husband.
- In 1792, during the early portion of the French Revolution, Washington was among 17 individuals who were made honorary citizens of France. This honor came to them because they were deemed to be "men, who

through their writings and their courage, have served the cause of liberty and prepared the freedom of the people."

- Because of wrangling between political leaders of the Revolution, Washington had misgivings about becoming president. He wrote to a friend, saying, "my movement to the chair of Government will be accompanied with feelings not unlike those of a culprit who is going to the place of his execution."
- Washington was the only sitting president who was involved, as an officer, in military conflict.
- In 1798, Washington had a distillery installed at Mount Vernon. It produced rye whiskey and two flavors of brandy, and it was exceedingly profitable.
- To attract more men into the military, the second U.S. president, John Adams, appointed his predecessor, Washington, to the position of "Commander of Chief."
- Washington, whose height was 6 feet 2 inches, was one of America's tallest presidents.
- A law was passed in 1976 giving Washington the highest military rank anyone had had or could have: General of the Armies of the United States.

Boxed Washington quotation at top of previous page: Excerpt from a letter Washington sent on Sunday, December 5, 1790, to his nephew George Steptoe Washington.

Criteria for becoming honorary citizens of France: Statement of the National Assembly of France on August 26, 1792.

Washington's stated misgivings about becoming president: Excerpt from page 559 of Ron Chernow's 2010 book *Washington: A Life*, New York: Penguin Press.

Photo credit/attribution: Title: Photo of 1794 portrait of George Washington; Source: https://commons.wikimedia.org/w/index.php?search=george+washington&title=Spe cial:MediaSearch&go=Go&type=image; Artist: Adolf Ulrik Wertmüller; Photo is in the public domain; Original color image has been cropped and made black-and-white.

> *What matters most are the simple pleasures*
> *so abundant that we can all enjoy them....*
> *Happiness doesn't lie in the objects*
> *we gather around us. To find it,*
> *all we need to do is*
> *open our eyes.*

Antoine de Saint-Exupéry, 1900-1944. Born into a wealthy family in Lyon, France, Saint-Exupéry grew up to become one of his country's— and the world's—most beloved authors. Saint-Exupéry was a newspaper journalist, poet, and author of magazine articles. However, it was his book, *The*  *Little Prince*, that made him incredibly famous both at home and abroad.

The Little Prince is a story about a pilot stranded for eight days in a desert after making a crash landing. The pilot meets a young boy (nicknamed "Little Prince") who has fallen to Earth from a tiny asteroid. During their conversations while the pilot tries to fix his damaged plane, the Little Prince describes several aspects of his life: his love of a rose, his previous encounters with six adults who worry about silly things, and a fox who points out that what's truly important in life can be seen only with your heart, not your eyes.

Parts of *The Little Prince* likely were based on Saint-Exupéry's own life experiences. He was a pilot who once crashed his plane in the Sahara Desert. Also, Saint-Exupéry had raised a desert sand fox (called a fennec) that probably was the inspiration for the fox's character in the book. Even the asteroid's number was similar to that on Saint-Exupéry's mail delivery plane.

Regardless of how much of the book was drawn from the author's background, no one can doubt the enormous impact of *The Little Prince*. It has been translated into more than 300 languages and dialects. It has been transformed into plays, movies, board games, and a ballet. And, the book's handwritten manuscript and artwork (painted by Saint-Exupéry himself), when put on display, draw overflowing crowds of admirers.

Saint-Exupéry became a national hero in France, partly because of the books he wrote and partly because of his aircraft exploits both before and during World War II. He is honored in many ways. For example, an inscription in the Panthéon in Paris praises him; he was made a Knight in France's Légion d'honneur; the Lyon airport is named after him, and his picture has appeared on a banknote and a commemorative coin.

Although most people are aware of Saint-Exupéry's *magnum opus* book, few know that he died during WWII when his plane crashed into the Mediterranean Sea. Even fewer know the full name he was given at birth: Antoine Marie Jean-Baptiste Roger, Comte de Saint-Exupéry.

Boxed Saint-Exupéry quotation at top of previous page: Excerpt from his 1943 book, *The Little Prince* (Translated from French to English by Katherine Woods), New York: Reynal & Hitchcock.

Photo credit/attribution: Title: Photo of Paris Monument Commemorating de Antoine Saint-Exupéry; Source: https://commons.wikimedia.org/wiki/File:Monument_Com-memororating_Antoine_de_Saint-Exup%C3%A9ry_-_panoramio.jpg; Photographer: Unknown; Image is used here under the Creative Commons Attribution-Share Alike 3.0 Unported license (https://creativecommons.org/licenses/by-sa/3.0/deed.en) [CC BY-SA 3.0]; Original color image has been cropped and made black-and-white.

> *Never doubt that a small group of thoughtful,*
> *committed citizens can change the world.*
> *Indeed, it's the only thing that ever has.*

Margaret Mead, 1901-1978. Born and raised in Pennsylvania, Mead's parents were highly educated. Her father was a professor of finance; her mother was a sociologist. Following her parents' lead, Mead herself became highly educated.

After graduating from high school, Mead went to DePauw University in Indiana. She was there for a year and then transferred to Barnard College in New York City. After earning her B.A. degree from Barnard, Mead enrolled as a graduate student at Columbia University. Her primary mentor there was the highly respected cultural anthropologist Franz Boas (considered the "Father of American Anthropology"). With her Master's degree in hand, Mead traveled to Samoa in Polynesia to do the needed anthropological fieldwork for her doctoral degree.

After receiving her Ph.D., Mead wrote a book called *Coming of Age in Samoa.* In this work (which summarized much of her doctoral findings), Mead described how Samoan adolescents—especially the girls—transitioned from being children to having young-adult bodies and roles. This book was immensely popular and made Mead the most famous anthropologist in the world. It also gave respect to a relatively new method for conducting anthropological research: living in a foreign land and simply noting its people's customs.

In Mead's other written works and speeches, she argued for a more liberated role for women, both in families and in society. She also felt that alleged racial differences in intelligence were caused by biased tests of IQ. Although Mead spent much of her career observing people in distant domains, she also was a prolific scholar. She wrote 39 books, penned 1,397 other publications, and gave countless talks worldwide.

Because of her many achievements, Mead was tapped to be president of the American Anthropological Association, as well as the elected leader of the American Association for the Advancement of Science. In 1979, President Jimmy Carter posthumously awarded Mead the prestigious Presidential Medal of Freedom. Its citation said:

> *Margaret Mead was both a student of civilization and an exemplar of it. To a public of millions, she brought the central insight of cultural anthropology: that varying cultural patterns express an underlying human unity. She mastered her discipline, but she also transcended it. Intrepid, independent, plain-spoken, fearless, she remains a model for the young and a teacher from whom all may learn.*

Boxed Mead quotation at top of previous page: Excerpt from page 4 of Nancy C. Lutkehaus' 2008 book *Margaret Mead: The Making of an American Icon*, Princeton, New Jersey: Princeton University Press.

Medal of Freedom citation: Excer pt from pages 87-88 January 8, 1979 issue of the *Weekly Compilation of Presidential Documents*, Vol. 15, No. 1 (published by National Archives and Records Service, Washington, D.C.).

Photo credit/attribution: Title: 1962 photo of Margaret Mead; Source: https://commons.wikimedia.org/wiki/File:Margaret_Mead,_AMNH.jpg; Photo comes from page 47 of the 1969 book *A Brief Expedition into Science at the American Museum of Natural* History; Photo is in the public domain; Original image has been cropped.

> *Be not ungrateful for all that has been done for thee,*
> *for thou hadst nothing in the world*
> *of thine own to begin with.*

Michelangelo, 1475-1564. If asked to name the most versatile and talented artist who ever lived, many people would respond with just one word: Michelangelo. If then pressed to name a few of this famous artist's works, most people so queried would list three masterpieces: the marble statue of David located in Florence, the painted ceiling in the Vatican's Sistine Chapel, and the *Pietà*  (a small sculpture in St. Peter's Basilica in Rome). There is, however, much more worth knowing about this artistic giant of the Italian Renaissance.

Here are seven lesser-known facts about the creative genius Michaelangelo:

- Michelangelo's full name was Michelangelo di Lodovico Buonarroti Simoni. His first name comes from the Hebrew name "Michael" (he who resembles God) and the Greek name "Angelo" (messenger).
- Many of Michelangelo's well-known works were done early in his career; he finished *David* and the *Pietà* by age 25, and he finished painting the Sistine Chapel's ceiling by the time he was 37.
- Michelangelo believed that a sculptor's task was not to chip away at stone so as to "impose" an idea on what originally was just rock; instead, he considered every piece of marble to have a sculpture within it, with the job

227

of the sculptor being to chip away everything that wasn't part of that pre-existing sculpture.

- Michelangelo was a respected architect. Among his many commissioned projects, he designed much of Saint Peter's Basilica in Rome, including its famous dome.
- More than just a sculptor, painter, and architect, Michelangelo also was a prolific poet. He wrote more than 300 sonnets. A six-line excerpt from one of those poems contains this beautiful thought:

> *My soul can find no stair*
> *To mount to heaven, save earth's loveliness.*
> *For from the stars above*
> *Descends a glorious light*
> *That lifts our longing to their highest height*
> *And bears the name of love.*

- Michelangelo and Leonardo Da Vinci were not friends. According to one source, they had "a lifelong rivalry fueled by jealousy and ambition." Michelangelo also did not get along with Rafael.
- Michelangelo had an unusual way of signing his paintings: he wouldn't put his name on them but instead would paint himself into them. He did, however, chisel his name into his sculpture, the *Pietà*.

Boxed Michelangelo quotation at top of previous page: Excerpt from page 230 of the 1913 book, *Michelangelo: A Record of His Life as Told in His Own Letters and Papers* (translated and edited by Robert Carden.), Boston: Houghton Mifflin Co.

Poem excerpt: From "Gli occhi miei delle cose belle" (translated by George Santayana), *The Harvard Monthly*, Vol. 31, No. 4, January, 1901, page 134.

Photo credit/attribution: Title: Photo of 1682 engraving of Michelangelo; Source: https://commons.wikimedia.org/wiki/File:Michel-Ange_Buonarotti.jpg; Artist: Nicolas de Larmessin; Photo is in the public domain {{PD-US}}; Original tinted image has been flipped horizontally, cropped, and made black-and-white.

> *It is our own mental attitude*
> *which makes the world what it is for us.*
> *Our thoughts make things beautiful; our thoughts*
> *make things ugly. The whole world is in our own*
> *minds. Learn to see things in the proper light.*

Swami Vivekananda, 1863-1902. Born in Calcutta, India, Vivekananda grew up to become the leader of the Hindu religion. He helped introduce the philosophy of Yoga to the Western world, promoted the concept of "nationalism" in his countrymen (then ruled by England), and contributed to Hinduism becoming a major  world religion. In the words of B. R. Ambedkar—India's first Minister of Law and Justice, and considered to be the "Father" of India's constitution—"the greatest man India produced in recent centuries was not Gandhi but Vivekananda."

As a child, Vivekananda was a voracious reader who consumed works dealing with philosophy, history, art, literature, and religion. In college, he studied the ideas of many Western icons such as David Hume, William Wordsworth, Immanuel Kant, and Charles Darwin. Interested in religion since he was a young boy, Vivekananda came to believe that service to others is the most effective way to worship God.

When 25, Vivekananda gave up almost all personal belongings, took formal monastic vows, and became a monk. He toured America and various European countries, always talking about India's great spiritual heritage. In India, he argued against the caste system, the subjugation of women, and colonial rule. He argued for belief in science, an end to poverty, and tolerance toward others with differing beliefs.

Vivekananda had two important goals. On the one hand, he sought a "modern" interpretation of Hinduism wherein there is, for example, gender equality and belief in science. On the other hand, he wanted India to end its cultural isolation from the West. By achieving these goals, Vivekananda became a revered icon.

In 1893, Vivekananda represented Hinduism at a major Chicago event, the "Parliament of Religions." This convention was at the Art Institute and had an audience of more than 4,000 people. Vivekananda spoke of the good in all religions, and he advocated universal tolerance and acceptance. After finishing his speech, attendees responded with a thunderous, long-lasting ovation. The next day, "all the papers lionized him as the greatest figure and the best speaker of the Parliament," and "the young monk became known throughout the United States."

Vivekananda has been honored in various ways. Among these, two are most impressive and enduring. Each year, India celebrates his birthday as "National Youth Day." Moreover, the anniversary of Vivekananda's stirring speech at the Parliament of Religions is celebrated yearly as "World Brotherhood Day."

Boxed Vivekananda quotation at top of previous page: Excerpt from page 136 in the 2022 book *Greatest Speeches of Vivekananda*, New Delhi, India: Prabhat Publisher.

Comments about Vivekananda's Chicago speech: Excerpt from the 2015 book *Chicago Address by Swami Vivekananda*, Uttarakhand, India: The Adhyaksha.

Photo credit/attribution: Title: 1893 photo of Swami Vivekananda; Source: https://commons.wikimedia.org/wiki/File:Swami-vivekananda.jpg; Photographer: Thomas Harrison; Photo is in the public domain {{PD-US}}; Original color image has been cropped and made black-and-white.

> *Keep some room in your heart*
> *for the unimaginable.*

Mary Oliver, 1936-2019. Born and raised in a semi-rural setting on the outskirts of Cleveland, Ohio, Oliver spent many hours of her youth taking walks in the nearby woods. It was there that she developed a love of nature. Something in that undeveloped, rural setting prompted Oliver, at age 14, to start writing poems. Her  poetry focused on what she experienced during her strolls through forests and fields, near waterfalls and ponds, at sunrise and in moonlight.

Oliver focused most of her early poems on nature's flora and fauna. For example, Oliver wrote about swans, geese, turtles, daisies, lilies, mushrooms, and moths. Collectively, those works made the point that one can't truly see the extraordinary beauty of plants and animals and seasons during fast-paced treks wherein "getting to the destination" is the goal. One must stroll slowly and observe, she believed.

About midway through Oliver's adult life, her poetic focus shifted to a consideration of people's internal beliefs, hopes, and fears. In these poems, she seemed to be offering advice on how to live a meaningful life. In one such poem, she wrote: "You must not, ever, give anyone else responsibility for your life." In another, Oliver advised: "Instructions for living a life: Pay attention. Be astonished. Tell about it."

A particular pair of Oliver poems seem to be linked together. That's because Oliver asks her reader a question in the first poem, and then she tells, in the second poem, how she herself would respond to that initial query. In *A Summer Day*, Oliver asks:

> *Tell me, what is it you plan to do*
> *with your one wild and precious life?*

Then, in *When Death Comes*, she directs that question to herself, answering:

> *When it's over, I want to say*
> *All my life, I was a bride married to amazement*
> *I was the bridegroom, taking the world into my arms....*
> *I don't want to end up simply having visited this world.*

Several awards and honors came Oliver's way, including the Pulitzer Prize for Poetry, the National Book Award for Poetry, and honorary doctorates from several colleges and universities. She also received, from Harvard, honorary membership in the esteemed organization Phi Beta Kappa. Perhaps the highest honor given to Oliver came from fellow poet and critic Alicia Ostriker, who wrote that Oliver was

> *as visionary as Emerson and is among the few*
> *American poets who can describe and transmit*
> *ecstasy, while retaining a practical awareness of*
> *the world.*

Boxed Oliver quotation at top of previous page: Excerpt from page 43 of her 2009 book, *Evidence: Poems*, Boston: Beacon Press.

Ostriker comment about Oliver: Excerpt from the 2012 book, *A Study Guide for Mary Oliver's "The Journey"* (Volume 40 of *Poetry for Students*), Farmington Hills, Michigan: Cengage Learning.

Photo credit/attribution: Title: Photo of Mary Oliver; Source: Don Usner Photography, Santa Fe, New Mexico; Photographer: Don Usner; In an email message sent to this book's author on May 11, 2022, Don Usner gave permission to use here his photo of Mary Oliver; Original image has been cropped.

> *In whatever circle of influence you have, speak out on behalf of tolerance and diversity and respect... even when it's unpopular. Especially when it's unpopular.*

Barack Obama, 1961-. Almost everyone in the world knows that Barack Obama was elected the first biracial president of the United States, that he served two four-year terms (2008-2016) in the White House, that his wife's name is Michelle, and that he won the 2009 Nobel Peace Prize. However, 10 additional, lesser-known facts about Obama are worth noting:

- Obama's first name, Barack, means "blessed one" in his father's native language, Swahili.
- Both of Obama's parents were highly educated. His mother earned a Ph.D. in anthropology from the University of Hawaii; his father, a Master's degree in economics from Harvard.
- When he was six, Obama and his mother moved to Indonesia, where they joined his new stepfather. After being there for five years, Obama moved back to Hawaii, where he lived with his maternal grandparents.
- While at Harvard Law School, Obama was editor of the *Harvard Law Review* and graduated *magna cum laude*.
- Before being elected president, Obama served as a state senator in Illinois. He then was elected a U.S. senator, winning 70 percent of the vote and over 90 percent of the counties in Illinois.

- Obama twice won the Grammy Award for the best spoken-word album. He won these awards for his narration of the audio versions of his books *Dreams of My Father* and *The Audacity of Hope.* (Obama is the author of three other books: *Of Thee I Sing: A Letter to My Daughters*, *Change We Can Believe In*, and *Our Enduring Spirit*; he also co-authored—with his wife, Michelle—*Be Vigilant, But Not Afraid.*)
- Three of Obama's heroes are Martin Luther King, Jr., Gandhi, and Picasso.
- In 11 consecutive Gallop polls (2008-2018), Obama was named the most admired man in America. In 2009, he was seen as the most respected and famous person in the world.
- Most of Obama's legislative goals were achieved. They included health care reform, respect for same-sex couples, the Paris Agreement on Global Climate Change, and the reduction of nuclear weapons.
- On a personal level, what are some of Obama's favorite things? His favorite movies: *Casablanca* and *One Flew Over the Cuckoo's Nest*. His favorite game: *Scrabble*. His favorite book: *Moby Dick*. His favorite snack: ice cream or a protein bar. His favorite sport: basketball.

Boxed Obama quotation at top of previous page: Excerpt from a comment he made during a town hall meeting November 14, 2014 at Yangon University, Myanmar.

Photo credit/attribution: Title: 2012 portrait of Barack Obama; Source: https://commons.wikimedia.org/wiki/File:President_Barack_Obama.jpg; Photogra pher: Pete Sousa; Photo is in the public domain {{PD-US}}; Original color image has been cropped and made black-and-white.

> *Do you not see how necessary*
> *a World of Pains and troubles is*
> *to school an Intelligence and make it a soul?*

John Keats, 1795-1821. Born and raised in London, the great English poet Keats nearly spent his adult life in the medical field. He became a medical apprentice when he was 14, and a year later, he entered medical school. At age 21, Keats earned a license to work as a physician, surgeon, and apothecary. His  passion, however, was and always had been poetry.

In 1816, the first published poem by Keats—a sonnet—appeared in a popular magazine. Soon after that, a book (entitled *Poems*) was published containing nothing but works by Keats. Few copies of that book were sold, however, and the venture was considered a publishing failure. Undaunted, Keats changed publishers and continued with his poetic endeavors.

The most famous poems by Keats are "Ode on a Grecian Urn" and "Ode to a Nightingale," two of the six major odes he created. (An "ode" is a poem that takes the form of a conversation one might have with, or about, an object, animal, or idea.) His other odes are "...on Melancholy," "...to Psyche," "To Autumn," and "...on Indolence."

The Grecian urn poem comprises five stanzas with 10 lines per stanza, and its focus is a set of images on the side of a classical Grecian urn. The poem ends with this famous pair of lines: "Beauty is truth, truth beauty; that is all / Ye know on earth, and all ye need to know." The Nightingale work is a bit longer, containing eight stanzas. In it, the focus is not so much on the nightingale but instead on the thoughts one might have while listening to the bird singing in a tree. Such musings are about pleasure and pain, life and death, imagination and reality.

While he was alive, neither Keats nor his poems were famous. Following his death, however, he came to be viewed as one of England's most beloved poets. That people came to admire Keats is remarkable because he wrote poetry seriously for only six years. Having written just 54 poems, he died of tuberculosis when he was but 25 years old.

Just prior to his death, Keats was depressed about his work and said his tombstone should say, "Here lies one whose name was writ in water." How wrong he was! The *Encyclopedia Britannica* notes that "his reputation grew steadily throughout the 19th century [and] his influence is found everywhere…." The entry on Keats in the *Oxford Bibliographies* goes further, pointing out that Keats is "one of the most loved and widely read poets in the English language."

Boxed Keats quotation at top of previous page: Excerpt from a letter he wrote to George and Georgiana Keats on April 21, 1810. Located on page 54 of volume 5 of the 1901 set of books (edited by H. Buxton Forman) *The Complete Works of John Keats*, Glasgow, Scotland: Gowans and Gray Publisher.

Message on Keats' tombstone: Excerpt from page 18 of the 1913(?) book by H. Nelson Gray and Sir James Rennell Rodd *The Protestant Burial-Ground in Rome*, London: Macmillan & Company.

Photo credit/attribution: Title: Photo of a circa 1822 painting of John Keats; Source: https://commons.wikimedia.org/wiki/File:John_Keats_by_William_Hilton.jpg; Artist: William Hilton; Photo is in the public domain {{PD-US}}; Location of painting: National Portrait Gallery, London; Original color image was flipped horizontally, cropped, and made black-and-white.

> *Forget conventionalisms; forget what the world will say.... Think your best thoughts, speak your best words, do your best works, looking to your own conscience for approval.*

Susan B. Anthony, 1820-1906. While growing up, Anthony saw her parents and siblings engaged in social activism. The main lesson she learned can be summarized in just five words: get involved to correct injustices. This lesson became her life-long guiding principle.

As most people know, Anthony was involved in the effort to secure equal rights for women. She was far more than just "involved"; she was a passionate and influential leader in this cause. Anthony gave lectures, chaired the first meeting of the International Woman Suffrage Alliance, raised money, co-authored the six-volume book *History of Woman Suffrage*, and became president of the National American Woman Suffrage Association (now called the League of Women Voters).

Anthony died before the suffrage battle was won. However, she was a leading force that prompted the United States to adopt the 19th Amendment. This addition to the country's Constitution gave women the right to vote.

Anthony's involvement in the suffrage movement is well-known. However, she was a forceful activist in another arena: the anti-slavery movement. Anthony's efforts to end this form of injustice began when, as just a 16-year-old girl, she collected petitions against slavery. Later, Anthony was part of the Underground Railway and worked with Harriet Tubman.

237

More overtly, she was New York's representative for the American Anti-Slavery Society. She helped organize a massive petition to abolish slavery, an effort that helped bring about the 13th Amendment in 1865. Because she was known as an outspoken and influential abolitionist, Anthony was invited, at age 75, to speak to 2,000 mourners at the standing-room-only funeral service for Frederick Douglass.

Besides being an outspoken suffragist and abolitionist, Anthony worked to correct other social injustices. She called for the training of nurses to be standardized. She pressed for educational opportunities for all children. She wanted women to be treated fairly in divorce proceedings. She supported union efforts to improve women's (and men's) salaries and working conditions.

Anthony's accomplishments have been honored in many ways. She is in both the Hall of Fame for Great Americans and the National Women's Hall of Fame. Along with Elizabeth Stanton Cady and Adelaide Johnson, Anthony can be seen in the Portrait Monument sculpture that sits in the Rotunda of the U.S. Capitol. She has appeared twice on U.S. stamps. (The first of these stamps was issued on the 16th anniversary of the day American women gained the right to vote.) Moreover, Anthony was the first female to appear on any form of U.S. currency.

Boxed Anthony quotation at top of previous page: Excerpt from Chapter 14 of Ida Harper's 1899 book, *The Life and Work of Susan B. Anthony* (Vol. 1), Indianapolis, Indiana: The Bowen-Merrill Company.

Photo credit/attribution: Title: 1890 photo of Susan Brownell Anthony; Source: https://commons.wikimedia.org/wiki/File:SB_Anthony_from_RoRaWW.jpg; Photographer: Unknown; Photo is in the public domain; Original image has been cropped.

> *Show the whole world that you are not afraid. Be silent, if you choose; but when it is necessary, speak— and speak in such a way that people will remember it.*

Wolfgang Amadeus Mozart, 1756-1791. Born in Salzburg, Austria, Mozart grew up to become one of the world's greatest musical composers. He belongs in the same super-elite category of musical giants that's populated by Bach, Beethoven, Brahms, Haydn, Chopin, Vivaldi, Rachmaninoff, Grieg, Mussorgsky, Handel, and Tchaikovsky.

Although nearly everyone knows a little about Mozart, several lesser-known facts about Mozart are worth noting.

- Mozart's full name when baptized was Joannes Chrysostomus Wolfgangus Theophilus Mozart. Later, he called himself Wolfgang Amadeus Mozart.
- A child prodigy, Mozart created musical compositions when he was just five years old and wrote his first symphony when he was eight.
- Early in his career, Mozart was hired by Salzburg's ruler as the "court musician." Later, Roman Emperor Joseph II appointed Mozart as his "chamber composer."
- One of the most versatile and prolific composers in history, Mozart produced more than 600 works during his short, 35-year life. These include symphonies, sonatas, concertos, string quartets, chamber music, serenades, marches, minuets, operas, and organ music.

- In 1770, Pope Clement XIV made Mozart a member of the Papal Order of the Golden Spur (designed to honor people—like Raphael, Paganini, and Titian—who made impressive contributions to the Catholic faith).
- Mozart's six most famous works include *Symphony No. 41 ("Jupiter");* the operas *The Magic Flute, The Marriage of Figaro,* and *Don Giovanni*; the liturgical work, *Mass in C Minor,* and his *Piano Concerto No. 24.*
- Music historians assert that Mozart was the preeminent composer during the so-called "classical" period: 1730-1820. That epoch was characterized by lightness, the use of a piano (rather than a harpsichord), and concertos.

It is often said that one's peers are in the best position to evaluate a person's professional worth. If that is true, Mozart can rest easy. Tchaikovsky wrote his Orchestral Suite No. 4 as a tribute to Mozart. Referring to Mozart, Joseph Haydn stated that "posterity will not see such a talent again in 100 years." And the great Ludwig van Beethoven once said: "I have always reckoned myself among the greatest admirers of Mozart, and shall do so till the day of my death."

Boxed Mozart quotation at top of previous page: Excerpt from a letter Mozart sent his father July 4, 1781. Located on page 749 of the 1997 book (translated and edited by Emily Anderson) *Letters of Mozart and His Family*, London: Macmillan.

Haydn's comment about Mozart: Excerpt from page 131 of H. C. R. Landon's 1981 book, *Haydn: A Documentary Study*, London: Thames and Hudson.

Beethoven comment about Mozart: Excerpt from an 1886 letter sent by Beethoven to A. M. Stadler. Located on page 55 of the 1905 book (edited by Friedrick Kerst and Henry E. Krehbiel) *Beethoven: The Man and the Artist, As Revealed in His Own Words*, New York: B. W. Huebsch.

Photo credit/attribution: Title: Photo of Wolfgang Amadeus Mozart painting; Source: https://commons.wikimedia.org/wiki/File:Wolfgang_Amadeus_Mozart_portrait_(95 69258408).jpg; Artist: E. H. Schroeder; Image is used here without any copyright restrictions; Original tinted image has been cropped and made black-and-white.

> *You have your destiny in your own hands.*

Cyrus the Great, 600-530 BCE. Referred to as the Great King, the King of Kings, and the King of Persia, Cyrus also had other names. He was called King of the Four Corners of the World, King of Anshan, King of Media, King of Babylon, and King of Sumer & Akkad. These monikers strongly suggest that

Cyrus was far more than just an ordinary figure in antiquity.

As founder of the Persian Empire, Cyrus has had a lasting and influential legacy. Two hundred years after his death, he was admired by Alexander the Great. Over two thousand years later, Cyrus was a personal hero of both Thomas Jefferson and David Ben-Gurion. Jefferson studied a biographical book on Cyrus, and certain historians believe that what Jefferson learned about Cyrus found its way into America's Declaration of Independence.

Born in what now is Iran, Cyrus became a king at age 41 when his father died. In those days, kings oversaw the management of their subjects and assumed command of the military. Cyrus was talented in both roles.

Being a highly successful military leader, Cyrus created an expansive empire. First, he united two Iranian groups. Then, he conquered territories and opposing armies both near and far. Before long, his vast empire was the world's largest. It extended from the Aegean Sea on the east to the Indus River near the eastern border of Pakistan.

Cyrus was not just a military conqueror, however. In his role as his people's leader, he established a general policy of religious tolerance, restored statues of Babylonian gods, freed slaves, and made costly reparations. He created a multi-state organization, each headed up by a governor who possessed a degree of regional autonomy. Cyrus also formed a network of irrigation canals, and he built a postal system that included several "relay stations."

Because Cyrus was benevolent and supported the continuance of longstanding cultural traditions, the masses admired him, calling him "liberator" (rather than "conqueror") and "Father." He is praised yet today. In her acceptance speech when receiving the 2003 Nobel Peace Prize, Shirin Ebadi said:

> *I am Iranian, a descendant of Cyrus the Great. This emperor proclaimed at the pinnacle of power 2,500 years ago that he "would not reign over the people if they did not wish it." He promised not to force any person to change his religion and faith and guaranteed freedom for all.*

In 2006, Stanford's acclaimed scholar Patrick Hunt stated that Cyrus "affected the world" and deserves the label, "Great."

Boxed Cyrus quotation at top of previous page: Excerpt from page 137 of Jacob Abbot's 1904 book, *Cyrus the Great*, New York: Harper & Brothers Publishers.
Ebadi comment about Cyrus: Excerpt from her Nobel Lecture, December 10, 2003.
Hunt comment about Cyrus: Excerpt from the episode "Engineering an Empire: The Persians" shown on December 4, 2006, on TV's *History Channel*.
Photo credit/attribution: Title: Cyrus the Great, King of Kings and founder of the Persian Empire under the Achaemenid Dynasty; Source #1: Page 104 of Guillaume Rouillé's 1553 book *Prima Pars Promptuarii Iconum Insigniorum a Seculo Hominum Subjectis Eorum Vitis, Per Compendium Ex Probatissimis Autoribus Desumptis* (Publisher: Apud Gulielmum Rovillium); Source #2: https://commons.wikimedia.org/wiki/File:Cyrus_II_rex.jpg; Artist: Unknown; Image is in the public domain {{US-PD}}; Original tinted image has been rotated slightly, cropped, and made black-and-white.

> *Do not mistake yourself*
> *by believing that your being*
> *has something in it more exalted*
> *than that of others.*

Blaise Pascal, 1623-1662. Mainly educated by his father in his French home, Pascal was a child prodigy. In his teenage years, he was a mathematical genius. As an adult, Pascal was a preeminent physicist, inventor, philosopher, and theologian.

Pascal is known today primarily for his "triangle" of numbers. This triangle has a single 1 at the top, two 1s in the next row, and then entries in any lower row that begin and end with a 1, with each intermediate spot filled with a number formed by adding together the two numbers above that spot. Here are the triangle's top few rows:

(Row 0)				1		
(Row 1)			1		1	
(Row 2)		1		2		1
(Row 3)	1		3		3		1

The numbers in Pascal's triangle are useful in determining probabilities. For example, the numbers in the second row below the meaningless top row are 1, 2, 1. Because we're now focused on the *second* meaningful row of the triangle, let's imagine that you flip a fair coin *two* times. (Row 2; 2 coin flips.) There are four possible outcomes when you flip a fair coin twice: head/head, head/tail, tail/head, and tail/tail, as indicated by the sum of the numbers on row 2. The individual numbers on this row tell us that there's 1 way to get two heads (head/head), 2 ways to get a head and a tail (head/tail; tail/head), and 1 way to get two tails (tail/tail). Divide this row's middle number, 2, by the total number of possible outcomes, 4, and you get .50. This tells us that there's a 50% chance of ending up with 1 head and 1 tail in 2 flips of a fair coin. Using the same procedure, we can determine from row 4—not shown in our abbreviated rendering of Pascal's Triangle—that there's only a 37.5% chance of getting 2 heads if you flip a fair coin four times.

Besides developing his famous triangle, Pascal invented a mechanical calculator and the hydraulic press. He also created an early form of the roulette wheel as he tried to develop a "perpetual motion" machine. Not surprisingly, Pascal was a staunch defender of the scientific method.

The book entitled *The Thoughts of Blaise Pascal* was published posthumously. In it, one finds this wise admonition: "The world is full of good maxims. All that is needed is their right application."

Boxed Pascal quotation at top of previous page: Excerpt from page 476 of the 1859 book, *The Thoughts, Letters, and Opuscules of Blaise Pascal* (translated from the French by O. W. Wight), New York: Hurd and Houghton.

Pascal's comment about maxims: Excerpt from page 314 of the 1905 book (edited by M. Auguste Molinier and translated by C. Kegan Paul), *The Thoughts of Blaise Pascal*, London: George Bell and Sons.

Photo credit/attribution: Title: Drawing of Blaise Pascal; Source: https://commons.wikimedia.org/wiki/File:Mais_vale_saber_alguma_coisa_de_tudo, _que_saber_tudo_de_uma_s%C3%B3_coisa._Blaise_Pascal,_1623-1662_-pt.svg; Artist: Gérard Edelinck; Photo is used here under the Creative Commons Attribution-Share Alike 4.0 International license (https://creativecommons.org/licenses/by-sa/4.0/deed.en) [CC BY-SA 4.0]; Original color image has been flipped horizontally, cropped. and made black-and-white.

> *You can't develop a better appreciation of the art [classical music] merely by reading a book about it. If you want to understand music better, you can do nothing more important than listen to it. Nothing can possibly take the place of listening to music.*

Aaron Copland, 1900-1990. Born in Brooklyn to parents who came to the United States from Russia, Copland was around music when he was a toddler. His mother played the piano and sang; his oldest brother played the violin. Copland began piano lessons at age 13, and at 15, he decided to become a composer.

Copland had an excellent music teacher, and he regularly attended the New York Symphony and the Metropolitan Opera. After graduating from high school, he studied music in Paris for three years. There, his teacher was the gifted Nadia Boulanger. Returning to the United States, Copland continued to compose. His first work that gained widespread appeal was *Billy the Kid.* That same year, he wrote the music for the movies *Of Mice and Men* and *Our Town.* Soon after that, he composed three of his most well-known works: *Appalachian Spring, Fanfare for the Common Man,* and *A Lincoln Portrait.* The first of those three masterpieces contains music based on the melodic Shaker tune, "Simple Gifts."

There is a distinctive character to many of Copland's compositions, with musical critics describing his works as "authentically American." This positive critique is a reflection of three aspects of Copland's works:

- Listeners can hear the music of American folk songs, gospel music, and jazz in several compositions. One example is the hymn, *At the River.*
- Copland's works often prompt listeners to conjure up mental images of what they hear, as is the case with the "Hoedown" portion of *Rodeo.*
- People often feel a sense of patriotism when exposed to Copland's music.

Sadly, Copland was unfairly caught up in the McCarthy accusations of the 1950s, and he was blacklisted. His *Lincoln Portrait*—scheduled to be played at President Eisenhower's 1953 inauguration—was taken off the program. In protest, many in the musical community spoke out in defense of Copland's patriotism.

Copland received several honors, including a Presidential Medal of Freedom, a National Medal of Arts, a Congressional Gold Medal, and a Pulitzer Prize in Composition. Perhaps he valued most his informal title: "Dean of American Music." According to one source, he earned this moniker because he was a caring teacher who "was generous with his time with nearly every American young composer he met during his life."

Boxed Copland quotation at top of previous page: Excerpt from page 1 of Aaron Copland's 1939 book, *What to Listen for in Music*, New York: McGraw-Hill.

Final comment about Copland: Excerpt from "Copland Biography," *Lumen Learning: Online Materials and Resources for Higher Ed.*

Photo credit/attribution: Title: 1962 photo of composer Aaron Copland; Source: https://commons.wikimedia.org/wiki/File:Aaron_Copland_in_1962.jpg; Photographer: Unknown employee of CBS Television; Photo is in the public domain; Original image has been flipped horizontally and cropped.

> *Life is made up, not of great sacrifices or duties, but of little things in which smiles, and kindnesses, and small obligations, given habitually, are what win and preserve the heart and secure comfort.*

Sir Humphry Davy, 1778-1829. Born in Cornwall, England, Davy was thought to be a genius by many of his school teachers.

As a young man, he pursued three seemingly incompatible kinds of work: poetry, painting, and chemistry. Davy wrote over 160 poems, eight of which were published. He was also a painter (with three of his works currently hanging in the Penlee House Museum in Penzance). Despite Davy's creations in the written and visual arts, his main love was chemistry. This love became the driving force behind his highly influential career as a scientist, inventor, and professor.

Davy was the first scientist to isolate potassium and sodium, and he also discovered calcium, magnesium, barium, strontium, chlorine, and iodine. He achieved fame for inventing a safety lamp for use in coal mines. Before Davy's invention, miners used a regular candle to light their underground workspace. Explosions, however, would occur when the candle's flame came into contact with methane gas. The "Davy's Lamp" prevented such disasters and thereby saved countless lives.

In addition to being a great scientist, Davy had other interests. He enjoyed hiking in the mountains, and many consider him to be the "father of fly fishing." He was also friends with notable literary figures such as Samuel Taylor Coleridge and William Wordsworth, both of whom asked Davy to proofread their joint collection of poems, *Lyrical Ballads*, that included Coleridge's most famous work, "The Rime of the Ancient Mariner."

Davy's achievements earned him many honors and awards, including election to the prestigious role of president of the Royal Society. (Earlier holders of that position were acclaimed architect Christopher Wren and the scientific genius Isaac Newton.) Davy's discoveries and inventions brought him fame and wealth, and he was knighted in England. He also was invited to meet Napoléon's wife, Empress Joséphine. Soon after Davy's death, a white marble plaque honoring him was installed inside Westminster Abbey.

Today's teachers and professors might profit from reading what Davy had to say about schools: "Learning naturally is a true pleasure; how unfortunate then it is that in most schools it is made a pain."

Boxed Davy quotation at top of previous page: Excerpt from page 448 of the 1839 book by John Davy (Sir Humphry Davy's brother), *Memoirs of the life of Sir Humphry Davy* (Vol. II), London: Smith, Elder and Co.

Davy comment about learning: Excerpt from page 4 of the same book written by John Davy about his brother.

Photo credit/attribution: Title: Photo of 1849 engraving of Sir Humphrey Davy; Source: https://commons.wikimedia.org/wiki/File:Sir_Humphrey_Davy_1849_RGN-RGNb10408769.09.tif; Artist: Sir John Barrow; Photographer: Unknown employee of the Science History Institute; Photo is in the public domain {{US-PD}}; Original image has been cropped.

> *The true secret of giving advice is,*
> *after you have honestly given it, to be perfectly*
> *indifferent whether it is taken or not and never*
> *persist in trying to set people right.*

Hannah Whitall Smith, 1832-1911. Born into a wealthy and prominent Quaker family living in Philadelphia, Smith was married at age 19. Six years later, she put this self-assessment in her diary: "I am twenty-five years old, with I suppose average female abilities...." The success of her life's work and her impact on others clearly showed that her abilities were  anything but average. She developed a worldwide reputation, championed social issues, and socialized with luminaries such as Alfred Lord Tennyson and Bertrand Russell. She also received friendly handwritten letters from Walt Whitman and William James.

When Smith was 16, she had a religious "awakening" that changed her personality and life goals. She became a famous Christian evangelist, speaking at "camp meetings" and "tent revivals" in England and several locations throughout continental Europe. Huge crowds came to hear Smith, who was called the "Angel of the Churches." People described her that way because of her gaze, Quaker dress, and golden hair.

In addition to preaching, Smith wrote many religious books. Her most popular work was *The Christian's Secret of a Happy Life*. On page 230 of this 1888 book, Smith offered her readers this sound advice:

Everything that comes to us becomes a chariot the moment we treat it as such; and on the other hand, even the smallest of trials may be a Juggernaut car to crush us into misery or despair if we so consider them. It lies within each of us to choose which they shall be. It all depends, not on what these events are, but upon how we take them.

This book sold two million copies and was translated into several languages. Smith wrote several other religious texts, one of which was a memorial to her son, who died at 18 while attending Princeton.

In addition to her religious speaking and writing, Smith became involved in several social issues. For example, she argued that women should be allowed to attend college and vote. Regarding women's rights, Smith wrote:

I know nothing more absolutely unjust in itself nor more productive of misery to the woman than the assumption of the place of authority on the part of men. It reduces women at once in principle to the position of slaves.

It is worth noting that Smith's niece was America's first female dean and the second president of Bryn Mawr College.

Boxed Smith quotation at top of previous page: Excerpt from a letter she sent on May 3, 1902. Located on page 146 of Logan P. Smith's 1950 edited book, *Philadelphia Quaker: The Letters of Hannah Whitall Smith*, New York: Harcourt Brace & Co.

Smith's comment about being "average": Excerpt from her journal, March 16, 1857.

Comment from Smith about women's rights: Excerpt from a letter she wrote to Frank Costelloe in 1882. Reproduced in the 1994 book, *The Christian's Secret of a Holy Life: The Unpublished Personal Writings of Hannah Whitall Smith* (edited by Melvin E. Dieter), Grand Rapids, Michigan: Zondervan Publishing.

Photo credit/attribution: Title: Photo of Hannah Whitall Smith; Source: https://commons.wikimedia.org/wiki/File:Hannah_Whitall_Smith.jpg; Photographer: Unknown; Photo is in the public domain; Original image has been cropped.

> *What wisdom can you find*
> *that is greater than kindness?*

Jean-Jacques Rousseau, 1712-1778. Born in an upper-class section of Geneva, Switzerland, Rousseau grew up to become a famous writer, composer, and philosopher. He contributed to the "Enlightenment" period of Europe, greatly influencing how others thought about politics, economics, and education.

Rousseau had an atypical and sad upbringing. Within two weeks of being born, his mother died. When 10 years old, his father disappeared, leaving Rousseau with an uncle who sent him to a boarding school. At 15, Rousseau ran away and traveled for years through Italy and France, working at various jobs (such as tutor, servant, and secretary to the French Ambassador to Venice).

Things changed dramatically for Rousseau when he was in his 20s. A female friend and lover financially supported his study of music, philosophy, and mathematics. When 27, Rousseau moved to France and wrote articles on various topics such as political economy, art, music, and science. After being in France for 15 years, Rousseau returned to Geneva, where a nobleman, the Prince de Conti, supported him.

In 1762, Rousseau published his most famous work, *Emile, or On Education.* In that book, he articulated a philosophy of education (and child-rearing) that included these four beliefs:

- Children learn best in a child-centered environment wherein the focus is on character and moral development, not retention of memorized facts.
- Teachers should realize that children pass through five developmental stages between birth and adulthood.
- Reliance on "natural consequence" is a better teaching tool than the use of rewards and punishments.
- The goal of education is to get children to reason. As Rousseau put it, "if children understood how to reason, they would not need to be educated."

These ideas influenced later educational leaders such as Maria Montessori and John Dewey.

Rousseau is well-known primarily for his contributions to education and philosophy. However, he was also an accomplished music theorist and composer of music. He wrote seven operas, one of which was called *The Village Soothsayer*. This work contained a duet that Ludwig van Beethoven later rearranged into a stand-alone song!

Rousseau is buried in the Panthéon in Paris, a large Gothic church-like building that contains the remains of famous French citizens. Interred there with Rousseau are Victor Hugo, Voltaire, Antoine de Saint-Exupéry, and Marie Curie.

Boxed Rousseau quotation at top of previous page: Excerpt from page 43 of Book II of Rousseau's 1762 work *Emile, or on Education* (translated by Barbara Foxley), London: J. M. Dent & Sons.

Photo credit/attribution: Title: Photo of painted portrait of Jean-Jacques Rousseau; Location of painting: Musée Antoine-Lécuyer, Saint Quentin, France; Source: https://commons.wikimedia.org/wiki/File:JeanJacques_Rousseau_(painted_portrait). jpg; Artist: Maurice Quentin de La Tour; Photographer: Unknown; Photo is in the public domain {{PD-US}}; Original color image has been flipped horizontally, rotated slightly, cropped, and made black-and-white.

> *Love the earth and sun and the animals,*
> *despise riches, give alms to every one that*
> *asks, stand up for the stupid and crazy,*
> *devote your income and labor to others....*

Walt Whitman, 1819-1892. Born in New York, Whitman became one of America's most famous poets. However, the world nearly missed out on seeing the results of this poetic genius. That's because Whitman spent five years as a teacher and then eight more as a journalist. He could have spent the rest of his life in this  latter career, for he was good at founding, editing, and publishing newspapers. Despite that fact, he followed his heart and chose to write poems.

When he was 31, Whitman began writing a dozen long poems for an 1855 book he self-published called *Leaves of Grass*. The young Whitman received high praise for this work from the already established and highly respected author, Ralph Waldo Emerson. In a letter to Whitman, Emerson said, "I find it the most extraordinary piece of wit and wisdom that America has yet contributed. I am very happy in reading it [and so] I greet you at the beginning of a great career."

Spurred on by Emerson's glowing review, Whitman revised and expanded *Leaves of Grass* multiple times over the rest of his life. He chose to do this instead of putting each set of his newest poems into a separate book. By the time Whitman died, the final edition of his great work contained 383 poems, many of which were quite lengthy. Written in "free verse,"

Whitman's poems had no rhyming scheme like those of earlier English poets like Shakespeare and Keats.

The vast majority of Whitman's poems concerned America. They dealt with topics such as democracy, education, poverty, various types of work, the Civil War, and the U.S. landscape. Whitman deeply loved America. This devotion likely was an extension of his parents' admiration for the United States, for they named three of Walt Whitman's male siblings after notable Americans. They were christened Thomas Jefferson Whitman, George Washington Whitman, and Andrew Jackson Whitman.

One of the most famous poems in *Leaves of Grass* is the relatively short work, "O Captain! My Captain!" It was published seven months after the assassination of President Lincoln, a person Whitman greatly admired. This poem is filled with symbolism. The ship represents America, the Captain is Abraham Lincoln, and the "voyage" or "fearful trip" is the Civil War. According to reports, many audience members shed tears when they heard Whitman recite this poem.

Boxed Whitman quotation at top of previous page: Excerpt from page vi of his 1855 book *Leaves of Grass*, Brooklyn, New York: printed by James and Andrew Rome.

Emerson comment about *Leaves of Grass*: Excerpt from a letter Ralph Waldo Emerson sent to Walt Whitman on July 21, 1855. Located in William S. Kennedy's article "The Friendship of Whitman and Emerson" on pages 73-74 of the *Poet Lore: A Magazine of Letters* (edited by C. Porter and H. A. Clarke), Vol. 7-8, 1895-96.

Photo credit/attribution: Title: 1869 photo of Walt Whitman; Source #1: https://www.loc.gov/pictures/item/2002710165/; Photographer: H. Goldsmith; Source #2: https://commons.wikimedia.org/wiki/File:Walt_Whitman,_1819-1892_LCCN2002710165.tif; Location of photo: Library of Congress Print and Photographs Division; Photo is in the public domain {{PD-US}}; Original image has been cropped.

> *If you find many people who are hard and indifferent to you ... you will also find there are noble hearts who will look kindly on you, and their help will be precious to you beyond price.*

Thomas Carlyle, 1795-1881. Born in a farming village in Scotland, Carlyle was a famous historian, mathematician, essayist, and social critic.

After attending the University of Edinburgh, Carlyle first worked as a mathematics teacher, then as a minister. He considered other vocations as well. However, after getting married and moving to London, Carlyle turned his attention to writing. His first significant work was *The French Revolution*, a three-volume account of events in France from 1774 to 1795. Charles Dickens admired this work so much that it inspired him to write his masterpiece, *A Tale of Two Cities*.

It's a good thing that Carlyle was persistent and had a near photographic memory. That's because he lent his handwritten work on the first volume of *The French Revolution* to John Stuart Mill. One of Mill's servants, thinking it was nothing but trash, burned it up. Carlyle took the news of this catastrophe in stride, and he rewrote all that had been destroyed!

Another major work by Carlyle was *On Heroes, Hero-Worship, and the Heroic in History*. In this book, Carlyle discussed six types of heroes: prophet, poet, priest, ruler/king, man-of-letters, and divinity. A few of Carlyle's heroes were

Mohammad, Martin Luther, William Shakespeare, and Napoléon Bonaparte. Had he lived in the 20th century, Carlyle likely would have listed Mother Teresa, Winston Churchill, and many others as additional exemplars.

Carlyle's book on heroes established the "great man" theory of history. He maintained that the critical events of evolving history are mainly due to the impact of individuals gifted with advanced wisdom, courage, or divine inspiration. If such leaders had not existed, as the theory goes, historical events would have turned out differently. (Not everyone agreed with Carlyle's theory. In particular, Herbert Spencer argued that history's celebrated figures are simply products of their environment, and others could have filled their shoes.)

Two aspects of Carlyle's personal life are worth noting. One is impressive, the other not so flattering. On the one hand, Carlyle had a life-long friendship with "the sage of Concord," Ralph Waldo Emerson. On the other hand, Carlyle and his wife quarreled incessantly, with Samuel Butler once saying: "It was good of God to let Carlyle and Mrs. Carlyle marry one another and so make only two people miserable instead of four."

Boxed Carlyle quotation at top of previous page: Excerpt from his address delivered to the students of the University of Edinburgh, April 2, 1866; Included in Carlyle's 1877 book *On the Choice of Books*, Boston: James R. Osgood and Company.

Comment about Carlyle and his wife: Located in a letter written by Samuel Butler to Miss Savage, November 21, 1884. See page 429 of the 1919 book by Henry Festing Jones, *Samuel Butler, Author of Erewhon (1835-1902), A Memoir* (Vol. 1), London: Macmillan and Co.

Photo credit/attribution: Title: Photo of Portrait of Scottish writer Thomas Carlyle; Source: https://commons.wikimedia.org/wiki/File:NIE_Carlyle_Thomas.jpg; Artist: P. Krämer; Photo is in the public domain; Original image has been cropped.

> *That's what we're here on this Earth for,*
> *to help others—and if you can, you ought to do it.*

Elizabeth Bloomer "Betty" Ford, 1918-2011. Ford is known most of all for being First Lady when her husband, Gerald, was President of the United States. However, her work while in the White House and her earlier and later accomplishments show her to have been a hard-working, independent, wise, candid,

and courageous human being. She was far more than just "Gerald's wife."

Ford spent most of her youth in Grand Rapids, Michigan. When just 11 years old, she earned money by holding dance lessons for younger children. Following high school, she enrolled in the Bennington School of Dance in Vermont and became a student of the revered dancer and teacher Martha Graham. Ford moved to New York to further her dance opportunities, and she performed in Carnegie Hall as a part of Graham's famous troupe. Upon returning to Grand Rapids, Ford started her own dance company that offered classes to African American children and youngsters with hearing or visual impairments.

Betty Ford's route to the White House involved some unusual twists and turns. After her first marriage dissolved, she married Gerald. In 1973, he became Vice President when Spiro Agnew resigned that post after pleading "no contest" to a felony charge of tax evasion. One year later, Richard Nixon resigned from the presidency because of his involvement in the

Watergate scandal. When Gerald ascended to the presidency, Betty became First Lady.

During and after her time as First Lady, Ford was outspoken on many issues. She was a firm advocate of women's rights. She unabashedly supported the arts. She openly shared her need for a mastectomy after being diagnosed with breast cancer, thereby raising awareness of a disease that many people were reluctant to discuss. Perhaps Ford's most significant accomplishment was her creation of the Betty Ford Center, a place where alcohol and drug addicts could receive help. She started that Center after recognizing that she, herself, suffered from alcoholism.

Because of her many accomplishments, Ford received the Presidential Medal of Freedom, the Woodrow Wilson Award for Public Service, a Congressional Gold Medal, and the Award for Greatest Public Service Benefitting the Disadvantaged. She also was inducted into the National Women's Hall of Fame, and in 1975 *Time* magazine named her "Woman of the Year." While these honors likely meant a great deal to Ford, she may have been most honored by the respect and admiration she earned from the American public. When Gerald ran for re-election in 1976, a prized campaign button said: "Betty's Husband for President."

Boxed Ford quotation at top of previous page: Excerpt from a videotaped interview with Ford shown on TV during a tribute to her after she died. (It was broadcast on MSNBC during the "Way Too Early with Willie Geist" program July 15, 2011.)

Photo credit/attribution: Title: 1974 photographic portrait of First Lady Betty Ford; Source #1: http://loc.gov/pictures/resource/cph.3g02019/; Source #2: https://commons.wikimedia.org/wiki/File:Portrait_of_First_Lady_Betty_Ford_-_NARA_-_6923691.jpg; Photographer: Unnamed employee of the U.S. government; Photo is in the public domain; Original color image has been cropped and made black-and-white.

> *What matters in life is not what happens to you but what you remember and how you remember it.*

Gabriel García Márquez, 1927-2014. A life-long resident of Colombia, South America, Márquez became one of his country's most famous citizens. In fact, Colombia's president asserted that Márquez was "the greatest Colombian who ever lived."

At his father's urging, Márquez studied law and almost became an attorney. However, he chose instead to follow his passion, writing. Márquez became a successful journalist and screenwriter, but his worldwide fame came from his novels and short stories. As literary icon Carlos Fuentes put it, Márquez was "the most popular and perhaps the best writer in Spanish since Cervantes." Not surprisingly, Márquez received the 1982 Nobel Prize in Literature.

Beginning when he was 40, Márquez wrote six novels, four novellas, six collections of short stories, and nine works of non-fiction. His *magnum opus* was the novel *One Hundred Years of Solitude*. It has sold more than 50 million copies and appears in 46 languages. In this fictional work, Márquez described the fortunes (and misfortunes) of seven generations of a family living in Macondo, a fictitious isolated and primitive Colombian town. One of the main themes of this book is how history repeats itself across the generations of the focused-upon family.

Within the *Hundred Years* novel, Márquez employed a literary technique called "magical realism." In this writing style, fantastical, unnatural people or events occur within the normality of everyday life (and regular events often become uncanny). The mundane becomes magical; the magical becomes mundane. In this novel, magic realism occurred when

- certain characters grew old and died but returned as ghosts or reincarnated members of the next generation.

- all but one of the striking workers on a banana plantation were rounded up and killed; however, Macondo's residents didn't believe the survivor's account and instead chose to accept a newspaper "report" indicating that the strike ended peacefully.

Márquez has been honored in several ways. In praising him, the Nobel selection committee compared him to Balzac and Faulkner. Five Colombian presidents attended his 80th birthday celebration, as did Spain's King and Queen. He became friends with the U.S. and French presidents. Despite those flattering events, Márquez may have felt most gratified by his nicknames. He was affectionately called "Gabo" throughout Latin America, and in Colombia, people reverently referred to him as "Nuestro Nobel."

Boxed Márquez quotation at top of previous page: Comment made by Márquez to Gerald Martin (considered by Márquez to be his official biographer), author of the 2008 book *Gabriel García Márquez: A Life*, London: Vintage Books.

Comment about Márquez from Carlos Fuentes: Excerpt from Bob Minzesheimer's article "Author Gabriel García Márquez Dies," *USA Today*, April 17, 2014.

Photo credit/attribution: Title: 2002 photo of Gabriel Garcia Márquez; Source: https://commons.wikimedia.org/wiki/File:Gabriel_Garcia_Marquez.jpg; Photographer: Jose Lara; Photo is used here under the Creative Commons Attribution-Share Alike 2.0 Generic license (https://creativecommons.org/licenses/by-sa/2.0/deed.en) [CC BY-SA 2.0]; Original color image has been cropped and made black-and-white.

> *If we understood the world, we would realize that there is a logic of harmony underlying its manifold apparent dissonances.*

Jean Sibelius, 1865-1957. Born in southern Finland, Sibelius is considered by many Finns to be their country's greatest composer and someone who helped Finland's people develop a sense of national identity. To honor Sibelius, Finland celebrates a "Day of Finnish Music" each year on December 8. That date is the composer's birthday.

Like most countries, Finland has long had a national anthem. However, many of the country's residents consider a portion of *Finlandia*—a symphonic tone poem written by Sibelius—to be Finland's "national hymn." At first, *Finlandia* was the final part of a larger musical piece composed by Sibelius in 1899 to recount seven periods of Finland's history. The composer intended the last segment ("Finland Awakens") to be an optimistic gaze into Finland's future.

Because of the popularity of the final forward-looking and inspirational segment of *Finlandia*, Sibelius revised it into a stand-alone piece. When Finland boldly declared its complete independence in 1917—thereby renouncing its status as a "grand duchy" of Russia—*Finlandia* became the expression of long-sought autonomy. Noting this, Sibelius said: "We fought 600 years for our freedom [and] my *Finlandia* is the story of this fight. It is the song of our battle, our hymn of victory."

Finlandia is eight minutes long. It is both stirring and forceful during its first five minutes and its final 75 seconds. Sandwiched between those two rousing portions of music is a soft, hymn-like musical interlude. Lyrics were added to this section of music, and the resulting choir piece became known as "Finlandia Hymn," "This Is My Song," or "Song of Peace." Soon, different groups added religious lyrics, with the most well-known of these sacred versions called "Be Still, My Soul."

Despite the widespread and lasting popularity of the Finlandia Hymn, it would be wrong to think of Sibelius as a "one-hit-wonder." He composed seven symphonies, a violin concerto, 13 tone poems, 21 choral works, and more than 100 songs. Much of this music was inspired by his love of Finland's flora and fauna.

Finland has honored the achievements of Sibelius in various impressive ways. The concert hall in Lahti bears his name, and Turku is home to the Sibelius Museum. The enormous sculpture, *The Sibelius Monument*, sits in Helsinki's Sibelius Park. Most notably, almost all of Finland's populace considers Sibelius to be their country's "Musical Father."

Boxed Sibelius quotation at top of previous page: Part of a conversation Sibelius had in 1907 with Gustav Mahler. Documented on page 309 in Henry Thomas and Dana Lee Thomas' 1940 book *Living Biographies of Green Composers*, Garden City, New York: Blue Ribbon Publishers.

Comment from Sibelius about *Finlandia*: Excerpt from page 5 of the London Philharmonic Orchestra's *Programme Notes* for the performance held Wednesday, March 31, 2021 at Southbank Centre's Queen Elizabeth Hall.

Photo credit/attribution: Title: 1891 photo of Jean Sibelius; Source: https://commons.wikimedia.org/wiki/File:JSibelius_1891_(cropped).jpg; Photo is used here under the Creative Commons Attribution 4.0 International license (https://creativecommons.org/licenses/by/4.0/deed.en) [CC by 4.0]; Photographer: Daniel Nyblin; Original tinted image has been cropped and made black-and-white.

> *You will win [your] race. Don't let me down.*

Abebe Bikila, 1932-1973. One of Ethiopia's elite long-distance runners, Bikila twice etched his name into Olympic history books. His marathon victory in the 1960 Olympics made him the first black African athlete in any sport to win an Olympic gold medal. Four years later, he became the first runner from any country to win back-to-back Olympic marathon races.

Bikila's two Olympic victories are extremely notable for different reasons. During the 1960 marathon in Rome, Bikila ran the entire race without shoes. This astonishing feat created a nickname for him: "Barefoot Runner." (A book about Bikila has those two words as its title.) Even though he was shoeless, Bikila finished the 26.2-mile event in 2 hours, 15 minutes, and 16.2 seconds. This broke the existing world record.

In the 1964 Olympics held in Tokyo, Bikila was just like other marathon runners in that he wore shoes. However, he was superior to all other competitors in ability, determination, and grit. Bikila again won the marathon race, and he did so in a record-setting time: 2:12:11.2. Amazingly, he crossed the finish line a full four minutes and 12 seconds ahead of the second-place runner. Bikila's margin of victory—breathtaking as it was—was not the most remarkable thing about his second Olympic Gold Medal. What is truly astounding is that Bikila even agreed to run in the race. Just five weeks before the event, he was in a hospital having abdominal surgery for appendicitis!

Because of Bikila's status as a double gold medal winner in the Olympics, Ethiopian people understandably consider Bikila to be a hero. For a different reason, he is a role model to many people around the globe. In 1969, Bikila was involved in an auto accident that left him permanently unable to walk. Confined to a wheelchair, Bikila didn't complain or ask for sympathy. Instead, he said:

I accepted those [Olympic] victories as I accept this tragedy. I have to accept both circumstances as facts of life and live happily.

Bikila was honored in many ways because of his running accomplishments and how he handled his auto-accident injuries. A stadium in Ethiopia's largest city bears his name. Annually, the New York Road Runners club gives the Abebe Bikila Award to someone who has made a significant contribution to long-distance running. Perhaps the most impressive tribute to Bikila came in 2010, 37 years after his death. During that year's Olympic marathon, the winner (an Ethiopian) ran shoeless for the final 300 meters of the race. He did that to mark the 50th anniversary of Bikila's first Olympic victory.

Boxed Bikila quotation at top of previous page: Excerpt from Kenny Moore's article, entitled "Chasing Justice," published in *Runner's World* on June 20, 2018.

Bikila's comments after his auto accident: Excerpt from page 281 of Edward S. Sears' 2015 book *Running Through the Ages* (2nd ed.), Jefferson, NC: McFarland & Co.

Photo credit/attribution: Title: 1968 photo of Abebe Bikila in Amsterdam; Source https://commons.wikimedia.org/wiki/File:Abebe_Bikila_1968b.jpg; Photographer: Jac. De Nijs; Photo is used here under the Creative Commons Attribution-Share Alike 3.0 Netherlands license (https://creativecommons.org/licenses/by-sa/3.0/nl/deed.en) [CC BY-SA 3.0 NL]; Original image has been flipped horizontally and cropped.

> *Kindness can only be repaid with kindness.*
> *It can't be repaid with expressions*
> *like "thank you."*

Malala Yousafzai, 1997-. Born in Pakistan's picturesque Swat Valley, Yousafzai was taught by her father, who was an educator and social activist. Impressed with her father's way of running his schools, Yousafzai herself became a passionate education advocate. Like her father, she argued publicly that girls should  receive the same educational opportunities as boys.

Yousafzai felt it necessary to speak out because the Taliban—a radical, ultra-conservative terrorist group that had taken control of northwest Pakistan—banned girls from attending school. Starting at age 11, Yousafzai openly argued that girls had a right to an education, just as boys did. She voiced these concerns when she spoke at her local press club, in blog columns she wrote for BBC radio broadcasts, and during guest appearances on television. These efforts made Yousafzai well-known as a proponent for her cause.

Yousafzai's growing prominence infuriated the Taliban. In 2012, a Taliban member tried to assassinate the 15-year-old Yousafzai as she rode home from school on a bus. Hoping to kill her, the gunman shot her in the head. Taken to a hospital, Yousafzai underwent a five-hour operation to remove the bullet. Over the next few months, she endured two additional surgeries to deal with the physical trauma caused by the assassin's bullet. She also underwent painful physical therapy.

After Yousafzai recovered, she courageously resumed her crusade and became the world's leading spokesperson for girls having the right to an education. Among other things, she authored three best-selling books: *I Am Malala*; *We Are Displaced: My Journey and Stories from Girls Around the World*; and *Malala's Magic Pencil*. She also founded, with her father, "The Malala Fund," an international organization working to ensure that every girl receives 12 years of education.

Yousafzai's efforts earned her a long list of international awards, including the Anne Frank Award for Moral Courage, the Mother Teresa Award for Social Justice, Pakistan's National Youth Peace Prize, the Sakharov Prize for Freedom of Thought, and the Nobel Peace Prize. In 2013, 2014, and 2015, *Time* magazine listed Yousafzai as "one of the most influential people globally." And in 2022, Yousafzai received the LionHeart Award at the Cannes Lions International Festival of Creativity, honoring her as someone who "harnessed their position to make a positive difference in the world around us."

Notably, Yousafzai chose not to sit back and "rest on her laurels." Instead, she applied to the University of Oxford, was admitted, and studied philosophy, politics, and economics. She graduated with a Bachelor of Arts degree in 2020).

Boxed Yousafzai quotation at top of previous page: Excerpt from Yousafzai's 2013 book *I Am Malala*, New York: Little Brown and Co.

LionHeart Award citation: Excerpt from the top paragraph of the 17 May, 2022 online article "Cannes Lions honours Malala Yousafzai with the 2022 LionHeart Award."

Photo credit/attribution: Title: 2013 photo of Malala Yousafzai; Source: https://commons.wikimedia.org/wiki/File:Malala_Yousafzai_par_Claude_Truong-Ngoc_novembre_2013.jpg; Photographer: Claude Truong-Ngoc; Photo is used here under the Creative Commons Attribution-Share Alike Unported 3.0 Generic license (https://creativecommons.org/licenses/by-sa/3.0/deed.en) [CC BY-SA 3.0]; Original image has been cropped.

> *It is not the style of clothes one wears, neither the kind of automobile one drives, nor the amount of money one has in the bank that counts. These mean nothing. It is simply service that measures success.*

George Washington Carver, 1864-1943. Despite being born into slavery and raised in foster families, Carver possessed a burning desire to become educated. He worked hard on his studies. After graduating from high school in Missouri, he entered Simpson College in Iowa. An art professor there noticed Carver's interest and talent in painting plants and flowers. That professor  advised Carver to transfer to Iowa State University, where he could get advanced training in botany. Following this advice, Carver became the first black student admitted to ISU.

After receiving his B.S. and Master's degrees, Carver was invited to join ISU's faculty. He accepted that offer and became the university's first African American teacher and researcher. When Carver was 32 years old, Booker T. Washington lured him to Alabama's Tuskegee University, where Carver immediately became head of the agriculture department. He taught and did research at Tuskegee until his death at age 79.

Carver's research showed, among other things, that crop rotation—alternating, for example, cotton with legumes—could increase nutrients (such as nitrogen) in the soil. This improved cotton yields and generated other lucrative crops. Carver was far more than just a researcher, however. He initiated an agricultural extension program in Alabama, shared recipes in his agricultural bulletins, and wrote a syndicated newspaper column.

Of his many achievements, Carver became most famous for his research on peanuts and his opinion that peanuts should become a prime agricultural product in America. Carver's reputation as an agricultural researcher and peanut expert grew and grew. Three U.S. presidents set up meetings with Carver, as did the Crown Prince of Sweden. Henry Ford invited him to talk at a conference in Michigan, and Carver testified in Washington at Congressional hearings focused on peanut imports. He also visited Southern white colleges on behalf of the Commission on Interracial Cooperation.

Several honors and awards were bestowed on Carver. He was inducted into two "halls of fame": the Hall of Fame for Great Americans and the National Inventors Hall of Fame. He has appeared on two U.S. stamps and, along with Booker T. Washington, on a commemorative half-dollar coin. Two navy ships were named after him. Notably, the George Washington Carver National Monument, located in Missouri near his childhood home, was the first national monument constructed to honor an African American. It also was the first national monument to recognize someone other than a president.

Boxed Carver quotation at top of previous page: Excerpt from page 20 of Gary R. Kremer's 2017 edited book *George Washington Carver: In His Own Words*, Columbia, Missouri: University of Missouri Press.

Photo credit/attribution: Title: Photo of George Washington Carver; Source: https://commons.wikimedia.org/wiki/File:George_Washington_Carver_(722301494 6).jpg; Photographer: Unknown; Photo is used here under the Creative Commons Attribution 2.0 Generic license (https://creativecommons.org/licenses/by/2.0/deed.en) [CC BY 2.0]; Original image has been flipped horizontally and cropped.

> *You ought to do something to help those who are not so fortunate....*

Abraham Lincoln, 1809-1865. Many scholars, as well as a multitude of ordinary citizens, consider Lincoln to have been the greatest president of the United States. Because of this, most Americans know (as do many people living in other counties) these eight facts about him:

- Although Lincoln was born in Kentucky and lived 14 years in Indiana, his political career began in Illinois.
- Elected U.S. president in 1860 (and re-elected in 1984), Lincoln was his country's leader during the Civil War.
- Lincoln delivered the famous "Gettysburg Address" that begins with these six words: "Four score and seven years ago."
- Lincoln's Emancipation Proclamation freed more than 3.5 million enslaved African Americans.
- John Wilkes Booth shot and killed Lincoln while the president watched a play in Washington's Ford Theater.
- An imposing marble statue of Lincoln, seated in a chair, is inside the Lincoln Memorial that's located at one end of the Reflecting Pool in Washington, D.C.
- A facial image of Lincoln (along with those of three other U.S. presidents) is carved into Mount Rushmore in South Dakota.
- Lincoln's nickname was "Honest Abe."

In addition to the previously-listed eight facts about Abraham Lincoln, several lesser-known aspects of his life, work, and legacy are worth noting. For example:

- Lincoln hardly attended school at all, for he was busy helping with the family farm. He was mainly self-educated, even when he decided at age 27 to be a lawyer.
- Lincoln invented a system for moving riverboats off sandbars, and he secured a patent for it.
- In the 1860 presidential election, Lincoln won 57% of the electoral votes. In 1864, he won 91% of such votes.
- Just 272 words are in the famous Gettysburg Address.
- "The Great Emancipator" was a nickname given to Lincoln because of his efforts to end slavery.
- Family tragedies were no stranger to Lincoln. His mother and only brother died when he was nine, his sister died when he was 19, and two of Lincoln's four children died before he did.
- Lincoln was the one who established a "National Day of Thanksgiving" to occur each year in late November.
- More than 50 countries have issued stamps with Lincoln's image on them.
- Robert Todd Lincoln Beckwith, who died in 1985, was the last direct descendant of Abraham Lincoln.

Boxed Lincoln quotation at top of previous page: Excerpt from page 4 of Vol. 8 of the 1894 set of books entitled *Abraham Lincoln* (edited by John G. Nicolay and John Hay), Harrogate, Tennessee: Lincoln Memorial University Press. (Quote comes from an address Lincoln made in Washington, D.C. on August 14, 1862.)

Photo credit/attribution: Title: Photo of Abraham Lincoln; Source: https://commons.wikimedia.org/wiki/File:Abraham_Lincoln_head_on_shoulders_ph oto_portrait.jpg; Photographer: Unknown; Photo is in the public domain; Original image has been cropped.

Index of Quotation Authors

Index of Quotation Authors (continued)

Index of Quotation Topics

Made in the USA
Las Vegas, NV
09 February 2023

67218112R00173